Private Security, Public Order

The Outsourcing of Public Services and Its Limits

Edited by
SIMON CHESTERMAN
and
ANGELINA FISHER

A project of the Institute for International Law and Justice at New York University School of Law

OXFORD
UNIVERSITY PRESS

OXFORD
UNIVERSITY PRESS

Great Clarendon Street, Oxford, OX2 6DP,
United Kingdom

Oxford University Press is a department of the University of Oxford.
It furthers the University's objective of excellence in research, scholarship,
and education by publishing worldwide. Oxford is a registered trade mark of
Oxford University Press in the UK and in certain other countries

First published 2009

Published in the United States of America by Oxford University Press
198 Madison Avenue, New York, NY 10016, United States of America

British Library Cataloguing in Publication Data
Data available

Library of Congress Control Number: 2009031330

ISBN 978–0–19–957412–4

Acknowledgements

This book is the result of an ongoing research project at the Institute for International Law and Justice at New York University School of Law. Particular thanks are due to Benedict Kingsbury, Faculty Director of the Institute, who helped us to define and shape the research project. Further intellectual roots lie in the Institute's research project on Global Administrative Law, directed by Benedict Kingsbury and Richard B. Stewart. For more information, visit <http://www.iilj.org>.

Many of the ideas presented in this book were shaped and discussed at a conference at New York University School of Law in April 2008. Thanks are due to Surabhi Ranganathan and Alma Fuentes. The text benefited from close reading by, among others, Christen Broecker. The project would not have been possible without the generous support of Carnegie Corporation of New York. All views expressed in this volume, however, are solely those of the respective authors.

Summary Contents

Contents

List of Contributors

Alfred C Aman, Jr is the Roscoe C O'Byrne Professor of Law at Indiana University School of Law in Bloomington. He was a member of the Cornell Law School Faculty from 1977–1991; Dean of Indiana University Law School in Bloomington from 1991–2002; Director of Indiana University's Institute for Advanced Study from 2003–2006; and Dean of Suffolk University Law School from 2007–2009. His books include *The Democracy Deficit: Taming Globalization through Law Reform* (New York University Press, 2004); and *Administrative Law in a Global Era* (Cornell University Press, 1992). He was a founding editor of the Indiana Journal of Global Legal Studies in 1993.

Daphne Barak-Erez is Professor of Law and the Stewart and Judy Colton Chair of Law and Security at Tel-Aviv University. She serves as the chairperson of the Israeli Association of Public Law and is a member of the International Academy of Comparative Law and the American Law Institute. She was a Visiting Professor of Law at several universities, including Columbia Law School and the University of Toronto. Her recent books include *Exploring Social Rights: Between Theory and Practice* (edited with Aeyal Gross, Hart Publishing, 2007) and *Outlawed Pigs: Law, Religion and Culture in Israel* (Wisconsin University Press, 2007).

Simon Chesterman is Global Professor and Director of the New York University School of Law Singapore Programme, and a Professor of Law at the National University of Singapore. Educated in Melbourne, Beijing, Amsterdam, and Oxford, his books include *Shared Secrets: Intelligence and Collective Security* (Lowy Institute for International Policy, 2006); *You, The People: The United Nations, Transitional Administration, and State-Building* (Oxford University Press, 2004); and *Just War or Just Peace? Humanitarian Intervention and International Law* (Oxford University Press, 2001).

Olivier De Schutter is a Professor at the University of Louvain (Belgium) and at the College of Europe. He obtained a J.D. degree from the Université Catholique de Louvain and Université Paris-II (Assas) and an LL.M. degree from Harvard University. A member of the Global Law School Faculty at New York University and a Visiting Professor at Columbia University, he was appointed in 2008 the UN Special Rapporteur on the right to food. His recent books include *Transnational Corporations and Human Rights*, editor, (PIE Peter Lang, 2005) and *Monitoring Fundamental Rights in the EU: The Role of the Fundamental Rights Agency*, editor with Philip Alston, (Hart, 2005).

Rebecca DeWinter-Schmitt is a post-doctoral fellow and adjunct professor at American University's School of International Service. Her dissertation, '*Business as usual? The mobilization of the anti-sweatshop movement and the social construction of corporate identity*', examined the role of grassroots mobilization in the intersubjective constitution of corporate rights and responsibilities. Her professional experience includes four years on staff at Amnesty International USA. More recently, she has been advising the organization on its campaign on private military and security companies. In addition to her doctorate from American University, she received her master's degree in political science from the University of Marburg, Germany.

Angelina Fisher is a Program Director and Institute Fellow at the Institute for International Law and Justice at the New York University School of Law. She received her law degree from Osgoode Hall Law School, Canada and an LL.M. from New York University School of Law. She was one of the primary researchers and authors of the reports, 'Torture by Proxy: International and Domestic Law Applicable to "Extraordinary Renditions"' (New York: ABCNY & NYU School of Law, 2004), and 'Beyond Guantanamo: Transfers to Torture One Year After Rasul v Bush' (New York: NYU School of Law, 2005). Fisher is also a co-author of 'Tortured Logic: Renditions to Justice, Extraordinary Rendition, and Human Rights Law', *The Long Term View*, vol 6(4) (2006) 52–71.

Chia Lehnardt is a DFG fellow and research fellow at the Chair for Public Law, Public International Law and European Law, both at Humboldt University, Berlin. Educated in Berlin, Oxford, Florence, and New York, she was previously an institute fellow and program officer at the Institute for International Law and Justice, New York University School of Law. She is editor, along with Simon Chesterman, of *From Mercenaries to Market: The Rise and Regulation of Private Military Companies* (Oxford University Press, 2007).

Michael Likosky is based at New York University's Institute for Public Knowledge and is now working on a project on public-private partnerships supported by the Ford Foundation. He holds a doctorate from the Law Faculty of Oxford University, and is formerly a full tenured law professor at the school of Oriental and African Studies, University of London. Likosky has held fellowships and visiting posts at Oxford University as Markle Foundation Fellow; Hauser Global Law School Program at New York University School of Law as Global Crystal Eastman Research Fellow; Fordham Law School; Wisconsin Law School; and the University of Bonn. Likosky has published five books on the role of government in the economy: *Obama's Bank* (Cambridge University Press, 2009); *Law, Infrastructure and Human Rights* (Cambridge University Press, 2006); *The Silicon Empire* (Ashgate, 2005); *Privatising Development* (Martinus Nijhoff, 2005); and *Transnational Legal Processes* (Cambridge University Press, 2002). He has twice contributed to the Oxford Amnesty Lectures. He is an expert to the United Nations and a Member of the OECD Working Group on Infrastructure and extractives in Africa. Likosky actively advises financial institutions on public-private partnerships including Credit Suisse, Deloitte, D. E. Shaw, UBS, and the American Business Council.

Mariana Mota Prado is an Assistant Professor at the Faculty of Law of the University of Toronto. She received her LL.B. from the University of Sao Paulo, and LL.M. and JSD degrees from Yale University. In 2004, she worked for the Private Participation in Infrastructure Database Project at the World Bank, and in 2005 she was a fellow of the Olin Center for Law, Economics and Public Policy at Yale Law School. In 2004–2006 Prado was tutor-in-law at Yale Law School. From 2000 to 2007, she was a researcher for the Law and Democracy Project, Brazilian Center of Analysis and Planning in Brazil.

Jacqueline Ross is Professor of Law at the University of Illinois College of Law. She is currently engaged in a comparative study of undercover policing in the United States, Italy, Germany, and France.

Introduction

Simon Chesterman & Angelina Fisher

Private actors are increasingly taking on roles traditionally arrogated to the state. In the industrialized North and the developing South, functions essential to external and internal security and to the satisfaction of basic human needs are now routinely contracted out to non-state agents. In the area of privatization of security functions, attention by academics and policy makers tends to focus on the activities of private military and security companies (PMSCs), especially in the context of armed conflicts, and their impact on human rights and post-conflict stability and reconstruction. The first edited volume emerging from New York University School of Law's Institute for International Justice project on private military and security companies, *From Mercenaries to Market*, broadened this debate to situate the private military phenomenon in the context of moves towards regulation of activities through market and non-market mechanisms.[1] This second volume looks at the transformations in the nature of state authority.

In the past two decades, the responsibilities delegated to private actors—especially but not only in the United States—have grown in depth and breadth. The much-discussed role assumed by Blackwater (now rebranded 'Xe') and other contractors in Iraq is in many ways the tip of the privatization iceberg. Many sectors traditionally regarded as 'public' have experienced varying degrees of privatization, from the operation of public utilities to the administration of prisons, from intelligence activities to peacekeeping. Drawing on insights from work on privatization, regulation, and accountability in the emerging field of global administrative law,[2] this book examines private military and security companies through the wider lens of private actors performing public functions.

The book is organized around three sets of questions. First, how do PMSCs fit within the broader context of outsourcing of public functions to private entities, and what implications does this have for the possibility of holding them or other actors accountable? Secondly, what lessons can be learned from other cases of privatization of public services? Thirdly, should there be limits on the ability of governments to outsource traditionally 'public' functions?

[1] Simon Chesterman and Chia Lehnardt (eds), *From Mercenaries to Market: The Rise and Regulation of Private Military Companies* (Oxford: Oxford University Press, 2007).

[2] See Benedict Kingsbury, Nico Krisch, and Richard B. Stewart, 'The Emergence of Global Administrative Law' (2005) 68 *Law and Contemporary Problems* 15. Additional materials are available online at www.iilj.org.

Part I considers the problem of accountability posed by PMSCs. In chapter one, Michael Likosky describes the links between privatization of military civilian activities and the significance this has for efforts to hold PMSCs accountable for their conduct. Through examining the trajectory of privatization across time and across sectors, he outlines the important role that public-private partnerships played from colonialism to the 20th century industrialization of the United States. The link between nominally civilian privatization projects and violence is explored through a Peruvian natural gas pipeline project: the contract did not directly address security questions but its effect on an indigenous population was no less violent. The difficulty of dissociating public and private aspects of a given industry is seen in the modern high tech industry: though its archetype is the garage entrepreneur made good, the foundations of this industry lie squarely in the US Department of Defense. Both insights suggest the need to have a broader and more flexible approach to accountability. Among other things, this means looking not just to who is contracting for or carrying out a given service, but also determining who is financing it. It also means looking beyond court-based prosecution of wrongdoers to embrace a wider range of potential legal and political means of accountability.

The basic questions of *what kind* of accountability is being sought with respect to PMSCs and *to whom* are examined in chapters two and three. In chapter two, Olivier De Schutter looks at the varied efforts to use the international law of state responsibility to hold states in which PMSCs are registered or incorporated (home states) accountable for their conduct. In chapter three, Angelina Fisher considers the possibilities for ensuring that accountability takes into account the interests of those most affected by PMSC conduct.

De Schutter examines whether, under international law, the home state is obliged to control its companies. Must such a state allow its courts to adjudicate claims filed against these companies? If such duties do exist, how may they be implemented taking into account the sovereignty of the state on the territory of which the PMSC is operating? Home states can be held responsible for PMSC actions when the company is a mere fiction used to pursue state interest, if governmental authority has been delegated to it, or if it is in fact under state direction or control. Such 'easy cases' do not capture the growing instances of PMSCs being employed by private entities (rather than states), however. In those cases, if the state on whose territory the company operates is unable or unwilling to hold the company accountable, the home state should bear that responsibility either through the exercise of extraterritorial jurisdiction or through the use of incentives, such as selective public procurement schemes, reporting obligations, or other contractual terms.

Fisher continues the discussion of PMSC accountability but focuses on 'downward' accountability; that is, accountability of private companies to the victims of their conduct. She concludes that conditions under which victims of PMSC abuse may seek legal accountability of the companies are limited under many domestic regimes as well as under international law. Attention must therefore be shifted to creating grievance mechanisms as an alternative means of augmenting PMSC accountability to victims. She proposes a mechanism for PMSCs that draws on the experience of other private industries, including those discussed in the subsequent chapters. To be effective, such a mechanism must enjoy legitimacy with both the industry and the local populations, be accessible to the public, be transparent both with regards to process and the outcome, engage relevant multi-stakeholders in productive dialogue, have a predictable and fair process, and empower local populations.

Addressing these accountability gaps requires political will and institutional creativity that has, to date, been lacking in the private military and security sector. Part II therefore turns to what lessons may be learned from other sectors. The use of lethal violence by private actors is often identified as a uniquely troubling aspect of the PMSC phenomenon.[3] As Daphne Barak-Erez demonstrates in chapter four, however, our understanding will remain only partial if this is not discussed in the broader context of other privatization policies. Through the prism of domestic constitutional law, with recourse to comparative tools, Barak-Erez analyses the trend to privatize public functions and discusses the limitations on privatization in general and the limitations on privatization of security functions in particular. She argues that the realities of widespread privatization of public functions necessitate a rethinking of the basic principles of constitutional and administrative law beyond the mere adjustment of specific rules and doctrines. She proposes a framework for examining private initiatives, including the decision to outsource military and security functions, that is situated around three fundamental questions: What are the boundaries of privatization? What is (and ought to be) the administrative process of privatization? And what are (and ought to be) the outcomes of privatization and its regulation? Consideration must be given to whether certain types of actions or powers cannot be privatized because they represent core government functions. If this initial threshold is crossed, one must consider the process through which the decision to privatize is made. This, in turn, requires a level of transparency and participation frequently lacking in the military and security sector, but seen at least in part in other sectors. The other chapters in Part II build on this framework, considering the boundaries of privatization (chapter five), the administrative process of privatization (chapters five and six), and the outcomes of privatization and its regulation (chapters six and seven).

In chapter five, Alfred Aman describes the case of prison privatization in the United States. Prisons offer an interesting insight into debates over which coercive aspects of the state should be kept within government hands, and thus shed some light on the outsourcing of military functions. They also present a

[3] See generally Sarah Percy, 'Morality and Regulation', in Chesterman and Lehnardt (eds), *From Mercenaries to Market*, 11.

slightly more developed example of administrative oversight of outsourced functions. Aman argues that the question of what is and is not 'inherently governmental' is a decision that must be made democratically, through an open political process that meets standards of transparency and accountability set in place by legislatures and overseen by courts. A new kind of administrative law may need to be created to respond to the democratic deficit associated with modern privatization.

In chapter 6 Mariana Mota Prado also considers the question of how a decision to privatize is made and examines how such a decision impacts the choice of regulatory framework. By developing a comparative analysis of the privatization processes in infrastructure sectors as well as the military and security sector, Prado discusses the circumstances under which a regulatory framework is established, designed, and enforced. Drawing on her analysis, Prado develops a series of recommendations for the establishment of a regulatory process for PMSCs. She argues that a government contracting with PMSCs should not only justify why privatization is necessary but that any such claim should be assessed by an independent body (similar to the cost-benefit analysis of regulation performed by the Office of Management and Budget in the United States). Secondly, with limited exceptions, a competitive bidding process should be the default rule for contracting with PMSCs, allowing for limited exceptions. Thirdly, the contracting government needs to assess some of the broader national public policy concerns that are connected to privatization of military and security services and impose across-the-board regulation to address them, preferably through legislative intervention. Similarly, home countries need to assess broader international public policy concerns that are connected to privatization of the military and impose regulation that applies to activities of its PMSCs abroad. Echoing Barak-Erez and Aman, Prado calls for transparency in privatization of private military and security services, arguing that citizens should have access to all information related to the competitive bidding process and contractual provisions. These policy implications must be considered within the broader regulatory context of different countries, because the circumstances under which a regulatory framework is established are relevant to the content of such a framework and its effectiveness and, consequently, can have an impact on the success or failure of a privatization process.

A more in-depth look at the content of regulation is provided in chapter seven by Rebecca DeWinter-Schmitt. She examines the evolution of regulatory regimes in the apparel industry as a comparison with efforts to regulate PMSCs. Lessons learned from the efforts of the Fair Labor Association and the Workers Rights Consortium might provide a road map for creating a hybrid public-private regulatory regime for PMSCs that contains all the necessary elements of high standards, implementation guidelines, independent monitoring, an enforcement mechanism, and public reporting. Incentives could be established by giving companies an industry seal of approval that would indicate their adherence to ethical business practices. DeWinter-Schmitt posits that this could be attractive to non-state customers, like NGOs and other companies that need security and are worried about the reputations of their providers. The existence of a hybrid regulatory regime would not, however, alleviate the state's responsibility to conduct ongoing assessments of the human rights impact of such an effort, including an examination of the global structure and operations of the PMSC industry. Part of those assessments should include whether the provision of certain security services should be limited to government actors.

This question of limits is the focus of Part III, drawing on three extreme cases of outsourcing that have been controversial in their own way: the use of private informants in domestic criminal investigations, the use of private companies in the collection and analysis of intelligence, and the use of private security companies in peacekeeping operations.

In chapter eight, Jacqueline Ross considers the circumstances in which a state can use private informants in criminal investigations. Informants raise concerns of abuse and lack of accountability similar to those posed by PMSCs, but Ross argues that the unique nature of informants as criminal insiders (that is, members of a criminal enterprise) makes the delegation of investigative functions to them particularly troubling. Criminal insiders recruited as informants often remain in place in their targeted organizations and continue to participate in crimes in order to provide investigators with information about the organization's activities. In doing so, informants may purchase and sell contraband undercover, or participate in other offences with their criminal associates. Ross looks closely at the German approach to regulating informants through promises of confidentiality under a series of conditions (including that the informant cannot participate in the crime he or she is investigating) and concludes that German confidentiality regulations not only guard against many of the risks identified with the use of criminal insiders but also provide an instructive example of how regulators set outer limits on the outsourcing of security operations, intelligence gathering, and criminal investigations. Confidentiality regulations may enable the state to keep the police from delegating police investigative functions to those who are structurally unreliable without some compensating mechanisms of accountability.

Unlike the domestic context, safeguards against the risks associated with the use of private parties in intelligence functions are lacking in the international context. In chapter nine, Simon Chesterman surveys the manner in which US intelligence functions have been outsourced in collection activities such as electronic surveillance, rendition, and interrogation, as well as the growing reliance on private actors for analysis. Chesterman focuses on three challenges to accountability specific to the privatization of intelligence: secrecy, incentives, and the difficulty of defining what activities should be regarded as 'inherently governmental'. Secrecy is inherent to intelligence tasks but undermines effective oversight in predictable ways even when those tasks are performed by government agencies. This suggests the need to avoid further removal of intelligence activities from democratic structures. The different incentives that exist for private and public employees also call for wariness in determining whether and to what extent intelligence functions should be outsourced. The simplest way of containing some of the accountability-related problems would be to forbid certain activities from being delegated or outsourced to private actors at all. A determination of which activities to forbid, however, is far from simple. In the United States, this question is framed in the language of 'inherently governmental' functions: those to be carried out by government employees only. There is, however, great uncertainty over the meaning of the term and little prospect of intelligence agencies adopting a robust definition of 'inherently governmental' functions. The significance of this limitation may be diminished by the ability to outsource even inherently governmental functions in so far as they could be construed merely as 'implementing' policy with some form of oversight. Nonetheless, a transparent definition of what functions should be 'inherently governmental' is the most effective way to achieve clarity, thus echoing the voices of other authors in this book.

Peacekeeping has long presented a troubling frontier for outsourcing. States—in particular Western states—may be reluctant to send their troops on humanitarian missions. Kofi Annan noted a decade ago that the world was probably not ready to 'privatize peace'.[4] Nevertheless, the role of PMSCs in peacekeeping operations has been increasing. In chapter ten, Chia Lehnardt surveys the roles that PMSCs have taken on and the more ambitious possibilities that have been proposed. There is, at present, little guidance on what functions can be outsourced in the implementation of a UN Security Council mandate. In fact, PMSCs have been engaged in a broad spectrum of activities, including some of the more ancillary aspects constituting peace consolidating measures or post-conflict measures, such as the recruitment and training of troops and the clearing of mines. At the same time, the status of PMSCs under international humanitarian law is murky at best. The situation is compounded by the questions of who ultimately bears responsibility for company misconduct. Despite these concerns, suggestions have been made for the expanded use of PMSCs, such as employing them as UN blue helmets or even as UN-mandated or UN-led troops carrying out military operations. The implications of taking further steps towards a more active role for PMSCs extend beyond questions of law or operational feasibility as the privatization of peace would also amount to the outsourcing of the international community's most basic commitments under the UN Charter.

[4] Kofi Annan, 35th Ditchley Foundation Lecture, 26 June 1998, UN Press Release SG/SM/6613.

The privatization of public functions thus raises important legal and political issues in the governance of private actors, but also calls into question the nature of what functions should be 'public'. The concluding chapter by the editors draws together findings from the various chapters and outlines the key elements of a governance framework for private military and security functions.

PART I

ACCOUNTABLITY GAPS

1

The privatization of violence

*Michael Likosky**

We paint privatization in primary colours. However, such political messaging not only distorts our understanding of the underlying legal structures of privatization, it also undermines attempts to devise effective instruments of accountability. We mistakenly tend to think of the privatization of prisons, school construction, bridges and roads as raising a distinct set of issues from those ones raised by the US military using mercenaries to wage war or private contractors to run detention facilities. One is about civilian functions, the other military. The first is about the modernization of government, the second its regression. One is about the public interest, while the other is about contracting away the laws of war. One seems suitable for civilian oversight, the other to criminal prosecution.

While it is important to identify material distinctions, we must also recognize that these two trajectories of privatization have common roots and contractual approaches; have circulated together transnationally for centuries; and also share many common thematic approaches. This chapter focuses on one commonality evidenced in certain instances of privatization found within each branch, civilian and military, of the tree—what I call 'the privatization of violence', denoting the public-private partnership based foundations of violence, organized through a particular set of institutional, regulatory, and contractual means. Privatization is

* This chapter has been presented at Yale University within the International Development Policy Series, International Affairs Council (sponsored by the International Affairs Council, the African Studies Council, The MacMillan Center; funded by Edward J and Dorothy Clarke Kempf Memorial Fund); New York University School of Law; Columbia University School of Law; the Law and Society Association Annual Meeting in Montreal; and the University of Wisconsin at 'The Privatization of Security and Human Rights in the Americas: Perspectives from the Global South' sponsored by the A E Havens Center for the Study of Social Structure and Social Change and organized by Katherine McCoy. I am grateful to participants and organizers of these events for the feedback. The chapter draws on an argument developed in expanded form in a forthcoming book publication and I would particularly like to thank the following people for discussions and comments on draft material: Judge Dennis Davis, Eleanor Fox, Katherine McCoy, Joy Mooberry, Sally Falk Moore, Susan Rose-Ackerman, Saskia Sassen, Joanne Scott, Francis Snyder, Ruti Teitel, and William Twining. It builds upon early arguments I made in various forms in previous publications, including: *Obama's Bank* (Cambridge: Cambridge University Press, 2009); *Law, Infrastructure and Human Rights* (Cambridge: Cambridge University Press, 2006) and *The Silicon Empire* (London: Ashgate, 2005).

invariably justified as advancing the public interest. In practice, however, the means chosen at times orchestrate violence, intentional or incidental. We contract out not only government functions, but also the government's monopolistic power over legitimate violence. What results is a splintering of sovereign power and thus an unsurprising accountability deficit.

This production of violence through public-private partnerships has long occupied scholars, politicians, civil society groups, and others. Resistance to it formed the basis of decolonization. While the logic and practice of these partnerships is not always visible and thus amenable to oversight, we do know violence when we see it: from the pictures circulating from Abu Ghraib or Blackwater in Iraq to the execution of Ken Saro-Wiwa in Nigeria.

Nonetheless, the visibility of this privatized violence does not necessarily mean that accountability follows. Transparent violence does not equal accountability. In fact, it is a particular testament to the power of transactional law, both domestic and international, which facilitates these partnerships that it is capable of outflanking attempts at rule of law oversight.[1]

Within a court-preoccupied United States, this rebalancing of power in which transactions trump litigation seems like a particular usurpation of power. International law has been the subject of much scepticism regarding even its status as a legitimate form of law so how is it that international law has, through its transactional branch, proven itself more powerful than the United States judiciary? To tie the 'rule of law' to the 'rule of courts' is not only a jurisprudential provincialism, it is also a recipe for continuing our inability to hold public-private partnerships to account.

Transnational partnerships arise out of a web of public and private law. Our accountability strategies must accordingly be attuned to the realities of how these deals are structured—not just to our legitimate affront to the violence produced, which gives impulse to turn to the courts for redress. When we look to the legal infrastructure of the partnership, to tailor and thus exert accountability, then the road project looks increasingly like the private military contractor. Perhaps then we will rebalance our own efforts away from mainly trying to file effective court actions (however important and essential) and toward thinking through capital markets and contracts.

In both the military and civilian situations, public-private partnerships emerge out of a 'molten mass of public and private, domestic, foreign and international law.'[2] They concern widely disparate areas of law such as commercial, foreign direct and indirect investment, procurement, labour, customs, taxation, construction, operation and maintenance, among others. Whether civilian or military,

[1] On civilian and military privatizations and contract see Michael Likosky, *Law, Infrastructure and Human Rights* (New York: Cambridge University Press, 2006). On military ones see Simon Chesterman and Chia Lehnardt (eds), *From Mercenaries to Market: The Rise and Regulation of Private Military Companies* (Oxford: Oxford University Press, 2007).

[2] Likosky, *Law, Infrastructure and Human Rights* (n 1 above, 7).

we must look at the particular set of laws—both regulatory and contractual—that travel with the jet-set that finance, construct, and operate these partnerships.

If bankers and businessmen do not see the sectors as inherently distinct, then should we? If so, what distinctions are important to maintain? And, if accountability is our goal, what is the best means for achieving it? Is it court or agency, regulation or contract, US law or international law, international cooperation and coordination or competition and extraterritorial assertion? Perhaps it is some combination of these, but when should our accountability strategies diverge, both between and within categories of privatization?

Although the privatization of violence emerged many centuries ago as an idea and practice, here our main concern is its 20th century re-emergence, refinement, and large-scale government production during the Second World War. Since then, it has taken hold within the United States and abroad. This chapter concerns itself with that evolution. Its purpose is threefold: first, to place privatization of war in a broader context, thus seeking to understand it as a branch of a tree that has also given life to the civilian branch; secondly, to highlight how violence is produced through public-private partnerships in a way that calls into question the usefulness of terms like 'privatization'; and, thirdly, to propose a series of questions that we might ask about the privatization of war, violence, and security—both civilian and military; that is, to devise modes of accountability that will assist the consideration of accountability more broadly.

The trajectory of privatization

In the United States, privatization has a long history dating back at least to the 19th century railroads. We see it also in the colonial chartered companies, the public-private foundations of *lex mercatoria*. We see it in the Roman free ports. However, my story starts in the 20th century. Nonetheless, a brief discussion of earlier public-private partnerships, particularly ones with a security dimension will be first briefly elaborated. We next turn to the 20th century privatization of the US defence function during the Second World War. After, we move to the Cold War period and into the public-private partnership basis of the high technology economy, itself an important ongoing aspect of defence privatization.

Early privatizations: From colonial chartered companies to railroads

Both colonial chartered companies and railroads were at their foundations transnational public-private partnerships. They form the basic template for today's partnerships and also offer accountability lessons.

An early form of partnership, highly oriented toward a security model was the colonial charted company. These companies have a long history and varied in form and extent both between colonial empires and within specific ones. The

French and German companies, for example, presented themselves as universalizing whereas the British and Dutch companies thought themselves more accommodating of local circumstances. In reality, both forged security-oriented public-private partnerships that employed a mix of force, coercion, and cooperation to advance interests.

In proto-Malaysia, when the British landed on what would eventually be called Penang, they declared it *terra nullius*. Although they recorded no inhabitants for legal purposes, in reality the island had a pre-existing population. Thus, at its foundation the first contact was marked by an erasure of existence that carried with it certain expansionary and control-based legal privileges. In other words, an act of violence was the foundation of the chartered companies' multi-nationality among other public-private colonial corporate forms.

Many colonial chartered companies had limited military capacity and, in places like China, faced more powerful land-based armies than they could themselves muster. Where settlement colonies were not desired or feasible, what emerged were commercial colonies. Many of these were formulated through the laws of unequal treaties.

Colonial chartered companies—themselves partnership-based—often extended their partnership composition to include local inhabitants into their governance structures. This extension, sometimes referred to as indirect rule, meant a broadening of the partnership dynamic to accommodate the real practical limits of a solely violence-based model. Nonetheless, it was often the threat of force of the partnership itself, combined with the added coercive power of local allies, that aggrandized and maintained the charter companies' powers. Thus these partnership-based institutions were prototypical institutions of privatized violence.

Moreover, they were prototypical in their ultimate demise. One of the central features of partnership-based models is a convergence of interests among partners at the outset of a project. Convergence may be the product of cooperation, coercion, or force. Over the life of a partnership, however, interests may begin to diverge. The ability to retain the partnership basis by adapting to this tendency to unravel is an indicator of its durability. Once divergence comes into play, the partnership may disaggregate and prior allies may have an interest in asserting oppositional stances towards one another. This was true with national independence movements; it was also the case during the French Revolution when free zones, another institution of public-private partnership, were shut down. There, the free zone system had been formulated and maintained to advance transnational commercial interests. However, French citizens, opposed to the concession to foreign commerce that the zone system represented, drove the domestic political machinery to exit the partnership and thus extinguish the country's free zone system.[3]

[3] Richard S Thoman, *Free Ports and Foreign-Trade Zones* (Cambridge, MA: Cornell Maritime Press, 1956) 16.

Railroads are another early partnership-based example. They came into play and thrived in the mid 19th and early 20th century throughout the world. Railroads gave rise to the Gilded Age capitalists and also helped move the US stock market from a small gathering under a tree into a fundamental pillar of the US and global economy. Although geographically dispersed, they often shared common financiers or were carried out by construction firms that sought opportunities unbounded by geography. The control over labour migration with the railroads too often crossed national borders. For example, groups of Chinese workers were delivered to Malaysia and to the United States to lay lines. Notably, projects cycled from public to private, private to public, many times, almost everywhere. Furthermore, it was the excesses of these partnerships, their structural inefficiencies that led the United States to seriously curtail their use during the New Deal period.

When railroads were extended through public-private partnerships, mixing nationalities of firms and financiers, into South America, they often usurped indigenous land. For instance, in Mexico, as John Coatsworth has shown, companies and governments partnered to break up communal indigenous land that was needed for rail expansion. Communal land posed a challenge for railways that had difficulty negotiating with a consolidated block of indigenous interests. Thus, through land reform, they broke up the land holdings, individuating plots. As a result of this partnership-based land reform effort, railway companies were able then to buy up land from individuals. Although this particular effort ultimately failed when a challenge was brought to local courts, this mode of individuating land was used elsewhere effectively.[4] Thus, transnational partnership-based railways, made their business plan conditioned upon breaking up communities and undermining social ties through coercive means.

Moreover, the history of railroads is characterized by this convergence of interests among financiers, railway firms, and governments. It is equally a narrative of their inability to keep this alliance together. As populations grew increasingly intolerant of the negative externalities of the railway partnerships, politicians found themselves reined in by their constituencies. The partnerships ultimately unravelled in part because of a basic principal-agent problem, a point revisited in the conclusion of this chapter.

Privatization, the Second World War and after

The most significant 20th century US privatization occurred in the defence sector with the mass privatization of the military during the Second World War. The scale of the wartime effort was unprecedented in the United States and involved an extensive contract-based effort whereby private companies carried

[4] John Coatsworth, 'Railroads, Landholding, and Agrarian Protest in the Early Porfiriato', *The Hispanic American Historical Review*, vol 54, no 1 (1974) 48.

out the defence function.[5] The war effort itself would have been inconceivable without this use of companies to wage it. The government and its military were not sufficiently built-up to fight a war at the needed scale. As a result, entrepreneurs quickly adapted from a civilian to a military economy.

This privatization did not end after the war, although many post-war lawsuits were filed arising from outstanding disputes between the government and the firms with which it contracted during the war. This model of privatization persisted into the Cold War period. Here, too, the government made extensive use of federal contracts with private companies. The resultant public-private network of enmeshed government agencies and firms spread across sectors and products.

The impact of this relationship on the public interest was debated within the academy and in politics. It was the central theme of President Dwight Eisenhower's famous 'military-industrial complex' speech in which he called for transparency, scrutiny and accountability.[6]

Regardless of the normative assessment, the mixing of public and private resulted in a system of 'federalism by contract', a term used by Don K Price to refer to the parallel mixing within the science sector.[7] Here, the defence function was carried out through a pyramidal system in which the government sat at the apex and sequential downward layers were administered by private firms, sometimes in partnership with the government. In situations in which a limited number of private firms were given responsibility by government overseers to carry out defence functions through large numbers of subcontractors, these companies, as Michael Reagan argues, served as de facto anti-trust administrators. Reagan further charted how private companies often sat on government committees devoted to handing out contracts as well as how the United States financed lobbying efforts to win awards.[8]

During the reconstruction efforts that followed the 2003 Iraq war, we saw a return of this basic pyramidal contractual scheme. A small number of construction companies, notably Bechtel and Halliburton, appeared to monopolize control over the reconstruction effort. However, this cartelization of control over Iraq reconstruction was belied by the existence of a vast subcontracting system. The United States Agency for International Development's second contract with Bechtel, for example, mandated subcontracting out almost 90 percent of its work to Iraqi firms.[9]

[5] For a bibliography of legal literature on Second World War defence procurement see Law Branch, The Army Library, *Bibliography on Government Procurement and Contractual Procedure and Related Materials* (March 1953/Revised March 1954).

[6] President Dwight D Eisenhower, 'The Military Industrial Complex Speech' (1961), available at <http://avalon.law.yale.edu/20th_century/eisenhower001.asp>

[7] Don K Price, *Government and Science: Their Dynamic Relation in American Democracy* (New York: New York University Press, 1954) 65–94.

[8] Michael D Reagan, *The Managed Economy* (Oxford: Oxford University Press, 1967) 193.

[9] Contract No SPU-C-00-04-00001-00 between USAID and Bechtel National Inc (1 May 2004) H15 Safety of Contractor Personnel.

At the same time, the history of the privatization of violence within the Cold War period is not a simple story of inefficiencies, lack of accountability, and public interest shortfalls. The Internet emerged out of a public-private partnership. Indeed, the growth of the US high tech economy is traceable in large part to the licensing schemes established between defence agencies and private firms that allowed for the commercial use of the products of military contracts. Thus, the foundation of the late 20th century and early 21st century United States and, arguably, global economy is in large part a defence-based public-private partnership. We sometimes call this the 'peace dividend'.

At the same time, this history is also a cautionary tale of the security threats produced by the privatization of the defence function, of security and the production of violence, alongside its commercialization. Eisenhower was not the only one to make vocal calls for accountability. Efforts to hold public-private relationships accountable to the public interest date back to the New Deal Functionalists and Realists who concerned themselves with non-defence-sector public-private partnerships, from Morris Cohen's famous work on the public basis of private contract[10] to Robert Hale's argument that private law emerges out of public power[11] and even into the subsequent work of Louis Jaffe with his trenchant critique of *Carter Coal*.[12]

After the Cold War, the government's role as provider of welfare state functions has declined (at least in the United States). At the same time, however, there has been a resurgence of this defence- or security-based model of public-private partnering. It has spread to almost every corner of the world and throughout virtually every sector of our global economy.

Since the late 1970s, this defence sector mode spread more widely with the onset of what we now call Thatcherism. The model was adopted within the United States by Ronald Reagan, and then adapted under Bill Clinton as a part of Al Gore's efforts to modernize government. It has spread globally not only through the use of private military and security companies (PMSC), but also throughout emerging economies with the help of foreign aid and pushed gently along by International Monetary Fund conditionalities. In the United States we see it in the birth of Silicon Valley and Route 128, as well as in US foreign commercial policy towards South-east Asia in particular. Thus privatization has driven a dramatic extension of the Second World War partnership-based model into most walks of life. These privatizations of civilian and military life are mutually reinforcing and highly integrated at the commercial level.

[10] Morris R Cohen, 'Property and Sovereignty', *Cornell Law Quarterly* vol 13 (1927–8) 827; Morris R Cohen, 'The Basis of Contract', *Harvard Law Review* vol 46 (1932–3) 562.

[11] Robert L Hale 'Coercion and Distribution in a Supposedly Non-Coercive State', *Political Science Quarterly*, vol 38 (1923) 470; Robert L Hale, 'Force and the State: A Comparison of "Political" and "Economic" Compulsion', *Columbia Law Review*, vol 1935 (1935) 149.

[12] Louis L Jaffe, 'Law Making by Private Groups', *Harvard Law Review*, vol 51 (1937–8) 201.

Privatization in the 21st century is thus premised upon public-private partnerships whereby governments and firms share responsibilities for financing, building, and operating initiatives. In both defence and security, these partnerships are typically transnational.

Producing violence through public-private partnerships in civilian context

Even if we retain the term 'privatization', we should see privatization itself as created by public-private partnerships, rather than a move of activities from the 'public' and into the 'private' domain. Nominally privatized projects include a mix of public and private participation in financing, construction or operation of a privatized enterprise.[13]

The most obvious contractual example of this point is the common privatization form, the build-operate-transfer (BOT) agreement. Its characterization as a privatization device is belied by the fact that the contract form moves the provision of public services into the private sector for a period only to return them ultimately back into public hands. Another example of the blending of public and private functions is a common privatization arrangement in which the financiers include a government as well as a private investment bank or a hedge fund. The construction and operation stage might also involve a mix of government and private companies, contractors and subcontractors. Places like Iraq and elsewhere highlight the transnational nature of these partnerships with the integration of public and private militaries. Kate McCoy has demonstrated how the multinational makeup of these security forces adapts itself to specific regional exigencies creating a distinctly multinational aspect to operations in which language skills and cultural currency become criteria for security force composition.

Considerations of security and privatization also need to broaden the conception of what counts as 'security'. It is far from clear where responsibility productively lies when we refer to the 'privatization of security'. That is, if the sector itself is created through public-private partnerships, then it might not make sense to single out one or two aspects of this partnership. We tend to focus, for instance, on firms and governments, but ignore the financing of these activities by private investment entities by private equity, or the advice given by law firms that may service multiple sectors supplying common contractual forms. Moreover, it may be that large firms charged with carrying out projects, such as construction firms or service providers, have integrated their practices to encompass a range of sectors.

[13] See generally Likosky, *Law, Infrastructure and Human Rights*, n 1 above.

The need to ascertain the nature of this blend of public and private is of more than empirical importance. It is also central to conceiving an accountability strategy. If we seek social change, then which actor(s) should we target to drive it? Should we hold Blackwater or the US government accountable? What about the banks and the law firms that service them, or the multinational consultancy firms? Does an argument of service providers strike us as absurd? If so, then why? Is it rooted in our notion of professionalization? Does it make sense to revisit codes of professional ethics as a wedge for driving greater accountability? What of the international capital markets that in part finance this activity? Is it appropriately rule-bound or inappropriately based upon arbitrage? And, what of permissive securities regulation that creates a dynamic that encourages and indeed incentivizes this model of public-private-organization?

Two short case studies help explore these questions. The first is a natural gas pipeline project in Peru that did not, on its face, have a security component. The second is the US high tech economy, which persists in its narrative of garage engineers yet in fact has its foundations firmly in the Department of Defense.

Privatized violence and pipelines: Camisea[14]

The Camisea pipeline would appear to be a generic non-military privatization scenario. However, violence played a foundational role. The project was to build a natural gas pipeline running through the Peruvian rainforest to bring gas from reserves in the rainforest to the capital city of Lima, and then to distribute this gas domestically as well as internationally. The project was a transnational public-private partnership financed by a group of international investment banks with loans from various governments, including the United States, and intergovernmental organizations, notably the Inter-American Development Bank, to sweeten the pot. The companies that carried out the project were Italian, French, and Brazilian among others. Private investment banks such as Citigroup also played a prime role. Companies like Shell and Mobil contributed as did Tractebel. Many protests targeted these partners. The campaigns were spearheaded primarily by international non-governmental organizations (NGOs) and Peruvian civil society groupings. This targeting was made all the more difficult because banks and companies entered and exited the scene throughout the project lifecycle. This created the convergence/divergence dynamic discussed above.

The entrance and exit of major players within a privatization project is significant. That is, if we seek to locate accountability responsibilities on a particular security company or financial institution, are we confident that they might not just exit the project? This would leave a situation in which large

[14] This section is largely based upon chapter six of Likosky, *Law, Infrastructure and Human Rights*, n 1 above (see references within that text).

amounts of capital have been invested into a campaign that no longer has a fixed target. For example, what happens if too many eggs get put in the Blackwater basket and the industry itself along with government simply adapts and sustains, evading accountability for the mercenary enterprise itself? Furthermore, it might be that these campaign energies are not easily transferable to secondary targets. The organic nature of public-private partnerships has bedevilled campaigners throughout the world.

In the case of Camisea, one campaign by NGOs argued that the project planners aimed to have a pipeline run near an isolated indigenous group. Campaigners made a case that this community would be vulnerable to the spread of disease from pipeline workers, because they had lived in geographic isolation and thus had not built up resistance to diseases—much in the same way that initial encounters with indigenous groups in the Americas resulted in the decimation of indigenous populations as much by disease as swords.

Camisea's planners ignored this warning. They proceeded with the pipeline along the planned geography. Over 50 percent of the indigenous community died of resultant disease. This is then an instance of the privatization of violence occurring squarely in the civilian realm.

Where is the locus of responsibility when the partnership is transnational and the makeup changes over time beyond the practicalities of effective targeting? The Camisea case study underscores the strategic difficulties faced by reformers and opponents. Given the massive scale and financial resources of Camisea, campaigners must pick their battles. Moreover, while actor-based targeting often proves the most effective means for driving concessions through naming and shaming strategies, it also brings with it significant challenges as demerits affix to actors, who may exit the scene, rather than projects. Nonetheless, Camisea also demonstrates the effectiveness of partnership-directed campaigns, as NGOs and their local allies drove the establishment of an ombudsman to hear complaints and also forced the incorporation of local groups into project decision-making.

Privatizing security: Dual-use technologies

As indicated earlier, one of the main products of the Cold War defence build-up was the creation of the US high tech economy. Ownership of many of the high tech commodities was shared at the time between government and industry, deployed for public and private purposes. It was more than garage entrepreneurs. Law was central—for instance, intellectual property law. In other words, the government granted companies the right to commercialize these defence subsidized technologies. The Department of Defense then used them for its own purposes.

When the Cold War ended, the peace dividend resulted in a shift in the nature and function of the US military generally, but also in the US government's active promotion of US military technology, notably under President

George H W Bush and, more significantly and prolifically, under the Clinton and George W Bush administrations.

So-called 'dual use' technologies are those designed and produced for military purposes as well as civilian. This promotion became a basic feature of US foreign commercial policy. It is a partnership-based model promoted not only through the Department of Defense, but also through the United States Export-Import Bank and through its Overseas Private Investment Corporation, as well as through intergovernmental organizations like the World Bank Group, the United Nations Industrial Development Organization, the United Nations Conference on Trade and Development, the Organization for Economic Cooperation and Development, and others. Public partners, namely the United States, also revised tariff laws and allowed loopholes in environmental regulations to facilitate a de facto export subsidy. The relaxing of export controls and government subsidies for US firms going abroad put this partnership into practice.

Similarly, when telecommunications technologies were mobilized by US multinational firms to build a fibre optic cable around the globe to facilitate the global information highway, it happened with a government boost through the US Export-Import Bank. In other words, telecommunications companies went abroad and were able to capitalize on opportunities because of this partnership foundation. The US Export-Import Bank underwrote crucial political risks that would have otherwise crippled the business plan itself.

In 2007, the media was full of accounts of how democratic activists and religious leaders used blogs, emails and uploads to fight for freedom against the military state in Myanmar (Burma). Activists used the Internet to connect with allies around the world and to convince others to take notice, successfully coalescing international pressure. Embarrassed and exposed to public scrutiny, the Burmese military shut down the channel of communications—the Internet.

When President Bush responded in an address to the UN General Assembly, he reinforced the idea that a battle is underway between US-supported dissidents overseas and foreign dictators. Soon thereafter, the Burmese Foreign Minister took the bait, calling foreign intervention into his state the 'ugly head of neo-colonialism'. However familiar this recurring foreign policy narrative sounds, in reality, the protagonists prove far more enigmatic, the reality far more complex and disturbing. The international media outlets and democratic activists have pointed to the role of Total, the French oil company enmeshed with its own government on the partnership-based model, in propping up the Burmese junta. Caught up in its own freedom narrative, the United States overlooked the role of its own Silicon Valley firm, Fortinet, manufacturer of the technological arms used by the junta to limit internet access in the first place. This was accomplished through a series of licensing agreements designed to establish a 'don't ask don't tell' system. Thus, US licensing law, the public foundation of these transnational commercial high tech activities, helped forge a partnership between US technology and the Burmese junta.

Whereas colonial chartered companies sometimes travelled with the flag of their country of origin flying from their ships, today's multinationals offer themselves up as autonomous private actors. In reality, however, these firms are partners with government.

Another example can be seen in the lead up to the 2008 Beijing Olympics. At the time, somewhat timid concern was expressed at the export of US high technology surveillance equipment to China to ensure security.[15] This included defence-subsidized products migrating through licensing agreements into the private sector.

The roots of the Olympic controversy are traceable to the Clinton administration. Although President Clinton worked hard to open up trade relations between the United States and China through the granting of permanent most-favoured-nation status and a negotiated entrance of China into the World Trade Organization, he had to overcome serious Congressional concerns with greater openness in light of the 1989 Tiananmen Square incident. Under a sanctions regime adopted after Tiananmen, the export of such security-based products into China had been forbidden. Another trade-off was increased broadcasting of the democracy/freedom message into China by Radio Free Asia. Together, commercial engagement and the promotion of democracy, formed the cornerstone of the US foreign policy of peaceful evolution.

In the run up to the Olympics, US high tech security firms expressed concern that they might miss out on commercial opportunities to European rivals who did not face similar constraints. Under the US Tiananmen sanctions regime, a waiver of the export control could be granted by the Commerce Department. At the time of the Olympics, within the Commerce Department, the Bureau of Industry and Security was delegated the authority to refuse or grant waivers. US security firms applied for waivers and many were granted. As a result, controversial biometric technology now allows the Chinese government to employ face-recognition software to track potentially disruptive individuals. Many worry that this securitization of privatized technology will result in many post-Olympic uses.

Focus during the Olympics was mainly centred around a number of high tech firms actively seeking out Olympic contracts, such as Honeywell, General Electric and United Technologies. Once again though, these are transnational public-private partnerships. Hedge funds, presumably bringing together multinational pools of government and private money, are financing these technologies, which are also, at least in part, traceable to the Department of Defense Cold War build-up and tied to more recent 'war on terror' contracts.

As within almost all walks of privatization, the circulation of individuals between the public and private sectors only reinforces the synergies. William

[15] The organization Human Rights in China has extensively documented the human rights issues tied to the Olympics.

Reinsch, for example, was Under Secretary of Commerce during the Clinton administration and is now president of the industry association in this area. In 2008 he expressed concern that the government must take care not to develop rules which limit US opportunities, ceding them to foreign competitors.[16]

Conclusion: Accountability, privatization, and violence

Given this web of public and private activity, how do we determine the locus of accountability for privatized violence from mercenaries to road projects? This chapter has attempted to place the PMSC issue into a broader context. It suggested that this issue is also traceable to both defence sector and post-Cold War privatizations. It argued that, in focusing on those aspects of public-private partnerships that produce violence, a comparative approach is best suited to identify and define culpability and thus inform our decisions about accountability.

Privatization of the armed forces is also carried out through transnational public-private partnerships. In addition, to determine the actual responsibility of the various partners, we must also think about the strategic issue. That is, should we be targeting companies, governments, hedge funds, investment banks, or others? And, within these classes of actors, what do we do when some enter and then exit the scene briefly over the life of a project? Unless one focuses on the transnational aspects of these activities—both in the sense of the geography as well as the participants—then even the most vigilant internal or external reformer risks being outmanoeuvred.

Many of the fundamental questions about accountability of public-private partnerships were asked by the Functionalists, Cohen, Hale, Jaffe, and others in the early 20th century. The approach devised by them and refined by subsequent generations of politicians and academics is usefully applied to today's military and civilian privatizations.

First, we must start from the premise that both public and private involvement in the economy is inherently political and thus justified upon their abilities to promote the public interest. They are simply different means to accomplish the same ends. Importantly, for these transnational security projects, we must figure out, at least operationally, how to define the 'public interest'. That is, are we talking about the US public interest when it contracts a firm to provide security operations in Iraq? Or, are we talking about the Iraqi public interest? Is it important to scrutinize how these interests may at times legitimately diverge and its consequence for accountability?

Secondly, we need to overcome our empirical deficit. We know very little about how these partnerships are put together. We do not know, at least in a systematic way, who finances them. We have a growing number of security firms

[16] Keith Bradsher, 'Keeping an Eye on China's Security', *New York Times*, 31 January 2008.

but do we know who gives them bank loans and who underwrites their activities? We know that they live, in part, on government contracts, but most also rely upon private financiers. Are these private financiers simply investment banks and hedge funds and so wholly private? Or is the money sitting in these banks and funds itself not only multinational but also inclusive of government cash? Moreover, what about the firms themselves? Have we systematically produced knowledge of the similarities and differences between the firms, both where they are incorporated and their staffing choices? Do we track the mix of governments and firms involved in certain security operations as they evolve over time? Do we know which firms work primarily for one government versus another? Do we know the geographical reach of all firms, their strategic business plans?

Thirdly, we must examine the empirical record to determine whether it promotes or retards the public interest. This involves a retrospective effort as well as a forward looking one. For this reason, we must take care to engage in a discussion about what is the optimal institution (or group of institutions) to accomplish accountability, both forward and backward. Is it the courts or the executive, domestic agencies or foreign or international, contracts or regulations, public or private?

This inquiry into the transnational public-private basis of violence and security, both in the civilian and military contexts, is nascent. The public interest remains vaguely defined, the partial empirical record is mainly journalistic with some important help from government inquiries, and we have yet to figure out how to determine accountability effectively *ex post*, while our *ex ante* approach is clearly wanting. Partnerships have long been vulnerable when they produce violence illegitimately. At these points principal-agent relationships tend to become attenuated and opportunities for usurpation of control over public partners become increasingly available.

2

The responsibility of states

Olivier De Schutter

In March 2008, Mr José Luis Gómez del Prado, President of the Working Group on the Use of Mercenaries as Means of Violating Human Rights and Impeding the Rights of Peoples to Self-determination, made the following appeal to governments:

> Keeping in mind the difficulties experienced by war-torn States in regulating and controlling private military and security companies, a considerable part of the responsibility falls upon States from which transnational companies export military and security services. We therefore call upon States where exporting companies are registered to regulate and oversee private military and security companies; not to grant immunity to their personnel; and to investigate and bring to justice those security guards who may have committed crimes and human rights violations in Iraq or in other places.[1]

The relationship between governments and private military and security companies (PMSCs) can take a number of forms. PMSCs can be registered in one state and provide services to another state, for example, by assisting the armed forces of that other state in the performance of their duties, whether on the territory of that state or on the territory of a third state. Alternatively, PMSCs may be providing services to the armed forces of the state in which they are incorporated, whether at home or abroad. They may also be recruited by private actors, particularly corporations in need of better security than that which can be provided by the state on the territory of which they operate.[2] Following upon the suggestion of Gómez del Prado, this chapter examines a question which is raised in a subset of those situations, where a PMSC operates in a state other than that of its nationality, referred to here as its 'home state'.[3]

[1] José Luis Gómez del Prado, President of the Working Group on the use of Mercenaries as Means of Violating Human Rights and Impeding the Rights of Peoples to Self-determination, Statement before the Human Rights Council, 7th session, 10 March 2008, Geneva.

[2] For an attempt to stipulate the principles to be observed in such a situation, see See Bureau of Democracy, Human Rights, and Labor, US Department of State, Voluntary Principles on Security and Human Rights (2000), available at <http://www.voluntaryprinciples.org> (adopted at the initiative of the governments of the United States and Britain, companies in the extractive and energy sectors, and non-governmental organizations).

[3] For the criteria for the determination of the nationality of a legal person, see the discussion of the active personality principle below.

The chapter asks whether, under international law, the home state of a PMSC is obliged to control that company; whether that state must allow its courts to adjudicate claims filed against such a company or its employees for any violations of human rights or of international humanitarian law; and, if these duties do exist, how they may be implemented taking into account the sovereignty of the state on the territory of which the PMSC operates (the 'host state'). Whether or not they are 'transnational corporations' in the classic meaning of the expression,[4] companies operating across jurisdictions can only be effectively controlled if the home state contributes to the efforts of the host state at regulating their activities. This is particularly true as regards PMSCs. These companies typically operate in conflict and weak governance zones, where the regulatory apparatus is weak or nonexistent and therefore unable to effectively prevent abuses of human rights by private actors. The role of the home state of PMSCs is therefore crucial in order to ensure that there is no impunity for these abuses.

In rather exceptional situations, the employees of a PMSC may be considered as organs of the state whose armed forces they assist. That would be the case, for instance, when they form part of such armed forces within the meaning of Article 4(A)(1) of the Third Geneva Convention[5]—that is, when they constitute armed forces, a militia or a volunteer corps within the official armed forces. In such cases, and quite independently of the question of whether the Geneva Conventions apply, their acts are those of the state of whose armed forces they form a part: there is no doubt that the state may be responsible for such acts under international law. However, the employees of PMSCs will not be considered agents of the state if they form an independent militia, as in the situation envisaged by Article 4(A)(2) of the same Convention, or if they are 'civilians accompanying the armed forces without being members thereof' under Article 4(A)(4).[6] In these far more frequent situations, the question of state responsibility appears in a totally different light. For, in the current state of international law, it is only under narrowly defined conditions that private persons or entities—persons or entities who are not state organs according to the internal law of the state concerned—may engage the responsibility of that state.

[4] Transnational corporations are traditionally defined as corporations which own, control, and manage assets in a state other than their country of origin. See Peter Muchlinski, *Multinational Enterprises and the Law* (London: Blackwell, 1995) 12. Private military and security companies, which are the focus of this paper, may fall under this definition. In most cases however, the 'transnationalisation' of their activities does not result in the establishment of an investment nexus between the company, headquartered or incorporated in one state, and another state where it operates: instead, services are provided in that other state's territory, simply by the posting of employees in that state, often for short-term missions.

[5] Geneva Convention Relative to the Treatment of Prisoners of War (12 August 1949) 75 UNTS 135, entered into force 21 October 1950 (Third Geneva Convention).

[6] PMSCs recruited in order to provide surveillance of civilian infrastructures, for instance, would fall under this category.

What are these conditions? In certain rare instances, a private person or entity may be under the 'complete dependence' of the state. It may then be treated as a de facto state agent.[7] Apart from that hypothesis, the Articles on Responsibility of States for Internationally Wrongful Acts, adopted in 2001 by the International Law Commission (ILC)[8] (hereinafter 'Articles on State Responsibility'), identify essentially four instances where the acts of a private actor may be attributed to the state for the purposes of engaging its international responsibility. Such attribution may occur where the private entity 'is empowered by the law of that State to exercise elements of the governmental authority [provided that entity] is acting in that capacity in the particular instance' (Article 5); where the private entity 'is in fact acting on the instructions of, or under the direction or control of, that State in carrying out the conduct,' which may give rise to international responsibility (Article 8); where the entity 'is in fact exercising elements of the governmental authority in the absence or default of the official authorities and in circumstances such as to call for the exercise of those elements of authority' (Article 9); and, finally, conduct which is not attributable to a state under any of the preceding doctrines 'shall nevertheless be considered an act of that State under international law if and to the extent that the State acknowledges and adopts the conduct in question as its own' (Article 11).

This seems relatively meagre, especially insofar as PMSCs are most often hired by private entities, and not governments, which limits the usefulness of the ground of imputation referred to in Article 8.[9] However, if we move from the realm of general international law to the province of international human rights law, not one, but two distinct obligations of the state appear to be at stake: apart from the obligation not to commit any violation of the human rights which that state is internationally bound to respect—which then leads to the question of whether the behaviour of the PMSC is imputable to the state of origin, according to the principles of state responsibility—a second and distinct obligation is the positive obligation of the state to adopt measures that protect human rights from the threats posed by the acts of private actors, including PMSCs. These two obligations ought to be clearly distinguished from one another. By definition, the failure to protect human rights (that is, the failure to comply with the latter of these obligations) consists of an omission on the part of state organs—whether legislative, executive, or judicial—and no question of

[7] This is discussed further below.

[8] Report of the International Law Commission on the Work of Its Fifty-Third Session, 2001, UN Doc A/56/10.

[9] It has been stated by a member of the International Committee of the Red Cross that 80% of the contracts of PMSCs are in fact with non-state entities. See Emanuela Gillard, 'The Position Under International Humanitarian Law', in Marc Vuijlsteke and Peter Stroobarts (eds), *Proceedings of the Bruges Colloquium: Private Military/Security Companies Operating in Situations of Armed Conflict* Collegium No 36 (2007) 32, available at <http://www.coleurop.be/file/content/publications/pdf/Collegium%2036.pdf>.

attribution is raised. Just as a state may be responsible for failing to adopt the measures that could have reasonably been expected to prevent a loss of life under its jurisdiction, without the implication that the act of any particular murderer will be attributed to the state, so can the state be responsible for failing to control the private contractor effectively, without it being necessary to attribute to the state the acts of that private entity.[10] If the notion of 'imputability' is invoked in this context, it should be treated as little more than a metaphor: what is meant is simply that the behaviour of the private entity has brought to light a failure of the state itself, in that it did not do enough to prevent the behaviour from occurring.

Thus, in order to identify any responsibility of the home state in controlling the behaviour of the employees of a PMSC, we need to ask whether the behaviour of that corporation can be attributed to the state and, if it cannot, whether the state is under an obligation to protect human rights that are affected by the acts of that corporation. Whether we follow the first or the second branch of this alternative affects the way we think about the other issues related to identifying the contours of such state responsibility. The next section discusses conditions under which the acts of PMSCs may be attributed to a state. The subsequent section then examines the scope of states' obligations to protect human rights outside their national territory by virtue of extraterritorial jurisdiction.

Attribution to the state

The international law of state responsibility defines restrictively the conditions under which persons or entities who are not state organs according to the internal law of the state concerned[11] may engage the responsibility of that state. Our concern here is to clarify the kind of relations which may exist between a state and a PMSC justifying imputing to the former the acts of the latter.[12] As regards PMSCs, both the state which the PMSC assists and the state under the jurisdiction of which the PMSC is registered could potentially be found liable where the PMSC:

[10] See Robert McCorquodale and Penelope Simons, 'Responsibility Beyond Borders: State Responsibility for Extraterritorial Violations by Corporations of International Human Rights Law', *Modern Law Review*, vol 70 (2007) 618.

[11] As mentioned above, the employees of PMSCs which are integrated into the armed forces of the state should be considered as organs of that state, which is therefore responsible for their conduct.

[12] For earlier attempts in doctrine, see McCorquodale and Simons, 'Responsibility Beyond Borders', 598–625; Danwood Mzikenge Chirwa, 'The Doctrine of State Responsibility as a Potential Means of Holding Private Actors Accountable for Human Rights', *Melbourne Journal of International Law*, vol 5, no 1 (2004); Chia Lehnardt, 'Private Military Companies and State Responsibility', in Simon Chesterman and Chia Lehnardt (eds), *From Mercenaries to Markets: The Rise and Regulation of Private Military Companies* (Oxford: Oxford University Press, 2007) 139.

(1) is under the 'complete dependence' of the state;

(2) is empowered by the law of the state to exercise elements of governmental authority and acts under those powers in the particular instance concerned; or

(3) is in fact acting 'on the instructions of, or under the direction or control of', the state in carrying out the conduct that allegedly gives rise to international responsibility, as stipulated in Article 8 of the Articles on State Responsibility.

All three grounds of attribution may be invoked in order to impute the acts of the PMSC to the state that has hired the services of the company, or to the state where it is registered, depending on the circumstances of each case.

Two other grounds of attribution should be mentioned. First, where the PMSC 'is in fact exercising elements of the governmental authority in the absence or default of the official authorities and in circumstances such as to call for the exercise of those elements of authority',[13] its acts may be attributed either to the territorially sovereign state, whose failure to fulfil its functions leads to the void which private actors seek to fill, or to the foreign state that deployed its armed forces on a portion of the territory and acquired the status of an Occupying Power.[14] Secondly, as recalled by Article 11 of the Articles on State Responsibility, conduct that in principle is not attributable to a state 'shall nevertheless be considered an act of that State under international law if and to the extent that the State acknowledges and adopts the conduct in question as its own'. While this doctrine has a solid foundation in general international law,[15] it too will have only a marginal role to play in the kinds of situations we are concerned with here, since it requires that the state authorities approve of the abuses committed by the corporation and encourage it to perpetuate them. In what follows, we leave aside these subsidiary doctrines of attribution, and focus instead on the three doctrines of attribution that are most relevant to the situation of PMSCs.

Complete dependence

Where a private person or entity is under the 'complete dependence' of the state, it may be treated as a de facto state agent. This proposition was put forward by

[13] Articles on State Responsibility, n 8 above, art 9.

[14] This is without prejudice to the direct liability of such private actors, which could be engaged in such situations. See 'Risk Awareness Tool for Multinational Enterprises in Weak Governance Zones', Organisation for Economic Co-operation and Development, adopted 8 June 2006, available at <http://www.oecd.org/dataoecd/26/21/36885821.pdf> (guiding companies' behaviour in such circumstances).

[15] *United States Diplomatic and Consular Staff in Tehran (United States v Iran)*, ICJ Reports 1980, 3.

the International Court of Justice (ICJ) in the *Bosnian Genocide* case, where it noted that

> persons, groups of persons or entities may, for purposes of international responsibility, be equated with State organs even if that status does not follow from internal law, provided that in fact the persons, groups or entities act in 'complete dependence' on the State, of which they are ultimately merely the instrument. In such a case, it is appropriate to look beyond legal status alone, in order to grasp the reality of the relationship between the person taking action, and the State to which he is so closely attached as to appear to be nothing more than its agent: any other solution would allow States to escape their international responsibility by choosing to act through persons or entities whose supposed independence would be purely fictitious.[16]

Although this position goes beyond the previous case law of the ICJ, it nevertheless was seen as a compromise position in the context in which it was put forward. In 1999, the International Criminal Tribunal for the former Yugoslavia (ICTY) had used an 'overall control' test in order to decide whether the Bosnian Serbs were parties to an international armed conflict for the purposes of applying certain provisions of international humanitarian law. The ICTY had asked what degree of state control was required under international law over organized military groups for the application of such provisions of international humanitarian law to be justified. According to the ICTY, in order for an armed conflict to be considered 'international', it is required that a state 'wields overall control over the [private group waging war], not only by equipping and financing the group, but also by coordinating or helping in the general planning of its military activity'; however, the ICTY considered that 'it is not necessary that, in addition, the State should also issue, either to the head or to members of the group, instructions for the commission of specific acts contrary to international law'.[17]

While it does not go as far, the 'complete dependence' test referred to by the ICJ in the *Bosnian Genocide* case nevertheless constitutes a departure from the strict doctrine adopted in *Nicaragua v United States* (and subsequently reaffirmed in Article 8 of the Articles on State Responsibility).[18] Indeed, the 'complete dependence' test allows the attribution of acts by a private entity to a state even though it might be impossible to identify any instructions given by the state to that entity, or any direction or control exercised by the state, in the particular instance concerned.[19] This doctrine thus could be relied upon if it

[16] *Case Concerning the Application of the Convention on the Prevention and Punishment of the Crime of Genocide (Bosnia and Herzegovina v Serbia and Montenegro)* ('the *Bosnian Genocide* case'), ICJ Reports 2007, paras 391–4, particularly para 392.

[17] *Prosecutor v Tadic*, International Criminal Tribunal for the former Yugoslavia, 15 July 1999, IT-94-1-A, para 120.

[18] *Military and Paramilitary Activities in and against Nicaragua (Nicaragua v United States)*, ICJ Reports 1986, para 115.

[19] See also, for a similar criterion, European Court of Human Rights, *Ilascu and ors v Moldova and Russia*, App No 48787/99, 8 July 2004, paras 393–4.

could be proven that a particular PMSC constitutes a mere façade used by the state in order to pursue its interests. It would not be sufficient to demonstrate that the PMSC has been supported by the state, for instance, through insurance guarantees or diplomatic efforts in support of the bids of the company. It would need to be shown that the state is in fact acting through the company that lacks any will of its own, and whose commercial interests, for instance, are secondary to the interests of the state which its activities serve. Attribution of violations of international law to the state whose armed forces the PMSC assists may occur, for example, when the 'private' contractor is a mere fiction behind which that state seeks to shield itself from accusations of committing such violations directly through its armed forces, as through the use of paramilitary forces closely linked to the state apparatus.[20]

Empowered by law

In addition to the circumstance of being under 'complete dependence' of a state, attribution of PMSC acts to the state may be justified where the private entity 'is empowered by the law of that State to exercise elements of the governmental authority [provided that entity] is acting in that capacity in the particular instance'.[21] This provision ensures that the state will not escape liability by privatizing certain public or regulatory functions.[22] Although what constitutes 'governmental' functions will depend on a set of circumstances, including 'the particular society, its history and traditions',[23] it seems that even under the narrowest understanding of such functions, they should comprise law enforcement activities and the activities of the armed forces. Functions related to the maintenance of law and order may thus be considered to constitute elements of governmental authority for which the state should be held responsible even if it has chosen to delegate these functions to private entities. The acts of PMSCs whose agents are authorized to bear arms and use them in self-defence or in defence of private property or to arrest individuals and bring them to the police should therefore be seen as attributable to the state that chose to delegate such powers to the companies.

[20] See, eg, Maria McFarland Sánchez-Moreno, esq., 'Hearing Testimony, United States House of Representatives Committee on Foreign Affairs, Subcommittee on International Organizations, Human Rights, and Oversight, Subcommittee on the Western Hemisphere and the House Committee on Education and Labor, Subcommittee on Health, Employment, Labor and Pensions, and Subcommittee on Workforce Protections', 28 June 2007, available at <http://edlabor.house.gov/testimony/062807MariaMcFarlandTestimony.pdf>; Human Rights Watch, 'The "Sixth Division": Military-paramilitary Ties and US Policy in Colombia', September 2001, available at <http://www.hrw.org/reports/2001/colombia/>; *'Mapiripán Massacre' v Colombia*, Series C, No 132, Inter-American Court of Human Rights, 15 September 2005 (testimony of Federico Andreu Guzmán).

[21] Articles on State Responsibility, n 8 above, art 5.

[22] James Crawford, *The International Law Commission's Articles on State Responsibility. Introduction, Text and Commentaries* (Cambridge: Cambridge University Press, 2002) 100.

[23] Ibid. 101.

There is one important limitation to this principle, however. In order for the private entity's acts to be attributed to the state, the entity must have been explicitly empowered to exercise elements of governmental authority. Thus, a PMSC would not engage the liability of the state if it is simply acting in accordance with the general regulations which, in that state, define the conditions in which private citizens may use arms or which define the conditions for self-defence. For instance, where PMSC forces hired by corporations have used excessive force or intimidation against trade unionists or local communities—a pattern of abuse which is sadly common[24]—this could reveal a failure by that state to protect the rights of populations under its jurisdiction,[25] but this does not imply that the acts of those forces should be treated as if they were those of the state itself. On the other hand, for its acts to be attributable to the state, it is sufficient that the private entity has been explicitly delegated elements of governmental authority, whether or not this delegation of powers was effectuated through formal legislation defining their scope and conditions of exercise. As an illustration, the United States is responsible for the torture, intimidation, and humiliation of detainees by private contractors at the Abu Ghraib prison in Iraq, even in the absence of delegating legislation.[26]

Acting on instructions, or under direction or control

Another instance that allows for attribution of a private entity's actions to the state is where the private entity 'is in fact acting on the instructions of, or under the direction or control of, that state in carrying out the conduct' (Article 8). The rule has its origin in *Nicaragua v United States* where the Court considered that despite the strong support provided by the United States to the contras, the acts of the latter could only be attributed to the former if it could be proved that

[24] For instance, it has been reported that companies in Indonesia's pulp and paper industry have employed private gangs who intimidate or assault members of neighbouring communities. Human Rights Watch, 'Without Remedy: Human Rights Abuse and Indonesia's Pulp and Paper Industry' (2003). It has also been reported that private security forces have been involved in the use of excessive force against striking workers in China's heavy industries. Human Rights Watch, 'Paying the Price: Worker Unrest in Northeast China' (2002). Private security forces have also been involved in repressing protesters demonstrating against the exploitation of oilfields in Nigeria. Human Rights Watch, 'The Price of Oil: Corporate Responsibility and Human Rights Violations in Nigeria's Oil Producing Communities' (1999).

[25] On the obligation to protect human rights, see the section entitled 'Due diligence' below.

[26] Human Rights Watch, 'By the Numbers: Finding of the Detainee Abuse and Accountability Project' (2006); on the failure of the US to effectively combat the impunity of private contractors working in Iraq and Afghanistan, see Human Rights First, 'Private Security Contractors at War. Ending the Culture of Impunity' (2008). Therefore, the jurisdictional gaps in the Military Extraterritorial Jurisdiction Act should be filled, beyond the improvements of the Ronald W Reagan National Defence Authorization Act for FY 2005. US Congress, Military Extraterritorial Jurisdiction Act, PL 106–523, 18 USC § 3261, 114 Stat 2488 (22 November 2000); Ronald W Reagan National Defence Authorization Act for FY 2005, PL 108–375, 39 WCPD §1081, 118 Stat 1811(2004), amended by 18 USC §3267 (Supp IV 2004).

the United States 'had effective control of the military or paramilitary operations in the course of which the alleged violations were committed'.[27] It follows from this rule that however strongly a company is supported by the state, and however close its connections to the state may be, the conduct of the company will be attributable to the state only if the state controls the company's conduct in a specific instance.[28] This could be the case, for instance, if specific interrogation techniques are prescribed to be performed by private contractors under the agreement between them and the state, or if private contractors are encouraged, under rules of engagement agreed with the state, to commit violations of international humanitarian law or to use force disproportionately.

The question whether the acts of a corporation may be attributed to a state under the doctrine codified in Article 8 of the Articles on State Responsibility is entirely distinct, however, from the question of whether the state should exercise jurisdiction over the corporation—in other words, to regulate and adjudicate the conduct of the corporation in order to protect human rights. The next section examines the obligation to protect human rights as another, distinct source of state obligations.

Due diligence

In principle, the territorially competent state on whose national territory PMSCs operate—the host state—is obliged to effectively control their activities.[29] A state may fail to discharge this obligation, however. In so-called 'weak governance zones', the governmental apparatus may not be functioning, resulting in the host government being unable to exercise its authority effectively. The failure of the host state to control a PMSC may also be deliberate: the state may be itself the prime violator of human rights, and the PMSC present on its territory may be useful to the state (whether it acts under its direction or under those of another entity, for instance a private corporation) as an accomplice in the repression of the local communities.[30] When the host state is unable or unwilling to effectively protect the rights of its population against the acts of a

[27] *Nicaragua v United States*, n 18 above, para 115.

[28] Crawford, *State Responsibility*, n 22 above, 112–13.

[29] See, eg, *Social and Economic Rights Action Center and the Center for Economic and Social Rights v Nigeria*, Comm No 155/96, African Commission on Human and People's Rights (2001); *Velàsquez Rodrígueze*, Series C, No 4, Inter-American Court of Human Rights (1988); see also Stephanie Farrior, 'State Responsibility for Human Rights Abuses by Non-State Actors', *Proceedings of the American Society of International Law*, vol 92 (1998) 299.

[30] Occasionally, the degree of collaboration between the private agents and the armed forces of the state may be such that the failure of the state to effectively protect the rights of populations under its jurisdiction will be almost indistinguishable from its active implication in the violations committed, for instance, by paramilitary groups. See, eg, *'Mapiripán Massacre' v Colombia*, n 20 above, para 123.

PMSC registered abroad, is the home state under a duty to act? This question requires examining whether the obligation of states to protect human rights may apply to violations committed outside their national territory and whether states may seek to influence situations located outside their national territory, particularly by the exercise of extraterritorial jurisdiction, in order to discharge their obligation to protect human rights.

The extraterritorial obligation to protect human rights

The home state of a private corporation may be under an obligation to protect human rights even outside its territory to the extent that it may adopt measures compatible with the Charter of the United Nations in order to control such a corporation whose conduct might threaten or violate human rights. Although occasionally based on the human rights treaties to which the states concerned have acceded, such extraterritorial obligations to protect may also be derived from general international law, particularly under Article 56 of the UN Charter, and general principles of law. Such obligations to protect human rights outside the state's national territory are not limited to situations of foreign occupation; nor do they presuppose that the foreign state necessarily exercises effective control on a person or property, as has sometimes been asserted in judicial opinions.[31] A restrictive view of the situations in which the extraterritorial obligation to protect may be imposed fails to see that 'jurisdiction' may extend not only to situations over which the state exercises 'effective'—or physical—control, but also to any situation which, within the limits of international law, a state may influence. This includes all situations which a state may reach by exercising extraterritorial jurisdiction, by adopting legislation seeking to affect behaviour abroad (prescriptive extraterritorial jurisdiction), or by giving its courts the power to adjudicate situations having occurred abroad (adjudicative extraterritorial jurisdiction).

Indeed, as members of the United Nations, all states have pledged to 'take joint and separate action in cooperation with the Organization for the achievement of the purposes set forth in Article 55' of the UN Charter, which imposes on the United Nations a duty to promote 'universal respect for, and observance of, human rights and fundamental freedoms for all without distinction as to race, sex, language or religion'. The law of the UN Charter is not limited territorially any more than customary international law or the 'general principles of law recognized by civilized nations' mentioned in Article 38(1)(c) of the Statute of the ICJ [32] as

[31] See, eg, *The Queen (on the application of Mazin Mumaa Galteh Al-Skeini and ors) v The Secretary of State for Defence* [2005] All ER (D) 337, paras 48–53 (London Court of Appeal, Civ Div) (distinguishing 'effective control of an area' and 'state agent authority' as two distinct grounds justifying the extraterritorial reach of the European Convention on Human Rights, in order to extend its requirements to the behaviour of the British armed forces in Iraq).

[32] 3 Bevans 1179; 59 Stat 1031; TS 993; 39 AJIL Supp 215 (1945).

sources of international law—both of which, arguably, may be seen to include at a minimum a core set of the rights explicated in the Universal Declaration of Human Rights.[33]

States should be considered bound to contribute to the aims of the UN Charter and to respect human rights, either as customary international law or as general principles of law, in all their activities, regardless of whether these activities affect the human rights of their own population or affect the enjoyment of human rights abroad. Any proposition that human rights obligations would only apply between a state's authorities and the population of that state would place human rights apart from other norms of general public international law: just as a state has no right to allow the use of its territory to cause environmental damage on the territory of another state,[34] it should not allow a company domiciled under its jurisdiction to operate abroad in a way which causes violations of human rights. In the *Corfu Channel* case, while accepting that an activity cannot be imputed to the state by reason merely of the fact that it took place on its territory, the ICJ nevertheless noted that 'a State on whose territory or in whose waters an act contrary to international law has occurred, may be called upon to give an explanation.'[35] Where the state knew or ought to have known that activities unlawful under international law (that is, activities that would constitute a violation of international law if they were imputed to the state in question) are perpetrated on its territory and cause damage to another state, the first state is expected to take measures to prevent them from taking place or, if they are taking place, from continuing.[36] Ian Brownlie comments on this basis that the state 'is under the duty to control the activities of private persons within its State territory and the duty is no less applicable where the harm is caused to persons or other legal interests within the territory of another State'.[37]

This section explores the implications that follow for the authorities of the home state, defined as the state where a PMSC is registered and from which, therefore, it operates. By agreeing to a PMSC being incorporated under its laws, is a state accepting a responsibility to ensure that it complies with human rights wherever it develops its activities? There are strong arguments to suggest that the only limits to the obligation of states to protect human rights that may be

[33] See, eg, Theodor Meron, *Human Rights and Humanitarian Norms as Customary Law* (Oxford: Clarendon Press, 1989) 93; Bruno Simma and Philip Alston, 'The Sources of Human Rights Law: Custom, Jus Cogens, and General Principles', *Australian Yearbook of International Law*, vol 12, no 82 (1988–9).

[34] *United States v Canada* ('the *Trail Smelter* case'), 3 RIAA 1905 (1941) (arbitration); as regards environmental damage, see *Legality of the Threat or Use of Nuclear Weapons*, Advisory Opinion, ICJ Reports 1996 (Dissenting Opinion of Judge Weeramantry).

[35] *United Kingdom v Albania* ('the *Corfu Channel* case'), ICJ Reports 1949, 18.

[36] Ibid.

[37] Ian Brownlie, *System of the Law of Nations: State Responsibility* (Oxford: Clarendon Press, 1983) 165. See also Nicola Jägers, *Corporate Human Rights Obligations: In Search of Accountability* (Antwerpen-Oxford-New York: Intersentia, 2002) 172.

threatened by the activities of private actors operating across borders—for instance, PMSCs providing services in foreign states—are those imposed by international law itself, insofar as the law restricts the possibility for any state to exercise extraterritorial jurisdiction. The scope of these limits, however, has been long contested.[38] The following subsection seeks to summarize the debate. It concludes that there is no obstacle to require the states where the PMSC is registered to discharge its obligation to protect human rights by regulating the activities of that company, wherever it operates.

Discharging the obligation to protect by exercising extraterritorial jurisdiction

The use of extraterritorial jurisdiction to impose criminal or civil liability is one way in which states may influence the behaviour of companies operating overseas. Other means by which a state can fulfil its obligation to protect human rights include the use of non-binding tools, such as inserting clauses in public procurement schemes referring to human rights obligations, imposing reporting and other obligations on publicly listed or government-certified companies, and including conditions in project financing agreements with export credit agencies. Reliance on such incentives does not pose any question of extraterritoriality per se. Such incentives do not prescribe a certain form of conduct. They simply encourage companies to act according to certain norms if they wish to benefit from certain advantages (or not to be denied certain advantages) in their relationships with the state. In that sense, they do not constitute the exercise by the state of its extraterritorial jurisdiction at all.

Even within the notion of extraterritorial jurisdiction itself, a distinction should be made between adjudicative and prescriptive extraterritorial jurisdiction. A state may attribute to its jurisdiction a power to adopt decisions that concern situations having arisen abroad (adjudicative extraterritorial jurisdiction). This occurs either where criminal procedures may lead to convictions for acts committed abroad or where civil courts declare themselves competent to adjudicate proceedings that relate to extraterritorial situations. Alternatively, a state may adopt legislation intended to have an extraterritorial effect—that is, establishing norms governing persons, property, or conduct outside the national territory (prescriptive extraterritorial jurisdiction). It may, for instance, provide that certain forms of behaviour will constitute offences, wherever they take place, and decide that it may seek to prosecute such offences if the person suspected of having committed such offences is found on the national territory, or to request the extradition of that person.

[38] See, eg, Bernard H Oxman, 'Jurisdiction of States', in Rudolf Bernhardt (ed), *Encyclopedia of Public International Law*, vol 3 (Amsterdam: Elsevier Science Publishers, 1997) 55–60.

These two forms of extraterritorial jurisdiction are not necessarily entailed with one another, and there is no necessary logical connection between them. They are nevertheless related where criminal proceedings are concerned, since the criminal law of the state in which proceedings are brought—the 'forum state'—will necessarily be applied, although in most cases under a condition of double criminality. In contrast, where civil proceedings concern extraterritorial situations, the applicable law will be either the law of the forum state or the law of the host state, depending on the rules relating to conflicts of laws contained in the private international law of the forum state. In sum, how the question of extraterritoriality arises will differ depending on the nature of the proceedings concerned:

Civil liability	Criminal liability
A1: Extraterritorial adjudicative jurisdiction with application of the foreign law (application of the *lex loci delicti*) A2: Extraterritorial adjudicative and prescriptive jurisdiction: application of the law of the forum to extraterritorial situations	B1: Extraterritorial prescriptive and adjudicative jurisdiction with requirement of double criminality B2: Extraterritorial adjudicative and prescriptive jurisdiction without requirement of double criminality

While the situations A1 and B1 are genuine forms of exercise of extraterritorial jurisdiction, they are not problematic under international law, and specifically under the principle of the sovereign equality of states and its corollary, the prohibition against interference with other states' domestic affairs. Indeed, in both these situations, the forum state has recourse to extraterritorial jurisdiction in order to give effect to the laws of the territorially competent host state—in fact, ensuring that its organs will serve the implementation of those laws. In contrast, the exercise of extraterritorial jurisdiction in situations A2 and B2 deserve a more detailed discussion.

The legal doctrine is divided on the question of whether such forms of extraterritorial jurisdiction are authorized under international law where a state seeks to regulate situations abroad by imposing forms of civil liability on actors for their behaviour outside the national territory (A2), or by extending the scope of application of its criminal laws to situations having occurred abroad without imposing a condition of double criminality (B2). Some authors take the view that, as long as they stop short from sending their organs abroad, states are free to exercise extraterritorial jurisdiction by adopting legislation that seeks to regulate behaviour in other states and by allowing their jurisdictions to adjudicate cases related to such behaviour.[39] That was the position adopted by judge ad hoc Van den Wyngaert in her dissenting opinion to the 2002 judgment of the ICJ in

[39] Patrick Dailler and Alain Pellet, *Droit international public* (7th edn; Paris: LGDJ, 2002) 506.

the *Arrest Warrant* case.[40] Indeed, in the 1927 *Lotus* case, the Permanent Court of International Justice had expressed the view that states were in principle free to regulate matters situated outside their national territory, unless specific rules of international law prohibited such exercise of extraterritorial jurisdiction.[41] However, *Lotus* is a particularly weak precedent to build upon. The statement commonly quoted was *obiter dicta*, at a time when the idea of state sovereignty was at its apex in international law. In addition, even if we agree to take the passage as authoritative then and as still reflecting the current state of international law, the question of which rules might impose certain prohibitions against adoption of extraterritorial legislation would remain open.

The mainstream view rejects the thesis of an absolute freedom of states to exercise extraterritorial jurisdiction in the absence of specific prohibitions. Instead, it insists on extraterritorial jurisdiction having to be justified by the existence of at least some connection between the state exercising such jurisdiction and the situation concerned. Two of the classical bases justifying the exercise of extraterritorial jurisdiction are relevant to the question of whether a state may seek to regulate the conduct of PMSCs operating outside its national territory.[42] First, the nationality of both the offender and the victim may form the basis for extraterritorial jurisdiction. Under the active personality principle in particular, a state may enact legislation which will apply to its nationals even as regards their conduct abroad.[43] Indeed, it has been extended beyond nationality to permanent residency in certain recent statutes.[44] Secondly, under the principle of universality, certain particularly heinous crimes may be

[40] *Case Concerning the Arrest Warrant of 11 April 2000 (Democratic Republic of the Congo v Belgium)* ('the *Arrest Warrant* case'), ICJ Reports 2002, Dissenting Opinion of Judge Van den Wyngaert, para 19.

[41] *The Case of the SS 'Lotus' (France v Turkey)*, PCIJ Reports 1928, Series A, No 10, 18–19 ('Far from laying down a general prohibition to the effect that States may not extend the application of their laws and the jurisdiction of their courts to persons, property and acts outside their territory, it leaves them in this respect a wide measure of discretion, which is only limited in certain cases by prohibitive rules; as regards other cases, every State remains free to adopt the principles which it regards as best and most suitable').

[42] In addition to the two bases for extraterritorial jurisdiction detailed here, it is generally admitted that a state may exercise jurisdiction with respect to persons, property or acts abroad which constitute a threat to the fundamental national interests of the state; and that it may seek to influence, by the adoption of legislation which has an extraterritorial reach, activities which have a substantial, direct, and foreseeable effect upon or in its national territory. See *Restatement (Third) of the Foreign Relations Law of the United States*, vol 2 (St. Paul, MN: American Law Institute, 1987) ss 402(1)(c) and 403(1)).

[43] Under the *passive* personality principle, a state may seek to protect its nationals abroad by the adoption of extraterritorial legislation. However, invocation of this principle has been met with some suspicion, as it could serve as a means to circumvent the rules of the exercise of diplomatic protection, the normal means through which a state may seek to protect its nationals under another state's jurisdiction.

[44] 'Extraterritorial Criminal Jurisdiction', Report prepared by the Select Committee of Experts on Extraterritorial Jurisdiction established by the European Committee on Crime Problems (CDPC) (Council of Europe, 1990), 13.

prosecuted by any state, acting in the name of the international community, where the crime meets with universal reprobation.

Reliance on the active personality principle may be particularly useful where the conduct of a PMSC operating overseas is concerned, especially if such conduct is considered a criminal offence by the laws of the host state. Indeed, just as the exercise of extraterritorial criminal jurisdiction on the basis of the active personality principle is justified as regards natural persons by the fact that states normally refuse to extradite their own nationals, the exercise of extraterritorial jurisdiction over legal persons will be all the more justified where the host state, on the territory of which the PMSC has committed criminal offences, is unable to prosecute that company effectively, for instance because the imposition of certain sanctions requires the cooperation of the home state of the company targeted. Indeed, even if a state were to convict a foreign PMSC, the under-developed character of international judicial cooperation in criminal matters, made even more problematic by the diverging approaches the different states have about the question of the criminal liability of legal persons, may make it difficult for such a conviction to be recognized and enforced in the home state of the PMSC. It might therefore be argued that by adopting legislation seeking to regulate the conduct of 'its' companies wherever they operate, the home state enhances the effectiveness of the criminal laws of the host state: far from constituting a form of interference with domestic affairs of the host state, it therefore may be seen instead as a means of international cooperation.

In order to rely on the active personality principle to justify extraterritorial jurisdiction, one must be able to define the 'nationality' of the legal person. In the *Barcelona Traction* case, the ICJ seemed to reject that the nationality of a corporation could follow from the nationality of shareholders at least as regards the determination of nationality.[45] But that proposition—based on the view that a distinction ought to be maintained between the legal situation of the corporation and that of the shareholders—was stated only for the specific purposes of the exercise by a state of its right to diplomatic protection.[46] Whether it will be determinative beyond that field remains to be seen.[47] In addition, aside from the question whether the nationality of a company can be determined as following from that of its shareholders (or controlling 'parent'), we are clearly witnessing an extension of the conditions under which a state may be authorized to exercise extraterritorial jurisdiction where it seeks to influence the behaviour of companies controlled by companies of its nationality.[48]

[45] *Case Concerning the Barcelona Traction, Light & Power Co. (Belgium v Spain)* ('the *Barcelona Traction* case'), ICJ Reports 1970, 3.

[46] Ibid. at 184.

[47] On the relevance of *Barcelona Traction* beyond the exercise of diplomatic protection, see the doubts expressed by Stanley D Metzger, 'Nationality of Corporate Investment Under Investment Guaranty Schemes—The Relevance of Barcelona Traction', *American Journal of International Law*, vol 65 (1971) 532.

[48] See, eg, *Restatement (Third) of the Foreign Relations of the United States*, American Law Institute, 1987, s 414.

International law does not impose any particular mode of determination of the 'nationality' of the corporation. The determination of the nationality of the company through the place of incorporation remains the dominant mode of determination of the nationality of the corporation in a large number of states, including the United States and Britain, the advantage of this approach being that it contributes to legal certainty, since the results when applying these criteria are highly predictable.[49] Yet, it has increasingly been criticized as inadequate. The links between the corporation and the state under the laws of which it has been established may be extremely weak,[50] particularly in the current modes of organization of multinational corporations. Lower communication and transportation costs, as well as the abandonment of regulations relating, for instance, to the nationality of the directors or the location of shareholder and director meetings, have relegated the place of incorporation to little more than a legal fiction, or to the choice, by the company's board of directors, of a regulatory regime, without this corresponding to any genuine link between the company and the state of incorporation.[51]

One risk resulting from this disconnect is the effect equivalent to the phenomenon of 'flags of convenience' flown by vessels, who choose under which 'flag' to register on the basis, *inter alia*, of the regulatory framework to which they will be subjected.[52] The danger is that states may register companies under their laws, perhaps for the purpose of taxing their benefits, but neglect their duty to regulate those companies effectively, as might be required under contemporary conceptions of international solidarity between states. In other terms, one question raised by the use of the place of incorporation as determinative of the nationality of the corporation in a context where this might not correspond to reality,[53] is that of an obligation imposed on states to regulate the activities of their nationals that goes beyond their liberty to do so.[54] Unless we impose on the state under the laws of which a company is incorporated that it effectively regulates the activities of that company, we run the risk of 'relocations of convenience', by companies seeking to operate under the laws of a 'home state'

[49] Yitzhak Hadari, 'The Choice of National Law Applicable to the Multinational Enterprises', *Duke Law Journal* (1974) 1.

[50] M Tedeschi, 'The Determination of Corporate Nationality', *Australian Law Journal*, vol 50 (1976) 521.

[51] See generally Linda A Mabry, 'Multinational Corporations and US Technology Policy: Rethinking the Concept of Nationality', *Georgetown Law Journal*, vol 87 (1999) 563.

[52] See, eg, Emeka A Duruigbo, *Multinational Corporations and International Law. Accountability and Compliance Issues in the Petroleum Industry* (Ardsley: Transnational Publishers, 2003) 28–40; R Tali Epstein, 'Should the Fair Labor Standards Act Enjoy Extraterritorial Application? A Look at the Unique Case of Flags of Convenience', *University of Pennsylvania Journal of International Business Law*, vol 13 (1993) 653.

[53] Note that under the Convention on the Law of the Sea there must exist a genuine link between the vessel and its flag state. Convention on the Law of the Sea (1982), 1833 UNTS 396, art 91(1).

[54] On the duties of control imposed on the flag state under the Convention on the Law of the Sea, see ibid. art 94.

imposing on them only low levels of regulation. This argument may be particularly important in the debate over the control of PMSCs. These companies often operate in weak governance zones or in conflict zones. It is thus vital that they be effectively controlled by their state of origin, since the host state often will not be able, or willing, to exercise such control.

The principle of universality constitutes a second important basis for the exercise of extraterritorial jurisdiction for regulation of PMSC activities. Certain particularly heinous crimes may be prosecuted by any state, because they are met with universal reprobation. Genocide, war crimes, crimes against humanity, torture, and forced disappearances—all of which are international crimes for which treaties impose the principle *aut dedere, aut judicare*—belong to this category.[55] In prosecuting these crimes, states are not seen to act in their interest; they act as agents of the international community. Indeed, states are obliged to establish their jurisdiction over such crimes, wherever they are committed and whatever the nationality of the perpetrators or the victims, insofar as those accused of such crimes are found on their national territory. This is an obligation to exercise both prescriptive and adjudicative extraterritorial jurisdiction, which, although stated in the relevant treaties as regards war crimes, torture, and forced disappearances, is widely considered to belong to customary international law.

This ground of extraterritorial jurisdiction is of limited usefulness as regards the obligations of states to control PMSCs. The category of 'international crimes' is much narrower than the full range of human rights abuses which PMSCs could commit in the course of their activities. In addition, the instruments or customary norms defining certain forms of behaviour as international crimes[56] only impose on the states an obligation to provide in their legislation for the possibility of prosecuting a person for war crimes or torture committed outside their national territory in the event the suspected perpetrator of an international crime is found on their territory: they do not require that the states parties assert a 'pure universal jurisdiction' (that they establish their jurisdiction over these international crimes even where

[55] See the *Arrest Warrant* case, n 39 above, para 46 (joint separate opinion by Judges Higgins, Kooijmans, and Buergenthal) (citing Cherif Bassiouni, *International Criminal Law*, vol 3 (2nd edn; New York: Transnational Publishers, 1999) 228); Theodor Meron, 'International Criminalization of Internal Atrocities', *American Journal of International Law*, vol 89 (1995) 576.

[56] These are the Convention on the Prevention and Punishment of the Crime of Genocide, signed in New York, 9 December 1948, UNTS, vol 78, p 277; Geneva Convention Relative to the Treatment of Prisoners of War, signed in Geneva on 12 August 1949, UNTS, vol 75; Geneva Convention for the Amelioration of the Condition of the Wounded, Sick and Shipwrecked Members of the Armed Forces at Sea, signed in Geneva on 12 August 1949, UNTS, vol 75; Geneva Convention Relative to the Protection of Civilian Persons in Time of War, signed in Geneva on 12 August 1949, UNTS, vol 75; Geneva Convention for the Amelioration of the Condition of the Wounded and Sick in Armed Forces in the Field, signed in Geneva on 12 August 1949, UNTS, vol 75; the Convention Against Torture and Other Cruel, Inhuman or Degrading Treatment or Punishment (1984); and the International Convention for the Protection of All Persons from Enforced Disappearance, UN Doc A/HRC/1/L.10 (2006) 32.

the suspected perpetrator is not present on the national territory).[57] As noted by President Gilbert Guillaume in his individual opinion appended to the judgment of the ICJ in the *Arrest Warrant* case, a review of the international texts establishing the principle *aut dedere, aut judicare* shows that 'none of these texts has contemplated establishing jurisdiction over offences committed abroad by foreigners against foreigners when the perpetrator is not present in the territory of the state in question. Universal jurisdiction *in absentia* is unknown to international conventional law'.[58]

In addition, none of the instruments implementing the principle of universality was drafted with legal persons in mind. It would therefore not be plausible to derive from these instruments an obligation, for instance, for states where a company is incorporated to launch an investigation against that company, leading possibly to the imposition of effective sanctions, if it appears on the basis of reliable information that the company had taken part in the commission of international crimes.[59] Moreover, while the international crimes discussed above call, per definition, for sanctions of a criminal nature, not all states have accepted the concept of criminal liability for corporate bodies.

The *aut dedere aut judicare* principle established for perpetrators of international crimes may nevertheless have implications for legal persons, including PMSCs. The principle was imposed in order to ensure that natural persons who perpetrate international crimes will not be allowed to seek impunity because of the obstacles facing their extradition. But the implication seems to be unavoidable that the imposition by a state of certain sanctions (for instance, the confiscation of assets or the imposition of financial penalties) against a corporation 'present' under that state's jurisdiction, even when the corporation is not considered to have the 'nationality' of the forum state under its law, should be considered allowable, if it is determined that the corporation has indeed committed or been complicit in an international crime. It should not matter that the crime was committed abroad and is not connected in any way to the forum state except by the 'presence' of the corporation on its territory. In addition, the principle *aut dedere, aut judicare* in fact is simply one dimension of a broader

[57] As noted by Judges Higgins, Kooijmans and Burgenthal, the so-called 'universal jurisdiction' as exercised, for instance, according to the principle *aut dedere, aut judicare* stipulated in art 5 of the 1984 Convention against Torture in reality is but a modality of the exercise by a state of its territorial jurisdiction, 'albeit in relation to acts committed elsewhere'. See the *Arrest Warrant* case, n 39 above, joint separate opinion of Judges Higgins, Koojimans, and Burgenthal, para 41.

[58] Ibid, separate opinion of President Guillaume, para 9.

[59] It would be tempting to say that, since legal persons are not, as such, subject to extradition, a state on the territory of which a corporation is 'present' through its assets or its business activities is under an obligation to prosecute that person if reliable indications exist that it may have taken part in the commission of international crimes. This temptation should be resisted, since it would stretch the reading of the treaties discussed above far beyond the intentions of their drafters. As argued immediately below, this is without prejudice, however, of the existence of an obligation to take certain measures vis-à-vis the corporation for its operations abroad, which may imply its criminal, civil or administrative liability, where the ability of the host state to effectively combat international crimes committed on its territory in which the corporation has been involved is limited due to the failures of international cooperation.

obligation of states to cooperate internationally in combating international crimes. The Principles of International Cooperation in the Detection, Arrest, Extradition and Punishment of Persons Guilty of War Crimes and Crimes Against Humanity adopted by the UN General Assembly in 1973, for instance, state explicitly that 'States shall co-operate with each other on a bilateral and multilateral basis with a view to halting and preventing war crimes and crimes against humanity, and shall take the domestic and international measures necessary for that purpose'; and that they shall 'assist each other in detecting, arresting and bringing to trial persons suspected of having committed such crimes and, if they are found guilty, in punishing them'.[60] Similar references to the obligation of international cooperation are found in the Preamble to the Statute of the International Criminal Court,[61] which notes that 'the most serious crimes of concern to the international community as a whole must not go unpunished and that their effective prosecution must be ensured by taking measures at the national level and by enhancing international cooperation', and that 'it is the duty of every State to exercise its criminal jurisdiction over those responsible for international crimes'.

What are the implications of this requirement of international cooperation, if we take into account the difficulties the host state may encounter in holding criminally liable a PMSC operating within its territory, but based in a foreign jurisdiction? Due to the obstacles to international legal cooperation in criminal matters, the risk is high that PMSCs will be left unpunished even in cases where they face prosecution under the laws of the host state. Indeed, the execution of sanctions imposed on the company may require, in order to be effectively imposed, the cooperation of the home state (for example, in instances where there is a need for judicial winding-up order or placement under judicial supervision). But such cooperation is rendered extremely problematic by the fact that states have widely diverging approaches as regards not only the principle of criminal liability of corporations, but also the nature of the legal sanctions applicable to offences committed by corporations. Such divergences may constitute an obstacle to inter-state cooperation in this area. The exercise by the home state of extraterritorial jurisdiction may be seen to compensate, in this respect, for the obstacles facing the territorial (host) state in the effective imposition of criminal liability on the foreign PMSC operating within its borders. Such exercise of extraterritorial jurisdiction is in the interest of international solidarity, rather than in the selfish interest of the state concerned: it is therefore a form of extraterritorial jurisdiction which is in principle easier to justify.[62] Moreover, the exercise of extraterritorial jurisdiction in these circumstances may be seen as a derivative of the obligation of international cooperation

[60] UN Doc A/9030 (1973) paras 3–4.

[61] Rome Statute of the International Criminal Court, signed in Rome, 17 July 1998, UNTS, vol 2187, p 3.

[62] See 'Extraterritorial Criminal Jurisdiction', n 43 above.

in the punishment of persons guilty of international crimes, at least in situations where the host state on the territory of which such crimes have been committed is unable to effectively engage the criminal liability of the PMSC involved.

Conclusion

This chapter has examined the conditions under which the acts of PMSCs may be imputed to a state. It illustrated that apart from the special case in which PMSCs are so closely integrated into the armed forces of a state that they ought to be treated as state agents, such an attribution could be justified in three situations. First, if it can be proven that a particular PMSC, in fact, constitutes a mere fiction which the state uses in order to pursue its interests, it should be considered under the 'complete dependence' of the state and its acts, therefore, treated as though they were the acts of the state itself. Secondly, if a state chooses to exercise elements of its governmental authority, particularly in relation to law enforcement, by delegating the exercise of such powers to a private entity, it must accept responsibility for the way such delegated powers are exercised. Thirdly, a particular behaviour of the private entity may be attributed to the state in situations where the private entity 'is in fact acting on the instructions of, or under the direction or control of, that state in carrying out the conduct'. The two latter doctrines especially may be useful to impute to the state having hired the services of the PMSC the acts of PMSC employees. To the extent the PMSC is hired to perform duties which are normally of a governmental nature—a notion that includes the maintenance of law and order, the surveillance of prisons, or the interrogation of detainees—the second doctrine ensures that the state does not evade its international obligations by privatizing certain public functions. And even if that doctrine fails, for instance, because the 'public function' is being exercised by a private company without any express delegation to that effect, the third doctrine may at least allow the imputation to the state of the specific acts that are adopted by the private agents under its supervision.

For PMSCs that do not work for governments, but are instead hired by private corporations, the above doctrines will be of limited use. The responsibility of states, then, is to discharge their obligation to protect the rights that could be violated by the acts of PMSCs. In principle, this should be primarily a responsibility of the host state. However, where the host is unwilling or unable to do so, the home state of the PMSC should accept that it has a responsibility to effectively control the PMSC. The exercise of extraterritorial jurisdiction constitutes one tool in this regard; the use of incentives, such as selective public procurement schemes, reporting obligations, or conditionalities imposed on the support of export credit agencies, may constitute other alternatives. Such forms of extraterritorial control, for the benefit of the population of the state where the PMSC is present, may help the host state itself to better comply with its obligations under international law. While, ideally, we would need to make progress towards the definition of a multilateral framework defining the respective responsibilities of the host state and of the home state in controlling the compliance of PMSCs with certain universal values, in the interim, there is no other way out of impunity.

3

Accountability to whom?

Angelina Fisher

Discussions of privatization of security and the rise of private military and security companies (PMSCs) are often accompanied by claims that such companies routinely operate within a legal vacuum, without any accountability, and with total impunity.[1] Calls are made for regulators to hold these companies accountable—usually to the home state or under international humanitarian law—but there has been little sustained analysis of what kind of accountability is necessary and to whom accountability should be owed. Most strikingly, accountability to those whose lives are harmed by PMSCs is virtually missing from the discussions. This chapter aims to fill this gap by exploring the need, basis, and possibilities for accountability of PMSCs to affected populations: individuals and communities in places of PMSCs' operations, including employees of PMSCs,[2] who are harmed by PMSCs' conduct.

The chapter begins by exploring the need and the basis for PMSC accountability to affected populations. The chapter argues that while justice may demand it, there is limited basis (and opportunity) under domestic and international laws for affected populations to demand legal accountability of PMSCs for harms inflicted. In order to vindicate the rights of the victims of PMSC abuse, any approach to PMSC accountability needs to focus not on sources of legal accountability, but on mechanisms for redress of violations.

Why accountability to affected populations?

Privatization of security functions and proliferation of PMSCs have taken place without a corresponding outsourcing of accountability regimes. A state bears responsibility for its actions (as well as inactions), under both domestic and international laws, to its citizens and, in some circumstances, even to individuals

[1] See Simon Chesterman and Chia Lehnardt (eds), *From Mercenaries to Market: The Rise and Regulation of Private Military Companies* (Oxford: Oxford University Press, 2007).

[2] The reason for the inclusion of PMSC employees is that their human rights can be violated by their employers even though the violations may be qualitatively different from those suffered by the populations of the state in which PMSC operates ('host state').

beyond its borders. Domestic courts, administrative procedures, and public participation processes provide venues for individuals to hold public officials to account. A person abused in a state prison can file a grievance application. A bystander injured by a rogue police officer can seek redress in civil court. A state may also protect the victim's interests through criminal prosecution if the police officer's behaviour amounts to a crime. Finally, a victim or his or her kin may also request (usually, via a state or other government representative) an administrative investigation into a police officer's conduct. Moreover, at least in states with functioning democracies, citizens can hold public officials to account through public elections or through lobbying their government representatives (eg, council persons, state senate members, and so on). These options, however, are largely unavailable for individuals harmed by PMSCs. PMSCs operate transnationally with a multinational work force. An individual injured in Iraq by a Peruvian employee of a British PMSC may have a difficult time finding a forum in which to seek redress for injuries. Adding to this difficulty is the fact that PMSCs often operate in states with weak or non-existing governance regimes or where, as in Iraq, PMSCs are granted immunity by the state in which it operates. In those situations victims of PMSCs have no ability to seek redress for harm suffered.

Why is the ability to seek redress important? The right to a remedy appears in numerous international documents, including the Universal Declaration of Human Rights, the International Covenant on Civil and Political Rights, the International Convention on the Elimination of All Forms of Racial Discrimination, the Convention against Torture and Other Cruel, Inhuman or Degrading Treatment or Punishment, and the Convention on the Rights of the Child.[3] In 2005, the UN General Assembly adopted Basic Principles and Guidelines on the Right to a Remedy and Reparation for Victims of Gross Violations of International Human Rights Law and Serious Violations of International Humanitarian Law.[4] The recognition of the right in international law is an acknowledgement that human rights become empty if the individual has no ability to enforce them.

The right to remedy is also a necessary component of justice. As Cherif Bassiouni notes, 'the existence of State duties to provide a remedy and reparations forms the cornerstone of establishing accountability for violations and achieving justice for victims'.[5] Justice also entails 'responding to, acting in the light of, what we know or perceive of victims of past wrongs. It involves extending victims the concern and respect due to them in virtue of what they

[3] Universal Declaration on Human Rights, GA Res 217A (III), UN Doc A/810 (1948) art 8; International Covenant on Civil and Political Rights (16 December 1966) 999 UNTS 3, entered into force 3 January 1976, arts 1–2; International Convention on the Elimination of All Forms of Racial Discrimination (21 December 1965) 660 UNTS 195, entered into force 4 January 1969, art 6; the Convention Against Torture and Other Cruel, Inhuman, and Degrading Treatment or Punishment (10 December 1984) 1465 UNTS 85, entered into force 26 June 1987, art 14; Convention on the Rights of the Child (20 November 1989) 1577 UNTS 3, entered into force 2 September 1990, art 39.

[4] GA Res 60/147 (2006).

[5] M Cherif Bassiouni, 'International Recognition of Victims' Rights', *Human Rights Law Review*, vol 6, no 2 (2006) 231.

are—wounded others, in our society—and of what they have suffered'.[6] Being subjected to torture, rape, or other invasions of one's body not only causes physical and psychological suffering but also represents a '*symbolic* devaluation' of the person. Preventing the person from seeking acknowledgement of the wrong committed perpetuates the devaluation.[7]

Where the violation of human rights is committed by a private entity and the state is unwilling or unable to fulfil its duty to provide effective remedies to individuals whose rights have been violated, as is often the case with PMSCs, the private entity should bear that duty.[8] Failing to require this would not only lead to the injustice for victims but would also allow states to dispense with their responsibilities as they continue to outsource their public functions.[9]

Although justice may demand it, the question of whether a private company is legally accountable to those it harms (and thus has a duty to provide a remedy for violations) is far from settled. The following section examines the basis on which individuals whose rights have been violated by PMSCs can hold the companies accountable.

Bases for accountability

Domestic law

In discussing direct accountability of PMSCs to affected populations, one must first ask *on what basis* the affected populations can hold a company accountable.[10] A funder of PMSC activities can exercise influence over the PMSC on the grounds that it provides financial support and a state that delegated authority to a PMSC can hold the company accountable on the grounds of the delegation, but citizens of the state in which a PMSC operates as well as employees of the PMSC are rarely, if ever, in a position to either delegate authority to the PMSC or to provide the company with resources. However, PMSC accountability to the affected populations will exist where the law recognizes such accountability.[11]

Under many domestic regimes, criminal and civil laws operate to secure accountability of PMSCs (as well as other private actors) to those harmed by

[6] Frank Haldemann, 'Another Kind of Justice: Transitional Justice as Recognition', *Cornell International Law Journal*, vol 41 (2008) 680.

[7] Ibid.

[8] Bassiouni, 'International Recognition of Victims' Rights', 223; GA Res 60/147 (2006) art 15.

[9] See chapter two of this volume by Olivier De Schutter.

[10] Robert O Keohane, 'Global Governance and Democratic Accountability', in David Held and Mathias Koenig-Archibugi (eds), *Taming Globalization: Frontiers of Governance* (Cambridge: Polity Press, 2003) 140.

[11] Keohane, 'Global Governance and Democratic Accountability', 141–2; see also Richard Stewart, 'Accountability, Participation, and the Problem of Disregard in Global Regulatory Governance', paper presented at the IILJ International Legal Theory Colloquium: Interpretation and Judgment in International Law, NYU School of Law, 7 February 2008, available at <http://iilj.org/courses/documents/2008Colloquium.Session4.Stewart.pdf>.

their actions. For example, if a PMSC employee negligently discharges a weapon and injures bystanders in the process, the individual would likely face criminal prosecution and may be further subject to civil law suits by victims or their families. In some instances, domestic laws may also punish conduct that takes place outside of the state's borders. In the United States, for example, a person who is a national of the United States or is present in the United States may be prosecuted in US courts for committing, attempting, or conspiring to commit an act of torture.[12] In addition, the War Crimes Act authorizes the prosecution of war crimes committed by or against a US national or member of the armed forces inside or outside of the United States.[13] Also, the Special Maritime and Territorial Jurisdiction (SMTJ) of the United States extends the jurisdiction of US courts over certain listed offences committed by or against a US national, to 'buildings, parts of buildings, and land appurtenant or ancillary thereto or used for purposes of [US government] missions or entities, irrespective of ownership in a foreign state'.[14]

In addition, a PMSC employee may also incur liability under domestic military laws. In the United States, for example, the Military Extraterritorial Jurisdiction Act (MEJA) gives US federal courts jurisdiction to prosecute civilians employed by or accompanying the armed forces outside of the United States—including contractors, subcontractors, and their employees—who commit acts abroad that are considered criminal offences and that would be punishable under federal law by imprisonment for more than a year had the conduct occurred within the United States.[15] Also, the Uniform Code of Military Justice (UCMJ) authorizes courts-martial trials for offences prohibited under the UCMJ for those 'serving with or accompanying an armed force in the field' during a 'declared war or a

[12] US Congress, US Code, Chapter 113C—Torture, 18 USC § 2340A (12 April 2006).

[13] US Congress, War Crimes Act, 18 USC § 2441(a) (2006).

[14] US Congress, Special maritime and territorial jurisdiction of the United States defined, 18 USC §7(9)(A) (12 April 2006); amended by US Congress, USA Patriot Act, PL 107–56, §804, 115 Stat 272, 377 (2001).

[15] As originally drafted, MEJA extended only to those contractors, subcontractors and their employees that were engaged by the Department of Defense. In the aftermath of the Abu Ghraib abuses, the US Congress expanded the breadth of MEJA to include employees and contractors of *all* government agencies 'to the extent such employment relates to supporting the mission of the Department of Defense', a term which congress did not define. US Congress, Military Exterritorial Jurisdiction Act of 2000, PL 106–523, §3261(a), 18 USC §3261, 114 Stat 2488; amended by US Congress, Ronald W Reagan National Defense Authorization Act for FY 2005, PL 108–375, §1081, 118 Stat 1811 (2004); amended by US Congress, 18 USC §3267 (Supp IV 2004). Although bills that would expand MEJA to apply to *all* contractors, regardless of whether they are 'supporting the mission of the Department of Defense' had been introduced in both the House and the Senate, no action on the bills has been pursued. MEJA Expansion and Enforcement Act of 2007, HR 2740, 110th Cong, 1st sess (15 June 2007); Security Contractor Accountability Act of 2007, S 2147, 110th Cong, 1st sess (4 October 2007).

contingency operation'.[16] The UCMJ was invoked for the first time in April 2008 to charge an interpreter for the L-3 Communications Titan Group with assault in connection with the alleged stabbing of a fellow contractor.[17] Domestic laws also generally cover treatment of employees by PMSCs,[18] although they may not apply to the extraterritorial operations of transnational corporations.[19] Laws of the state in which the corporation operates generally will apply, although there may be limitations on claims brought by non-nationals.

Domestic laws come up short when it concerns PMSCs. PMSCs are transnational not only by virtue of the diverse geography of their operations but also because of the diversity of their employees' nationalities. For example, a US firm operating in Iraq may employ Iraqis as well as South Africans or Colombians. Victims (or their families) could not bring these individuals into US courts for criminal prosecution; civil suits against them would be difficult and probably fruitless. Moreover, when an employee of a PMSC is accused of misconduct, the company can simply replace him or her and continue with its business, even if the employee's misconduct was a result of the company's policies (or its own misconduct). The dismissed employee is free to seek employment with another PMSC, which may not be aware of the individual's work history. On the other hand, if the victim can hold the PMSC itself accountable, not only would it ensure due redress, but the company's policies may be influenced going forward and the company's activities may be brought to light. Some domestic regimes provide for corporate accountability to victims (for example, via civil suits or fines), but where PMSCs operate in states that lack effective domestic accountability provisions, or where there are no institutions to support the rule of law, reliance on domestic regimes is futile. Given the inadequacy of domestic legal systems to address accountability of

[16] A 'contingency operation' is an operation 'designated by the Secretary of Defense as an operation in which members of the armed forces are or may become involved in military actions, operations, or hostilities against an enemy of the United States or against an opposing military force'. US Congress, 10 USC § 101(a)(13). An order to active duty of members of the armed forces under certain other statutory provision may also trigger a 'contingency operation'. Ibid. One of the authors of the amendment, Senator Lindsay Graham, intimated that the change in the legislation was designed to bring contractors under the scope of the UCMJ. Griff White, 'New Law Could Subject Civilians to Military Trial', *Washington Post*, 15 January 2007.

[17] David Isenberg, 'Dogs of War: Military justice and PMCs', *United Press International*, 11 April 2008.

[18] See generally David Kinley, 'Human Rights as Legally Binding or Merely Relevant?' in Stephen Bottomley and David Kinley (eds), *Commercial Law and Human Rights* (Burlington, VT: Ashgate, 2002).

[19] David Kinley and Junko Tadaki, 'From Talk to Walk: The Emergency of Human Rights Responsibilities for Corporations at International Law', *Virginia Journal of International Law*, vol 44 (2004) 934. In the United States there are a few exceptions to this rule: (i) the Age Discrimination in Employment Act extends coverage to US citizens employed abroad by US employers or their subsidiaries; and (ii) Title VII and Americans with Disabilities Act extend protection to US citizens employed in a foreign country by a US employer or a US-controlled employer. US Congress, Age Discrimination in Employment Act, PL 90–202, 81 Stat 602, 29 USC §§ 621–34 (15 December 1967); US Congress, Civil Rights Act of 1964, Title VII, PL 88–352, 42 USC 2000e – 2000e-17; US Congress, Americans with Disabilities Act, PL 101-336, 42 USC § 12101 etc (26 July 1992). These exceptions would not apply to a non-US national employed by a US PMSC to work, eg, in Iraq.

PMSCs to individuals they harm, attention must turn to international law. The next section examines the basis on which international law may support accountability of PMSCs (as corporate entities) to the affected populations.

International law

Increasingly, international law is recognizing the direct responsibility of individuals, including corporate officers, for crimes such as piracy, slavery, crimes against peace, war crimes, and crimes against humanity.[20] At the same time, while '[c]orporations increasingly are recognized as "participants" at the international level, with the capacity to bear some rights and duties under international law', international human rights instruments do not generally impose 'direct legal responsibilities on corporations'.[21] Although it has been suggested that some international human rights documents impose direct legal responsibility on transnational corporations, that point remains unsettled.

The preamble to the Universal Declaration on Human Rights (UDHR) provides that 'every individual and every organ of society . . . shall strive by teaching and education to promote respect for these rights and freedoms and by progressive measures, national and international, to secure their universal and effective recognition and observance'.[22] Louis Henkin has argued that '[e]very individual includes juridical persons. Every individual and every organ of society excludes no one, no company, no market, no cyberspace. The Universal Declaration applies to them all.'[23] Article 29 of the UDHR is more definitive in terms of establishing a duty of a corporation to populations at large: 'Everyone has duties to the community in which alone the free and full development of his personality is possible'.[24] Nonetheless, given that the UDHR is a non-binding declaration, it is not clear whether the referenced duty is legal or merely ethical.[25]

[20] Early examples include *United States v Krauch* ('the *IG Farben* case'), *Trials of War Criminals Before the Nuernberg Military Tribunals*, vol 8 (1997) 1187–92; *United States v Flick* ('the *Flick* case'), *Trials of War Criminals Before the Nuernberg Military Tribunals*, vol 6 (1997) 1202; *United States v Krupp* ('the *Krupp* case'), *Trials of War Criminals Before the Nuernberg Military Tribunals*, vol 9 (1997) 1–2; *United Kingdom v Tesch and ors* ('the *Zyklon B* case') 1 ILR 93 (1946) (UN War Crimes Commission, British Military Court, Hamburg).

[21] Report of the Special Representative of the Secretary-General (SRSG) on the Issue of Human Rights and Transnational Corporations and Other Business Enterprise, UN Doc A/HRC/4/035 (2007) paras 20 and 44 ('2007 SRSG Report').

[22] Universal Declaration of Human Rights, n 3 above, preamble.

[23] Louis Henkin, 'The Universal Declaration at 50 and the Challenge of Global Markets', *Brooklyn Journal of International Law*, vol 17 (1999) 25.

[24] Universal Declaration of Human Rights, n 3 above, art 29.

[25] Although some provisions of the UDHR are considered to have become part of customary international law, it is generally accepted that such provisions currently apply only to states (and, in certain cases, to individuals) and do not include its preamble or art 29. 2007 SRSG Report, n 21 above, para 38; International Council on Human Rights Policy, 'Beyond Voluntarism: Human Rights and the Developing International Legal Obligations of Companies' (February 2002), available at <http://www.reliefweb.int/rw/lib.nsf/db900sid/ASIN-7DBQ7F/$file/ICHRP_Beyond%20Voluntarism.pdf?openelement>.

Human rights bodies have intimated direct responsibility of corporations, while at the same time maintaining that private entities are not accountable under human rights treaties. In the General Comment on the Right to Work, the Committee on Economic, Social, and Cultural Rights has said that while private actors, including corporations, 'have responsibilities regarding the realization of the right to work' and 'have a particular role to play in job creation, hiring policies and non-discriminatory access to work', they are 'not bound' by the International Covenant on Economic, Social and Cultural Rights.[26] The Human Rights Committee takes a similar position.[27]

Lack of recognition of direct legal responsibility of corporations to individuals they harm translates into an absence of a direct legal accountability regime. At the same time, the intimation of human rights bodies that corporations have responsibilities vis-à-vis its victims can be viewed as attempts to push the envelope and bring in corporate responsibility within the realm of international law, but on what grounds?

At the outset, it must be pointed out that corporations possess a series of rights and duties under international law. For example, under the International Convention on Civil Liability for Oil Pollution Damage, corporations bear liability for pollution damage as owners of ships and enjoy rights as legal persons;[28] under the Council of Europe's Convention on Civil Liability for Damage Resulting from Activities Dangerous to the Environment, they have rights and responsibilities;[29] and under bilateral and multilateral investment treaties, they have a plethora of rights and obligations.[30] Corporations are also able to bring claims under a number of international tribunals, including the UN Compensation Commission.[31] The question is thus not whether corporations can have rights and obligations under international law—they do—but under what circumstances do they owe duties to individuals they harm. The first step in this inquiry is to identify circumstances that may give rise to corporate legal responsibility. Once that threshold is crossed, one must define the group of

[26] General Comment No 18, UN Doc E/C.12/GC/18, Committee on Economic, Social and Cultural Rights, 2006, para 52.

[27] General Comment No 31, UN Doc CCPR/C/21/Rev.1/Add.13, Human Rights Committee, 2004, para 8.

[28] International Convention on Civil Liability for Oil Pollution Damage (1969), replaced by the Protocol of 1992, as amended in 2000. From 16 May 1998, Parties to the 1992 Protocol ceased to be Parties to the 1969 Convention due to a mechanism for compulsory denunciation of the 'old' regime established in the 1992 Protocol. However, for the time being, the two regimes co-exist, since there are a number of states that are parties to the 1969 Convention and have not yet ratified the 1992 regime, which is intended to eventually replace the 1969 Convention. See <http://www.imo.org/Conventions/contents.asp?doc_id=660&topic_id=256#4>.

[29] Council of Europe, Convention on Civil Liability for Damage Resulting from Activities Dangerous to the Environment (1993) (not yet entered into force), available at <http://conventions.coe.int/treaty/en/Treaties/Word/150.doc>.

[30] Kinley and Tadaki, 'From Talk to Walk', n 19 above, 947.

[31] The UN Compensation Commission was established by SC Res 692 (1991) to process claims and pay compensation for losses resulting from Iraq's invasion and occupation of Kuwait.

people to whom the corporation would owe duties. The final stage is to identify the scope of a corporation's duties.[32]

What circumstances may give rise to corporate legal responsibility?

Steven Ratner draws on the theories of state responsibility and individual responsibility as grounds for corporate accountability to victims. He argues that direct corporate responsibility to victims exists (i) 'where an enterprise has close ties to the government' and, in particular, where a corporation is a *de facto* agent of the state, where a corporation's conduct can be attributed to the state under the 'control' doctrine of state responsibility or where the corporation exercises governmental authority,[33] and (ii) where the corporation is complicit with the state's wrongful conduct.[34] In the first case, as Olivier De Schutter notes in chapter two, state responsibility would also be present, creating a situation of joint responsibility. Importantly, only direct corporate responsibility, and *not* state responsibility, amounts to accountability *to victims.*

In the context of increasing privatization of public functions, reliance on the state-corporation relationship as a grounding for corporate legal duty is both compelling and too restrictive. As states continue to outsource their functions to private entities, and as those entities subsequently sub-contract those functions to other private entities, the ties between states and corporations become increasingly dubious. Yet, it is precisely in that circumstance that an accountability regime is needed. Take, for example, the case of a multinational PMSC that receives a security contract from the United States to operate in Iraq. The PMSC subcontracts various components to a group of unrelated corporations, some of which are not residents (in a corporate sense) of either state. If one of the subcontracting companies commits a violation of international human rights law in Iraq, who is accountable to the victims? In most cases, the subcontracting company would not be an agent of the United States (or Iraq, for that matter). Moreover, given the subcontracting web and realities of PMSC operations, it is unlikely that the company would be either under US or Iraqi control. State complicity may not be present; and if it is, it may be difficult to prove. Thus, unless the offending company can be said to exercise governmental authority, it would seem that under international law the offending corporation bears no legal responsibility for its actions. To be clear, such violation may also constitute a criminal violation under domestic law, but private contractors may be immune

32 Steven R Ratner, 'Corporations and Human Rights: A Theory of Legal Responsibility', *Yale Law Journal*, vol 111 (2001) 497.

33 Ibid. at 497–9. This argument draws on the doctrine of state responsibility, discussed in detail in chapter two of this volume by Olivier De Schutter.

34 Ibid, 500–4. Other scholars have reached similar conclusions. See, eg, Kinley and Tadaki, 'From Talk to Walk', n 19 above, 965; International Council on Human Rights Policy, 'Beyond Voluntarism', n 25 above.

from domestic legal provisions (as has been the case in Iraq) or a state may have too weak or non-existent a governance regime to allow for prosecution of the offender.

In some respects, and in particular with respect to the conduct of military activities, PMSCs provide one of the easier cases of exercise of governmental authority: what can be more 'inherently governmental' that the conduct of war and foreign relations?[35] Similarly, PMSCs acting as prison guards or contracted by the state to operate detention facilities may be considered engaged in exercise of governmental authority.[36] However, the scope of modern PMSC activities is far broader and it is not clear whether PMSCs—for example, providing supplies, guarding installations, or providing logistics training—engage in the exercise of governmental authority. More effort is needed to define 'governmental authority' in a way that reflects the realities of today's corporate market.

To whom does a corporation owe legal duty?

Assuming that a basis for a legal duty of a PMSC is established, it is necessary to circumscribe the group of people to whom the company would be accountable.

To identify the population to whom a corporate entity owes a legal duty, one theory draws on the proximity of the corporation to individuals: as the extent to which the enterprise and the population form a meaningful association increases, so does the degree of duties the corporation owes toward these individuals; as the proximity lessens, so do the duties.[37] This concept was endorsed by the UN Global Compact in 1999 and subsequently reflected in the Norms on the Responsibilities of Transnational Corporations and Other Business Enterprises with Regard to Human Rights, adopted by the Sub-Commission on the Promotion and Protection of Human Rights ('the Norms').[38]

[35] In an expert meeting on private military contractors, organized by the University Centre for International Humanitarian Law in Geneva, it was generally agreed that PMSCs hired by states will often be covered by article 5 of the ILC Articles, 'as military operations are functions which are inherently governmental.' University Centre for International Humanitarian Law, Expert Meeting on Private Military Contractors: Status and State Responsibility for Their Actions, convened at International Conference Centre, Geneva, 29–30 August 2005, text available at <http://www.adh-geneva.ch/events/pdf/expert-meetings/2005/2report_private_companies.pdf>. In 2001, the International Law Commission adopted its Draft Articles on the Responsibility of States for International Wrongful Acts, which address the fundamental questions of when a state breaches international law and what are the consequences of such a breach. The ILC Articles were subsequently commended to the attention of the states by the United Nations General Assembly. See GA Res 56/83, para 3 (12 December 2001).

[36] In discussing examples of instances where an entity is considered to be exercising governmental authority, the ILC commentary specifically notes that private security firms that are contracted to act as prison guards that exercise powers of detention and discipline. James Crawford, *The International Law Commission's Articles on State Responsibility: Introduction, Text and Commentaries* (Cambridge: Cambridge University Press, 2002) art 5.

[37] Ratner, 'Corporations and Human Rights', n 32 above, 508.

[38] UN Doc E/CN.4/Sub.2/2003/12/Rev.2 (2003).

As used by the Global Compact, '[t]he sphere of influence concept implies that the more control, authority or influence a business has over a situation giving rise to human rights abuses (or the means to improve respect for human rights), the greater the business responsibility to act . . . Ultimately the closer the company's relationship is with a group of rights holders (or perpetrators of rights abuse), the greater the need for an immediate business response.'[39] The Norms, in their broadest pronouncement, state that '*[w]ithin their respective spheres of activity and influence*, transnational corporations and other business enterprises have the obligation to promote, secure the fulfillment of, respect, ensure respect of and protect human rights recognized in international as well as national law, including the rights and interests of indigenous peoples and other vulnerable groups'.[40]

An alternative theory has been proposed by John Ruggie, the Special Representative of the Secretary-General (SRSG) on the issue of human rights and transnational corporations and other business enterprises. Ruggie proposes an inductive fact-based analysis in the course of which companies would consider three sets of factors:

(1) the country contexts in which their business activities take place, in order to highlight human rights challenges,

(2) what human rights impacts their own activities may have within that context, and

(3) whether they might contribute to abuse through relationships connected to their activities.[41]

Ruggie's framework is designed to support his contention that the baseline for corporate legal responsibility is the obligation to *respect* human rights and that to discharge this responsibility requires companies to undertake due diligence. The factors analysis defines the scope of the due diligence.

Although useful for that purpose, Ruggie's framework may be insufficient to define the group of individuals who have a right to hold a company accountable because a company may construe the impact of its actions narrowly, both in terms of the type of activities in which the company thinks it is likely to engage and in terms of the population it is likely to impact. For example, a company charged with protecting government officials may not consider that it could be affecting the civil and political rights of the local populations even though its zealous protection may prevent the population from gaining access to their

[39] Office of the United Nations High Commissioner for Human Rights, Human Rights and Business Learning Tool, 'Module 2: Sphere of Influence, Section: Sphere of Influence and the Global Compact Principles', available at <http://www.unssc.org/web/hrb/details.asp?mod=2&sec=1&cur=1>.

[40] UN Doc E/CN.4/Sub.2/2003/12/Rev.2 (2003) art 1 (emphasis added).

[41] Report of the Special Representative of the Secretary-General (SRSG) on the Issue of Human Rights and Transnational Corporations and Other Business Enterprises, UN Doc A/HRC/8/5 (2008) para 57 ('2008 SRSG Report').

political representatives. To be sure, the degree of duty that a PMSC would owe to individuals in various circumstances is not the same and some individuals would fall farther along the spectrum of 'sphere of influence' than others. Nonetheless, it is important to ensure that a framework for corporate responsibility does not disregard any potential right-bearers. To that end, the 'sphere of influence' approach is a helpful concept.

Assuming that corporate responsibility is triggered and the group of relevant right holders can be identified, there is a further question of the content of corporate duties.

What duties would corporations owe to the identified individuals?

Ratner suggests that 'the company's duties typically will be to avoid directly infringing upon the right based on the balancing test [of rights and corporate interests]. . . , including through some prophylactic measures', although he acknowledges that '[o]ther derivative duties might be appropriate where the nexus between the enterprise and the individual is particularly close'.[42] Ruggie takes a similar view, hesitating to go further.[43] Yet, in the face of increasing outsourcing of public functions, as the corporation's functions approximate those of a state, it is appropriate to insist that the corporation not only refrain from directly infringing upon human rights, but take on, to the extent feasible, positive obligations to respect, protect, and ensure human rights.[44] This proposition increasingly finds support in so-called 'soft laws'. For example, the Norms require corporations to inform themselves of the impact of their activities on human rights and to '*use their influence in order to help promote and ensure respect for human rights*'.[45] The Voluntary Principles on Security and Human Rights ('the Voluntary Principles'), a multi-stakeholder initiative established in 2000 to guide the operations of extractive companies, also impose a series of positive obligations on companies.[46]

The Organisation for Economic Co-operation and Development (OECD) Guidelines for Multinational Enterprises—an influential series of recommendations jointly addressed by governments to multinational enterprises—recommend that the firms 'respect the human rights of those affected by their activities consistent with the host government's international obligations and commitments', as well as 'abstain from any improper involvement in local

42 Ratner, 'Corporations and Human Rights', n 32 above, 519.

43 2008 SRSG Report, n 41 above, para 24.

44 Kinley and Tadaki, 'From Talk to Walk', 965, 972. See also chapter 2 of this volume by Olivier De Schutter.

45 UN Commission on Human Rights, Commentary on the Norms on the Responsibilities of Transnational Corporations and Other Business Enterprises with Regard to Human Rights, UN Doc E/CN.4/Sub.2/2003/38/Rev.2 (2003), A2(a) (emphasis added).

46 Voluntary Principles on Security and Human Rights, Fact Sheet Released by the Bureau of Democracy, Human Rights, and Labor, US Department of State, 20 December 2000, available at <http://www.state.gov/www/global/human_rights/001220_fsdrl_principles.html>.

political activities'.[47] The Guidelines cover topics such as disclosure, employment and industrial relations, environment, combating bribery, consumer interests, science and technology, competition, and taxation. Of course, it is telling that the Norms, the Voluntary Principles, and the OECD Guidelines are not binding legal documents. Nonetheless, these instruments have the potential 'to crystallize into harder forms'.[48]

Corporations' legal obligations toward their own employees, as opposed to other individuals who may be harmed by their actions, have more robust underpinnings. Employees are at the closest proximity to the corporation and therefore it makes sense that a corporation would owe greater duties to them. The International Labour Organization (ILO), an influential global body responsible for drawing up and overseeing international labour standards, has produced 187 conventions, which are binding legal documents on states that ratified them. Some of the ILO conventions have been interpreted as recognizing a duty of corporations 'not to interfere with the ability of employees to form unions'[49] and to 'ensure that, as far as is reasonably practicable, the workplaces, machinery, equipment and processes under their control are safe and without risk to health'.[50] In addition to the conventions, the ILO adopts recommendations, which are nonbinding but influential. In 1977, the ILO adopted the Tripartite Declaration of Principles concerning Multinational Enterprises and Social Policy (subsequently modified in 2000 and 2006), which states that all parties, including multinational enterprises 'should respect the Universal Declaration of Human Rights and the corresponding international Covenants', and provides recommendations in five areas of labour rights: general policies, employment, training, conditions of work and life, and industrial relations.[51]

The ILO has a complaint procedure that allows a member state or an International Labour Conference delegate or the governing body itself to bring a complaint, which is then investigated by a commission of inquiry. The concerned government may also refer the complaint to the International Court of Justice for final decision.[52]

[47] The OECD Guidelines for Multinational Enterprises OECD Doc DAFFE/IME(2000)20 (2000), available at <http://www.oecd.org/dataoecd/56/36/1922428.pdf>, II(2), II(11).

[48] 2007 SRSG Report, n 21 above, para 49. Other so-called 'soft norms' addressing corporate responsibility include the International Finance Corporation Environmental and Social Standards, the Equator Principles and dozens of other initiatives focused on a particular industry or company. See Natalie Bridgeman and David S Hunter, 'Narrowing the Accountability Gap: Toward a New Foreign Investor Accountability Mechanism', *Georgetown International Environmental Law Review*, vol 20 (2008) 187 fn 9.

[49] Ratner, 'Corporations and Human Rights', n 32 above, 479.

[50] Convention Concerning Occupational Safety and Health and the Working Environment, ILO No 155 (1981) art 16(1); see also Ratner, 'Corporations and Human Rights', n 32 above, 479.

[51] Tripartite Declaration of Principles concerning Multinational Enterprises and Social Policy, *ILO Official Bulletin*, vol 83, Series A, No 3 (2000).

[52] ILO Constitution (1919), entered into force on 28 June 1919, adopted by the Peace Conference in April 1919 as Part XIII of the Treaty of Versailles (28 June 1919), art 26, available at <http://www-ilo-mirror.cornell.edu/public/english/standards/norm/enforced/complnt/index.htm>.

It is noteworthy, however, that an individual victim of labour rights violations cannot bring a complaint.

The private military and security industry itself has started paying attention to labour rights and companies have begun to include labour-related provisions in their codes of conduct. In 2006, Securitas, a security company, signed a global labour rights agreement with Union Network International (UNI) covering 225,000 workers worldwide. The agreement provides for regular global dialogue between unions and Securitas and incorporates core labour rights and the Universal Declaration of Human Rights. It also provides for practical assistance to unions in organizing, including lists of and access to employees. Agreements like these, along with industry codes and contracts for provision of services, can also become sources of affirmative legal duties towards individuals who are not employees of PMSCs. As Laura Dickinson has argued, the inclusion of a third-party beneficiary clause in a contract between a PMSC and the contracting entity could allow the beneficiary—which, depending on the relevant circumstances, may be an individual from the community affected by PMSC conduct—to seek redress from the PMSC under the contract.[53] The scope of the duty to the beneficiary under these circumstances would, of course, depend on the content of the third-party beneficiary clause.

Summary

At a minimum, a PMSC has an obligation to respect human rights and is required to become aware of, prevent, and address adverse human rights impacts.[54] It can also be argued that a PMSC has a legal duty to:

(1) refrain from interfering with the enjoyment of human rights of those who are within its 'sphere of activity and influence' and promote compliance with human rights; and

(2) protect human rights and prevent abuse of those to whom PMSC has proximate ties[55]

[53] Laura A Dickinson, 'Contract as a Tool for Regulating Private Military Companies', in Chesterman and Lehnardt, *From Mercenaries to Market*, n 1 above.

[54] 2008 SRSG Report, n 41 above, para 57.

[55] In chapter two of this volume Olivier De Schutter reaches a similar conclusion with respect to state responsibility, arguing that a state is responsible for PMSC conduct if (i) the PMSC, in fact, constitutes 'a mere fiction which the state uses in order to pursue its interests' (this branch is not relevant to the discussion of corporate responsibility since in this scenario the corporation is a mere sham); (ii) a state exercises elements of its governmental authority by delegating the exercise of such powers to a private entity (this is similar to the case of corporation performing state functions); and (iii) the PMSC 'is in fact acting on the instructions of, or under the direction or control of, that state in carrying out the conduct' (this is analogous to the agency and control tests for corporate responsibility).

where:

(1) a PMSC has a close relationship to the state (either by virtue of being the state's agent or under the state's control, or by virtue of complicity with the state);

(2) PMSC is essentially performing a state's function; or

(3) a contract (or other legal document) or industry code so provides.

Victims of PMSC abuse may find these conditions limiting. PMSCs rarely act as state agents and often provide services through a web of subcontracts, effectively removing any argument that the ultimate violator is under any degree of control by the state. Contract provisions establishing legal duties to the affected populations are not common and the industry itself has not established a clear duty to the affected populations. Given that reliance on international law for accountability of PMSCs to victims of abuse is premature, attention must be turned to other means of augmenting PMSC accountability, such as creating grievance mechanisms. A number of such regimes already exist in other areas dominated by corporate actors. The following section examines some of the more relevant models with the goal of suggesting a mechanism, or a series of mechanisms, that can provide meaningful redress for victims of PMSCs.

Grievance mechanisms

Although both the notion of justice and numerous international documents require provision of redress to the victims of human rights violations, they do not specify the form such redress must take or the procedures by which it should be attained. For victims of PMSCs, redress can include monetary compensation, a change in the company's policy and actions, and/or an acknowledgement of the violation and apology to the victim. The type of appropriate redress may vary from situation to situation and may be specifically tailored to a particular dispute. This section discusses some of the complaint mechanisms that are used by private companies in other industries with the aim of identifying elements for a mechanism that would provide redress to victims of PMSCs. The discussion draws on the study of grievance mechanisms by the Corporate Social Responsibility Initiative at the John F. Kennedy School of Government at Harvard University.

Grievance panels, compliance investigative units, and other institutional grievance mechanisms

The intergovernmental agency model

Two models employed by intergovernmental organizations are considered here: one used by financial institutions to give voice to individuals affected by foreign-financed projects and another used by the OECD to respond to complaints of violations of the OECD Guidelines.

In the case of financial institutions, a complaint is usually reviewed by a designated person and subsequently referred either for consultation or problem-solving and compliance review.[56] Consultation (generally offered first) may include site visits, discussion with all relevant stakeholders, and mediation. If a resolution is reached through this process, a report with a recommended course of action agreed upon by the parties is usually submitted for approval to the board of directors (or the president) of the financial institution. If the process fails (or if a complainant is not satisfied with the process), the complaint may proceed to a compliance review, which is usually conducted by a panel of experts[57] and may include fact-finding, meeting, consultations, and site visits. At the end, the panel prepares a report, which it submits along with its recommendations to the board of directors (or the president) which decides whether to accept it or not.

For victims of PMSCs, the flexibility of such a mechanism, both in terms of modes of investigation and types of remedial actions offered,[58] is appealing. However, this type of grievance mechanism requires a lot of institutional support, and investigations may take several months to complete. This may not be feasible for PMSCs, whose employees may not be present in the state for that long. Moreover, such a process may be cumbersome to institute unless responsibility for it is placed on the home state.[59] This could be one way in which the home state could satisfy its responsibility to prevent its private entities from committing human rights violations, as discussed in chapter two of this volume by Olivier De Schutter. For example, the home state could be required to institute a grievance mechanism whereby upon receipt of a complaint, a dedicated person or a group of persons could be dispatched to the territory in question to facilitate a dialogue between the PMSC and the complainant. The home state could also require all companies, prior to engaging in a contracted mission, to place funds in escrow, which could be used if compensation to the complainant is an appropriate outcome.[60]

[56] The World Bank's Inspection Panel does not have the consultation/problem-solving phase.

[57] The experts are generally paid by the bank but are not formal employees of the bank. Some banks have a requirement that an expert cannot have been an employee of the bank for a specific number of years.

[58] The available outcomes vary depending on the institutions' policies but some include full compensation, independent monitoring and evaluation of the project, changes in the institution's policies, and recommendations for establishing project-level grievance mechanisms.

[59] Although theoretically, it is possible for the mechanisms to be administered by the host state, practically this would be no more effective than relying on the host state to hold PMSCs accountable under local laws. See chapter two of this volume by Olivier De Schutter.

[60] There already appears to be a precedent for this, albeit instituted by a host state. A study by Swisspeace reports that in 2007, the Afghan Ministry of Justice passed a regulation, which would, among other things, require all international companies to deposit a bond of 15 million Afghani (about $300,000), and national PMSCs to deposit 10 million Afghani (about $200,000), into the Afghan Central Bank as security that could be used for payment of damages caused by PMSCs and their staff. At the time of this writing, it is unknown whether the regulations have gone into effect. Ulrike Joras and Adrian Schuster (eds), 'Private Security Companies and Local Populations: An Exploratory Study of Afghanistan and Angola', Swisspeace Working Paper 1 (2008), 25, available at <http://www.swisspeace.ch/typo3/fileadmin/user_upload/pdf/Working_Paper/WP_1_2008.pdf>.

Possible obstacles include difficulty accessing relevant sites and obtaining information if the home state is not the same as the state that hired the PMSC; difficulty gaining trust of the local population by a foreign representative; difficulty in monitoring the PMSCs post-complaint behaviour if the home state does not have a permanent representative on the territory; and limited courses of action available to the home state where the alleged offender is a national of a third state (although a state could require the PMSC to dismiss the employee and award compensation to the complainant). The home state may be under political pressure to keep the process away from the public eye and its actions may not be transparent, even to the complainant. This would undermine the legitimacy of the process in the eyes of the aggrieved population, which then may be less likely to use it.

Some of these concerns are addressed by the grievance mechanisms that are community- or project-focused, such as the OECD model. For example, the OECD conducts reviews through National Contact Points (NCPs), which are set up by governments committed to the OECD Guidelines.[61] Some NCPs involve businesses, trade unions and even NGOs in addition to government representatives. Once an NCP receives a complaint that the OECD Guidelines have been breached and determines the complaint to be *bona fide*, it offers its good offices to help parties resolve the issue and may, subject to the parties' consent, facilitate access to conciliation or mediation. If an agreement is reached, the NCP can monitor the outcome if it wishes and the parties agree. The outcomes can vary, depending on what the parties agree, but may include compensation. If the parties cannot arrive at an agreement, the NCP issues a statement regarding whether, in its opinion, the OECD Guidelines were breached, and may make recommendations. OECD member-states and OECD business or trade union advisory bodies can request the OECD Investment Committee to express its view on whether the NCP has correctly interpreted the Guidelines. The process generally remains confidential but outcomes are normally public.

This process has the advantage of having a permanent local person handle the complaint and, particularly where NCPs include multiple stakeholders, the process enjoys legitimacy. For PMSCs, this model also has the advantage of assuring confidentiality of the process. The downside is that if the parties cannot reach an agreement, there is no additional recourse outside of local courts. Moreover, if the parties have agreed to confidentiality, the information about the conflict cannot be made public. Thus, there may be little incentive for PMSCs, and few advantages for the local population, to engage in the process at all. Even if the PMSCs engage with the process, the lack of mandatory

[61] OECD, 'National Contact Points for the OECD Guidelines for Multinational Enterprises', available at <http://www.oecd.org/document/60/0,3343,en_2649_34889_1933116_1_1_1_1,00.html>.

monitoring provides little assurance to the complainant that the company will comply with the terms of the agreement (and little incentive for the PMSC to comply), unless home states exert pressure on PMSCs to do so. Home states, however, may be unwilling to exert such pressure for political reasons. Alternatives to a government-led model include grievance mechanisms led by the industry itself as well as multi-stakeholder-led initiatives.

The industry association model

The International Peace Operations Associations (IPOA), a PMSC industry group, allows individuals and entities to lodge complaints against PMSCs that are members of the IPOA. A complaint must be submitted to the Standards Committee of the International Peace Operations Association (SCIPOA), which is tasked with monitoring PMSC compliance with the IPOA Code of Conduct. The SCIPOA will accept only those complaints that relate to the breach of IPOA's Code of Conduct and is not empowered to provide compensatory remedies to the victims of PMSCs. Instead, SCIPOA may put a company on probation, expel it from the IPOA, or subject it to some other disciplinary action, although it is not clear if it has ever exercised this function. Apart from the fact that the IPOA process provides *no* redress to the victim of PMSCs, the process suffers from a lack of transparency; it is not even known publicly how many complaints have been submitted to the IPOA.

Other industries have better grievance mechanisms. In chapter seven of this volume, Rebecca DeWinter-Schmitt makes an argument for drawing upon the regulatory experience of the apparel industry, specifically the Fair Labor Association (FLA) and the Worker Rights Consortium (WRC), in thinking about a regulatory regime for PMSCs. Indeed, the industries share a number of relevant similarities: the PMSC and apparel industries are both 'geographically mobile' and have the ability to 'relocate if they are unhappy with a nation's regulatory environment or reconstitute themselves into different corporate forms to avoid regulation and liability for their actions'.[62] Thus, grievance mechanisms instituted by the FLA and WRC may be instructive for PMSCs.

The FLA has a third-party complaint procedure for allegations of non-compliance with the FLA Code of Conduct or Principles of Monitoring.[63] The procedure is run entirely by the FLA, with the first phase after the initial assessment of the complaint being conducted internally by the company that is the subject of the allegations. The company must investigate the allegations, remediate non-compliance if the allegations prove true, and report back to the FLA Executive Director. If the grievance is not resolved at the company level, the FLA gets directly involved and may initiate an independent external

[62] See chapter seven of this volume by Rebecca DeWinter-Schmitt.
[63] Fair Labor Association, 'Third Party Complaints', available at <http://www.fairlabor.org/thirdparty_complaints.html>.

investigation, mediation, or arbitration, depending on circumstances. Enforcement and/or monitoring of the outcome must be agreed upon by the parties. The FLA reports publicly on the process.

In contrast to the FLA, the WRC's grievance mechanism is run by the WRC in collaboration with local experts. The primary process for the WRC is investigation and, once the complaint is accepted, the WRC builds an investigative team involving its staff, representatives from the local community, and independent experts. The investigation team issues a report of its findings and recommendations and continues to monitor conditions, issuing reports on progress. All reports are made public.[64]

An obvious advantage of an industry-run mechanism is that it has the presumptive buy-in of the industry. On the other hand, such mechanisms may be charged with lack of independence or a biased approach to the dispute. Both the IPOA and the FLA mechanisms can be critiqued on those grounds. The WRC model addresses some of these concerns by ensuring that its grievance mechanism is run collaboratively with local experts. Moreover, the WRC itself is a multi-stakeholder initiative, which renders it more akin to an independent body than a classic industry association.

Since, as DeWinter-Schmitt notes in chapter seven of this volume, industry associations hold the most promise in augmenting PMSC accountability, not the least because they enjoy the presumptive buy-in of the industry, serious thought should be given to situating a grievance mechanism within the PMSC industry. The process, however, must involve multiple stakeholders; be transparent; involve local populations; and, given the diversity of PMSC operations, be project-specific. The following section discusses some of the elements of grievance mechanisms that are tailored to specific projects.

Project-specific grievance mechanisms

A unique aspect of project-specific mechanisms is that applicable standards and processes can be custom-tailored. For example, the Baku-Tbilisi-Ceyhan (BTC) pipeline project focused its grievance mechanism on breaches of domestic law; voluntary standards adopted by the company, including its Code of Conduct; and standards required of the company by the International Finance Corporation, as well as a mix of tailored standards.[65] Gap Inc, an apparel retailer that sources products from third-party suppliers, has a mechanism to address violations of its Code of Vendor Conduct, which includes compliance with all applicable laws, including those against discrimination, forced labour, child

[64] A similar mechanism is also used by the Ethical Trading Initiative, an alliance of UK-based companies, NGOs and trade union organizations.

[65] Baku-Tbilisi-Ceyhan, 'Grievances and Dispute Resolution'. See 'BTC Pipeline/BP (ended in 2006)', BASESwiki, available at <http://www.baseswiki.org/En/2-GrievanceMechanisms/Fcompany_Mechanisms/BTC_Pipeline%2F%2FBP>.

labour, working conditions and freedom of association.[66] Xstrata Plc, a global mining group, has a mechanism for its operations in Peru that is based on human rights law and the company's own standards.[67] In all three instances, the grievance mechanisms are public-private hybrids, involving local government, communities, and/or NGOs in their processes.

BTC's grievance process was almost entirely community-led, with solutions to the complaint first being sought by one or more locally-hired community liaison officer(s) (CLOs). If the proposed solution was not acceptable to the parties, the CLO initiated a direct negotiation between all relevant parties, including local authorities, with the purpose of reaching a common settlement. If that process failed, and where the disputed issue related to land or compensation, the complainant could contact the Centre for Legal and Economic Education (CLEE), a local NGO engaged by the company to act as an arbiter. CLEE then reviewed all relevant information and opined on the appropriate outcome, which often included compensation. If the complainant was not satisfied with CLEE's opinion, he or she could petition the local courts.[68]

In contrast, factories in Lesotho that supply Gap Inc have a grievance mechanism that involves internal investigations coupled with government processes if an internal process fails to reach a solution. First, a Gap-Lesotho supervisor investigates and attempts to resolve the complaint within two days. If the complainant is not satisfied, he or she can proceed to the departmental head or manager who will convene a meeting between the aggrieved employee, a worker's representative, the supervisor, and human resources personnel. If the grievance is not resolved within three days, the complainant may proceed to the company's manager who, within five days, may make a decision based on the report from prior proceedings, or may instigate further investigation. If the complainant is not satisfied with the manager's solution, he or she can bring the complaint to the Lesotho National Development Corporation (LNDC), which brings parties together before any formal process is set in motion, or to the Directorate of Dispute Prevention and Resolution (DDPR), which can employ conciliation and arbitration to resolve the dispute. LNDC and DDPR are national institutions unaffiliated with GAP Inc.[69]

Xstrata's complaint mechanism is a combination of internal and community-led processes. Having received a complaint, the Head of the Xstrata's Coordination Office[70] appoints one or more persons to conduct the investigation and propose a solution. If the complainant is not satisfied with the solution, the complaint will pass to the Complaint System Defence Counsel, an individual who is chosen jointly by Xstrata and the leaders of local communities. Xstrata

[66] Caroline Reese and David Vermijs, 'Mapping Grievance Mechanisms in the Business and Human Rights Arena', Corporate Social Responsibility Initiative, John F Kennedy School of Government, Harvard University, January 2008, available at <http://www.hks.harvard.edu/m-rcbg/CSRI/publications/Report_28_Mapping.pdf>.
[67] Ibid. 19–21. [68] Ibid, 10. [69] Ibid, 12. [70] Ibid. 19–21.

pays for the Defence Counsel's costs as well as the costs of the investigation. After conducting his or her own investigation, the Defence Counsel proposes a solution. If the complainant remains unsatisfied *and* the complaint is supported by the community or is itself a community complaint, it may be advanced to an Arbitration Court consisting of three arbitrators. Xstrata and the community appoint one arbitrator each, and these two arbitrators appoint the third one. The arbitrators conduct their own investigation and propose a resolution, which may include compensation. Although there is no enforcement mechanism, there is a monitoring committee, which consists of one representative of Xstrata and representatives of each of the communities in the project's area.

Since legal accountability of PMSCs to affected populations under international law is at its nascent stage, the ability to adjudicate disputes on the basis of a combination of local laws, existing 'soft laws', and voluntary codes of conduct is of significant benefit to victims. Moreover, a project-specific regime, like Xstrata's, which relies heavily on the local community, diminishes claims that the mechanism is biased in favour of the companies and enjoys legitimacy among the local population. The mechanism should be financed by the industry; however, in order to avoid claims of bias, local community members should participate in the establishment of the complaint's panel and the selection of its members as well as in the selection of negotiators, mediators, and/or arbitrators. Community involvement increases the transparency of the process and assures a degree of independence.

Office of ombudsman

Yet another model of a grievance mechanism that may be of relevance to PMSCs and which may operate in tandem with the project-specific industry-and community-led grievance mechanism is the office of ombudsman.[71] Generally speaking, an Ombudsman's mission is 'to provide a confidential, neutral, and informal process which facilitates fair and equitable resolutions to concerns that arise in the organization' and to serve 'as an information and communication resource, upward feedback channel, advisor, dispute resolution expert and change agent' in a non-biased manner.[72] The office of ombudsman, for

[71] The Office of Ombudsman has its origins in the Swedish model created in 1809 to look 'after the legality of actions by all civil servants of the state' and to 'prosecute any individual of them who breaks the laws and regulations of the country'. Jan-Erik Lane, 'The Ombudsman in Denmark and Norway', in Philipp Giddings and Roy Gregory (eds), *Righting Wrongs: The Ombudsman in Six Continents* (Amsterdam: IOS Press, 2000).

[72] Larry B Hill, Address at the Spring Meeting of the American Bar Association Section of Administrative Law and Regulatory Practice, Washington, DC, 18 April 1997, cited in Christina M Kuta, 'Universities, Corporations; and States Use Them—Now It's Time to Protect Them: An Analysis of the Public and Private Sector Ombudsman and the Continued Need for Privileged Relationship', *Southern Illinois University Law Journal*, vol 27 (2003) 392.

example, is sometimes used for prisons, including private prisons, discussed in chapter five of this volume by Alfred Aman.

The office of ombudsman is an important mechanism for prison accountability in Britain, Australia, New Zealand and Canada.[73] In Britain, a Prisons and Probation Ombudsman has jurisdiction over both public and private prisons and is tasked with investigating 'complaints from prisoners, people on probation and immigration detainees held at immigration removal centres, deaths of prisoners, residents of probation service Approved Premises, and those held in immigration removal centres.'[74] The British Prisons Ombudsman is appointed by the Secretary of State for Justice and operates independently of the Prison Service, the National Probation Service and the Border and Immigration Agency.[75] The Complaints Team of the Ombudsman's office consists of the Assessment Team, which assesses the complaint to ensure it can be considered by the Ombudsman under his terms of reference, and the Investigators Teams, which conduct the investigation and report their findings to an Assistant Ombudsman.[76] Investigators may propose a resolution to the conflict; however, the implementation of that resolution depends on agreement by both parties.[77] If no resolution is achieved, the investigators make recommendations, which are sent to the parties to the complaint. In addition, recommendations can be made to the Prison Service, the National Probation Service, or the British Borders Agency. The Ombudsman office complements the office of Her Majesty's Inspectorate of Prisons, which is an independent inspectorate that monitors and reports on conditions for and treatment of those in prison.[78] The Chief Inspector of Prisons is appointed from outside the Prison Service. It has been noted that while the Ombudsman and the Chief Inspector only have the powers to make recommendations, 'their reports are followed closely by the media and play an important role in publicizing contractual violations and other performance problems'.[79]

The office of the Ombudsman by itself would not be a workable grievance mechanism for PMSCs and affected populations, especially if the scope of outcomes is limited to making recommendations and is not supported by additional accountability-augmenting regimes. Moreover, given the sensitivity surrounding some PMSC activities, it is unlikely that companies would be

[73] In the United States, litigation of prisoner rights, either individually or as part of class actions, is the most common way of addressing prisoners' concerns that are not resolved by on-site processes. Richard Harding, 'Private Prisons', *Crime&Justice*, vol 28 (2001) 320–1. In addition, a state may institute its own grievance mechanism both for public and private prisons.

[74] Prisons and Probation Officer for England and Wales, 'About Us', available at <http://www.ppo.gov.uk/about-us/index.html>.

[75] Ibid. [76] Ibid. [77] Ibid.

[78] Her Majesty's Inspectorate of Prisons, 'About Us', available at <http://inspectorates.justice.gov.uk/hmiprisons/about-us>.

[79] David E Pozen, 'Managing a Correctional Marketplace: Prison Privatization in the United States and the United Kingdom', *Journal of Law&Politics*, vol 19 (2003) 281.

willing to submit to a mechanism that publicizes both its process and its findings. On the other hand, an independent Ombudsman may be a useful actor in informal conciliation and mediation discussions between the PMSCs and members of communities within which PMSCs operate. The Ombudsman would need to be supplemented by mediation or arbitration, as well as a compliance monitoring mechanism, in the event that attempts at informal resolution are not successful.

Conclusion

In order for individual rights to be meaningful, victims of PMSC abuses must be able to hold the violators to account. Where domestic laws fail and international laws are inadequate, attention must be turned to other mechanisms that can provide individuals with due redress. Redress can take many forms: it can entail criminal prosecution, compensation, restitution, or any other appropriate resolution to a rights violation, but it must also entail the recognition of the pain and humiliation that victims experienced at the hands of offending companies. An accountability regime must be both rights-focused and complainant-focused. A successful PMSC grievance mechanism should be a multi-stakeholder initiative (like the WRC) with active participation by the affected communities in the investigatory and adjudication phases (like the Xstrata mechanism).

A purely governmental (or intergovernmental) process is unlikely to be effective because it will necessarily require dedicated institutional resources, involve a tremendous amount of bureaucracy, and have its efficacy and efficiency undermined by political pressures. At the same time, a purely industry-run mechanism will equally be ineffective since, as DeWinter-Schmitt puts it in chapter seven of this volume, it can create an impression that the 'fox is guarding the henhouse'. In particular, complaint mechanisms like the one introduced by the IPOA not only fail to deliver justice in all senses, but also represent a failed form of governance, lacking legitimacy, accessibility, participation, and transparency. Nonetheless, to be effective, the mechanism must have the industry's buy-in and must incentivize the industry to participate in and abide by the mechanism's process and results. The most effective means of establishing and running the process may be for an industry association, such as the IPOA, the British Association of Private Security Companies, or a local association such as the Private Security Company Association of Iraq to lead the establishment of a multi-stakeholder grievance mechanism to which its member companies would be required to submit. Alternatively, the industry association can simply require its member companies to establish such mechanisms themselves in collaboration with the local communities. Yet another alternative would be for contracting states to require companies to establish a grievance mechanism under the terms of the contract. For those companies that operate under long-term contracts, a more comprehensive mechanism may be appropriate. On the other hand, for those companies which are operating on a short mission, establishing a process for dialogue with local communities prior to, or at the beginning of, the mission and maintaining it throughout the mission may be sufficient.

For companies that operate covertly pursuant to contracts with states, none of the described grievance mechanisms may be workable. In those instances, a heavier burden should be placed on contracting and home states to ensure that victims of PMSC abuses are able to seek and obtain meaningful redress. One means of achieving this would be through contractual terms. As Laura Dickinson has argued, a contract with PMSCs could include requirements to abide by a series of standards. Should a breach of a listed standard occur, the contracting state could ask the company to remedy the breach or could sue it for breach of contract.[80] The contract could even require companies to include and enforce the same standards provision in contracts with sub-contractors. Finally, as in many investment treaties, a contract between a state and a PMSC can provide for third-party rights and can stipulate that all third-party disputes be resolved by an arbitration tribunal. If drafted thoughtfully, such provision could enable victims to hold PMSCs accountable for their violations.

A local ombudsman (preferably appointed jointly by the company and the members of the community within which the company operates) may play a useful role in establishing a dialogue between the community and PMSCs, even before a dispute arises. Dialogue, direct negotiations, and conciliation should form the primary stage of the PMSC grievance mechanism since the companies are more likely to be responsive if they believe the conflict can be resolved quietly and away from the media; at the same time, these informal processes may not only provide victims with a sense of recognition and respect but may also dispel the myths and misunderstandings that local populations may carry about PMSCs. Should informal dialogue not produce satisfying results, the complainant should be given an option to proceed to arbitration. As in Xstrata's case, arbitration tribunal members should be selected jointly by the company and the local community.

At the end of the day, meaningful redress for victims of PMSCs can be accomplished only through a mechanism that enjoys legitimacy with both the industry and the local populations, is accessible to the public, is transparent both with regards to processes and outcomes, engages relevant multi-stakeholders in productive dialogue, has a predictable and fair process, and empowers local populations.[81]

[80] Dickinson, 'Contract as a tool for regulating private military companies', n 53 above.

[81] Rights-Compatible Grievance Mechanisms: A Guidance Tool for Companies and Their Stakeholders, Corporate Social Responsibility Initiative', John F Kennedy School of Government, Harvard University, January 2008.

PART II

LESSONS FROM OTHER SECTORS

4

The privatization continuum

*Daphne Barak-Erez**

The privatization of military functions has become a focal point of the public and academic debate on privatization. It is argued that this type of privatization has special characteristics which make it especially troubling. Military functions call into use the institutionalized violence of the state and its organs.[1] As such, they touch on the very core of state sovereignty[2] and carry the potential for far-reaching infringement of the most basic human and civil rights—life and liberty. In addition, they often have implications not only for the citizens and residents of the state, but also for people who live beyond its territory and sovereignty[3] (and, accordingly, involve also the laws of war).[4]

Although it is important to acknowledge the special traits of military functions, the significance of privatization in this area will remain only partially recognized if not considered in the broader context of other areas of privatization.

First, military actions are often similar to those taken by other state organs which deal with security, mainly the police and corrections services.[5] Accordingly, this chapter also addresses privatization initiatives concerned with security functions that are beyond the military domain.

* I thank Gilad Barnea, Gabby Blum, and Aeyal Gross, as well as the participants at the 'Private Security, Public Order: Governance & Limits' conference, for their comments.

[1] The discussion focuses on the operation of military actions by private corporations, in contrast to the mere purchase of goods (and technologies) from private corporations.

[2] See Paul R Verkuil, *Outsourcing Sovereignty* (New York: Cambridge University Press, 2007).

[3] Indeed, in the context of modern warfare, military operations may be conducted also by people who do not leave the country (but rather operate technological systems from afar). However, even in these cases, their actions have implications outside the borders of the state.

[4] For a focus on the accountability to people who are affected by the activities of private military and security corporations (PMSCs), see chapter three of this volume by Angelina Fisher.

[5] Some military activities, such as controls at checkpoints, resemble actions taken by the police. When the army holds detainees it is, in fact, an operator of a prison. It is important to discuss the privatization of military actions with due distinction between the various aspects of military operations (among which some are special but some resemble operations of other government organs). Simon Chesterman points out that even the relatively narrower topic of intelligence services includes actions of a different nature (electronic interception, renditions, interrogations, analysis) which should be distinguished from one another for the purpose of discussing the implications of privatization in this area. See chapter nine of this volume by Simon Chesterman.

Second, it is important that the focus on the special concerns raised in the context of the privatization of military and security functions will not obscure the broader questions that should also be discussed with regard to other privatization initiatives: what are the appropriate limits of privatization in general, and which forms of regulation should accompany privatization initiatives? Accordingly, this chapter seeks to address the whole spectrum of privatization and not merely its most extreme ends. A better understanding of the legal regulation of this continuum will also enable us to better address such extreme cases as the privatization of security functions.

A word of warning is needed here. Viewing the privatization of military functions as the extreme end of a continuum is not intended to legitimatize this practice (by formulating it as 'just' another example of privatization). Nor is it intended to imply that a contextualized analysis of its special traits is redundant. Rather, it seeks to emphasize that one cannot address the tip of an iceberg without taking into account the whole of its body.

The prism of this analysis is that of domestic constitutional and administrative law, drawing also upon comparative tools. The chapter discusses the limitations on privatization in general and the limitations on the privatization of security functions in particular, from the perspective of national law rather than international law. However, international law can inform the development of domestic law—a point discussed further below.[6]

The Different Faces of Privatization

In order to propose a comprehensive framework for discussing privatization, it is necessary to start by describing the features and characteristics of this phenomenon. Part of the failure to address privatization properly is the tendency to focus each time on another type of privatization or another context in which privatization is implemented, without addressing the full picture and the inter-relations among the various forms of privatization. In general, the phenomenon of privatization includes any policy directed at reducing governmental involvement in economic and social life.[7] However, this broad definition comprises different forms of government policy. In some cases, privatization entails the withdrawal of government from activities in areas in which market forces are considered more efficient than centralized intervention. In other cases, privatization is manifested only in contracting out operational aspects of governmental activity, while retaining public responsibility for the privatized action. In yet other cases, privatization is the shift from the universal, free provision of public services to a

[6] See chapter two of this volume by Olivier De Schutter.

[7] For a review of the different meanings of the term, see also Paul Starr, 'The Meaning of Privatization', *Yale Law & Policy Review*, vol 6 (1988) 6.

more market-oriented provision of services, with price tags attached. Awareness of the different manifestations of the phenomenon of privatization is crucial for addressing it properly. Indeed, demarcating the parameters of a new phenomenon in the social and public reality is a precondition for addressing it and regulating it with legal tools.

The analysis offered here will address various types of privatization while pointing to the central features of this phenomenon, as manifested in many particular examples: an increased role of private entities in the operation of social and economic activities; intensive collaboration between public authorities and private entities; and the application of private-market logic to the authorities' activities.

Drawing on the experience of several systems, it is possible to identify at least nine basic types of privatization:

Establishing companies for the purpose of promoting business activities

Government-established companies that conduct business-like activity and operate autonomously and separately from the government bureaucracy should be considered a type of privatization.[8] Indeed, when the government decides to act through the operation of companies it is still highly involved in economic life, but this involvement is carried through the use of private law mechanisms.

Selling government assets

The policy of selling government assets, especially state-owned companies, is one of the better-known manifestations of privatization.[9]

Outsourcing government activities to private contractors

Outsourcing is currently a major feature of privatization (and it is also the type of privatization most relevant for the discussion of this phenomenon in the context of military and security functions). This type of privatization has started with the transfer of technical activities to private contractors in such areas as construction, rubbish collection, school bussing, and computer services. In time, contracting with external entities has gradually expanded to matters that are technical by definition but comprise discretionary elements, such as collection services. The next stage involved transferring governmental functions that comprised a significant dimension of discretion to private entities, as in the cases of the welfare-to-work programmes and the privately owned and operated prisons. Occasionally, this type of privatization has the potential to indirectly

8 In Israel, for example, the Government Companies Law provides that a government company should be guided by economic considerations (unless it is specifically directed otherwise by the government). See Government Companies Law 1975, s 4.

9 See, eg, Dawn Raines, 'Privatization of Telecommunications in Latin America', *Administrative Law Review*, vol 48 (1996) 479.

influence public service, as demonstrated by the privatization of the training of public service professionals.

Construction of public infrastructure by private investors

A unique form of contracting with private entities centres on constructing new infrastructure by means of private entrepreneurs, who undertake not only to execute the construction work but also to invest in and operate the infrastructures through special concessions once they have been constructed. In this context, government collaboration with private entrepreneurs stems mainly from a desire to secure private funding for constructing the infrastructures at the initial stages. The concession-owners, who bear the costs of the project, ensure a profitable return on their investment by way of long-term administration of the project, during which they charge the public a fee for the use of the infrastructure. In the framework of this model, known as Build-Operate-Transfer (BOT),[10] the private investor builds the infrastructure at his expense; operates it over an extended period of time, as promised to him in advance; and, in the end, transfers ownership or control of the infrastructure to the state. This type of privatization has been used for transportation projects and water infrastructure.[11]

Licensing and concessions

The expansion of private activity at the expense of government actions has also been enabled by the granting of licenses to private service providers. Accordingly, in the area of education, for example, a growing tendency to privatize could manifest itself in the licensing of new private schools and universities (thus partially avoiding the need to establish more public schools and public universities). In the area of telecommunications, licensing private companies to operate cellular phone networks (as this new technology became available) was a similar example of privatization, although no transfer of shares or other assets was involved.

Privatization through omission: constricted governmental activity

At times, the state's contribution to the privatization of certain activities is the result of the failure of the government and other public authorities to act effectively in that area, thereby making room for private initiatives. The areas of education and health are illustrative of this particular process. Thus, for example, when the education system provides fewer hours or lower quality teaching services, more parents opt for private education.[12]

[10] See chapter one of this volume by Michael Likosky.
[11] See, eg, Laura A Malinsky, 'Rebuilding with Broken Tools: Build-Operate-Transfer Law in Vietnam', *Berkeley Journal of International Law*, vol 14 (1996) 438.
[12] For a discussion of the opting out problem, see Clayton P Gillette, 'Opting Out of Public Provision', *Denver University Law Review*, vol 73 (1996) 1185.

Provision of services for a fee

The privatization of areas of government action also occurs when the relevant agency continues to operate the same activities but decides to collect a fee for the services it supplies (a growing trend in various public places such as museums and parks). As noted above, sometimes this phenomenon is combined with the transfer of an area of activity from the authority to a company it controls and operates as a closed budgetary unit based on business profit considerations. However, privatization of this type can also be effected through the direct collection of fees by the agencies themselves.

Voucher systems

The government may choose to provide services by subsidizing the buying of these services from private suppliers (such as private schools or private health care providers).[13]

Cooperation with third-sector bodies

Another type of privatization is the institutionalized collaboration between the state and third-sector Non-Governmental Organizations (NGOs) for the purpose of performing functions that the state is supposed to fulfil.[14]

Privatization: Between policy and law

The traditional starting-point for discussing the challenges posed by privatization used to be the statement that the decision to privatize is a matter of policy, not of law. Accordingly, the legal engagement with the phenomenon was limited to a few doctrinal 'islands' which were relevant to the privatization initiative at hand (such as the application of the state action doctrine to the operation of private prisons),[15] as opposed to a systemic analysis of privatization as a phenomenon which requires a process of re-thinking public law.

More concretely, this perception of privatization has promoted an underlying assumption of 'constitutional neutrality'. In other words, the traditional legal

[13] Michael J Trebilcock, Ronald J Daniels, and Malcolm Thorburn, 'Government by Voucher', *Boston University Law Review*, vol 80 (2000) 205; Klint Alexander and Kern Alexander, 'Vouchers and the Privatization of American Education: Justifying Racial Resegregation from *Brown* to *Zelman*', *University of Illinois Law Review* (2004) 1131.

[14] See Martha Minow, 'Partners, Not Rivals?: Redrawing the Lines between Public and Private, Non-Profit and Profit, and Secular and Religious', *Boston University Law Review*, vol 80 (2000) 1061.

[15] Applying the state action doctrine in such manner did not stop the privatization endeavour but rather subjected it to constitutional norms. See chapter five of this volume by Alfred Aman.

stance with regard to the boundaries of privatization was that the decision whether or not to privatize a given activity raises no constitutional issues.

Against this background of constitutional indifference, the policy of privatization has moved forward even in areas of traditional government action, such as the operation of prisons and policing (operated by private contractors).[16] With all these privatized activities in the background, it is currently very hard to question the relatively new trend of privatization in the area of military actions. Many of the privatized functions in the military domain are not very different in kind from other functions already privatized for a relatively long time. In other words, it may be that the re-thinking of the privatization of security functions should lead to the re-thinking of privatization initiatives that have already become part of public life, such as the privatization of prisons.

The legal analysis of the phenomenon of privatization should be based on three different questions. The first question considers the boundaries of privatization: are there any limitations on the types of actions or types of powers that can be privatized? The second question relates to the administrative process of privatization: what are the constraints that should apply to the implementation of a privatization decision (for example, is there a duty to set a privatization policy before proceeding with a concrete privatization initiative, or is there a duty to disclose information regarding privatization initiatives)? The third question refers to the outcomes of privatization and its regulation: which legal regime should apply to privatized activities, and will they be subject to special regulation or special duties?

This chapter aims at proposing a model of analysis of privatization initiatives based on these questions. The model is applicable to the immediate challenge posed by the privatization of military functions, but its scope is broader: it can apply and should be used also for the study of other instances of privatization along the privatization continuum.

The boundaries of privatization

As noted earlier, the traditional premise of public law has been that the choice of activities for privatization is a matter of policy and not of law. This premise warrants reconsideration. Indeed, it is indisputable that privatization decisions are an expression of policy and, normally, should not be removed from the political arena to the legal sphere. However, even given this premise, it is necessary to challenge the convention that a decision to privatize is solely a matter of policy, and consider whether this approach, too, has its limitations.

The question of the boundaries of privatization should be addressed through two discrete forms of analysis—an institution-based analysis and a rights-based analysis. The institution-based analysis focuses on the question of whether there are certain activities that cannot be privatized because they are an integral part of

[16] See chapter five of this volume by Alfred Aman.

the state. The rights-based analysis focuses on the question of whether the privatization mechanism at hand includes safeguards against infringements of fundamental rights by those private actors vested with the responsibility to execute functions formerly handled by public officials.

Institutional analysis

Setting the boundaries of privatization from the institutional perspective is a difficult task. There is no universal definition of the core activities of the state. There is a wide range of views on this matter, from the 'night-watchman' conception of the state as primarily providing for personal safety,[17] to rich notions of a developed welfare state, with a wide spectrum of additional approaches in-between (identifying the state with the use of violent force, with activities that signify sovereignty, or with supplying public goods, to mention only a few options).

The difficulty in formulating a legal stance on this matter also stems from the different understandings of the public missions being privatized. For example, in the area of education, advocates of privatization insist that instruction and educational services can be supplied by private entities, under state supervision, because they perceive education as a product.[18] In contrast, those opposing privatization emphasize the spirit of education, asserting that the values of equal and democratic civil education are likely to be eroded if educational services are supplied by private entities, even under state supervision.[19] At any rate, it is clear that given the relatively diverse traditions regarding the functions that have to be carried out by the state, the definition of core government functions that cannot

[17] See Robert Nozick, *Anarchy, State and Utopia* (New York: Basic Books, 1992).

[18] Milton Friedman, who espoused the application of free-market principles in education as well, proposed an action outline for running private education as follows: 'Governments could require a minimum level of schooling financed by giving parents vouchers redeemable for a specified maximum sum per child per year if spent on "approved" educational services. Parents would then be free to spend this sum and any additional sum they themselves provided on purchasing educational services from an "approved" institution of their own choice. The educational services could be rendered by private enterprises operated for profit, or by non-profit institutions. The role of the government would be limited to insuring that the schools met certain minimum standards, such as the inclusion of a minimum common content in their programs, much as it now inspects restaurants to insure that they maintain minimum sanitary standards.' Milton Friedman, *Capitalism and Freedom* (Chicago: Chicago University Press, 1962) 89.

[19] Realization of the civic-democratic objectives of education is contingent on the way in which schools are run. This includes the way in which integration is achieved in schools, not only in its formal aspect of accepting students into the school, but also at the ongoing administrative level, for example, the distribution of students into different classes and learning groups. See Amy Gutmann, *Democratic Education* (Princeton: Princeton University Press, 1987) 66. Under this approach, education is in itself a social objective, and therefore state intervention cannot be limited to the prevention of harm or fraud with regard to the quality of the service provided, in contrast to Friedman's example of state regulation of restaurants. As Gutmann explains, '[t]he analogy implies that our common educational standards consist only of preventing schools from physically harming children or fraudulently claiming to educate them. Were our public interest in regulating schools as analogous to our interest in regulating restaurants as Friedman suggests, it would be hard to explain why we should subsidize schooling for every child. A necessary condition for justifying public subsidy of schools—but not of restaurants—is the fact that citizens have an important and common interest in educating future citizens.' Ibid. 67.

be privatized under any conditions would be relatively narrow (and hence the majority of privatization initiatives will not be constitutionally precluded).

Some constitutional provisions may be interpreted as precluding privatization of certain activities, but even they may leave room for experimentation in privatization. For example, section 87a of the German Basic Law[20] states that 'The Federation shall establish Armed Forces for purposes of defence. Their numerical strength and general organizational structure must be shown in the budget'. This provision may fairly be interpreted as barring the possibility of privatizing the army as such,[21] but it does not imply anything concrete about possible contracting by the army with private actors for specific purposes, such as training, buying services and goods, and more. It is a common feature of constitutional texts that they include provisions defining the main branches of government—the executive, the legislature and the judiciary—and these provisions may be interpreted as implying that it would not be possible to completely privatize their functions (for example, in the US context, the Constitution probably implies that article III courts cannot be privatized,[22] and that the power to legislate cannot be delegated to private professionals).[23] At the same time, these general provisions do not say anything about the scope of the functions that the executive has to execute (for example, should the government guarantee the provision of education through a public education system, or can it also rely upon provision by private schools).

The relatively opaque nature of constitutional texts on such matters can be illustrated by reference to the example of prison privatization. Should constitutional texts on executive power be interpreted as implying that functions traditionally associated with sovereignty cannot be executed outside the executive branch?[24]

[20] The German Basic Law (Grundgesetz) is the German Constitution, available at <http://www.bundestag.de/htdocs_e/info/infomat/basic_english/basiclaw_artikel.html>

[21] In a similar manner, under Israeli law, '[n]o armed force other than the Defence Army of Israel shall be established or maintained except under Law'. Israeli Basic Law: The Army (1976) s 6, available at <http://www.knesset.gov.il/laws/special/eng/basic11_eng.htm>.

[22] It is interesting to note that despite Milton Friedman's capitalistic approach, which espouses minimal state intervention in social and economic life, under his view, one of the prominent functions of the state is to define and interpret property rights. He claims that coordinating economic activity through a free exchange is based on the premise that we have ensured, through the government, 'maintenance of law and order to prevent coercion of one individual by another, the enforcement of contracts voluntarily entered into, the definition of the meaning of property rights, the interpretation and enforcement of such rights, and the provision of a monetary framework'. Friedman, *Capitalism and Freedom*, 27, n 18 above. This view implies that there should be limitations on the possibility of privatizing judicial functions.

[23] It is possible that the non-delegation doctrine would apply here.

[24] This argument has been raised in *The Human Rights Section of the Academic College in Ramat Gan Law School v The Minister of Finance*, HCJ 2605/05 (Supreme Court of Israel) (pending), which challenges the first initiative aimed at establishing a private prison in Israel. In the United States, the question of which functions are 'inherently governmental' is not asked at the constitutional level, but rather is situated in the context of applying Circular A-76, which uses this terminology to define the limits on contracting-out. See Verkuil, *Outsourcing Sovereignty*, 125–7, n 2 above. For discussion of this limitation with regard to surveillance activities, see chapter nine of this volume by Simon Chesterman.

At any rate, it is clear that such an argument may be made only with regard to some 'core' activities (such as policing and intelligence services), but not with regard to many other matters that are at the centre of current privatization initiatives, such as education, health, and welfare. Moreover, defining the 'core' of executive actions poses the risk of indirectly legitimizing the privatization of all remaining functions that do not fall within the scope of the definition.

Privatization in the area of security should likewise be evaluated by referring to the questions regarding the 'core' activities of the executive. Under a theory that reserves to the state the monopoly over the use of force, the privatization of combat activities and other functions that involve the use of force (including the incarceration of enemy combatants) should not be privatized (because they touch on the core of government actions). It is important to note, however, that adopting such a theory and applying it to the privatization of security-related actions may have implications for the discussion of related or similar actions outside the military context—for example, with regard to the privatization of prisons and policing. In the United States, this analysis may prove to be difficult, since the privatization of prisons is already a living reality as discussed by Aman.[25]

With regard to the privatization of military actions, it is also worthwhile to take into consideration the views and perceptions of international humanitarian law on the use of private actors in combat roles. The law governing this matter can be inferred, at least partially, from the principles governing the status of mercenaries. Traditional mercenaries, non-nationals who take part in hostilities for financial gain, do not qualify as combatants or as prisoners of war.[26] Accordingly, nationals of the military forces who are hired to carry out military

[25] For an overview of the history of the privatization of prisons in the United States, see Martin E Gold, 'The Privatization of Prisons', *Urban Lawyer*, vol 28 (1996) 359. The privatization of prisons is based on the distinction between the allocation of punishment (in the judicial process), which is not privatized, and its administration, which may be privatized. However, in fact, even the administration of imprisonment involves discretionary decision-making that affects prisoners' everyday life and discipline.

[26] According to Protocol Additional to the Geneva Conventions of 12 August 1949 (Protocol I) (1977) art 47: '1. A mercenary shall not have the right to be a combatant or a prisoner of war. 2. A mercenary is any person who: (a) is specially recruited locally or abroad in order to fight in an armed conflict; (b) does, in fact, take a direct part in the hostilities; (c) is motivated to take part in the hostilities essentially by the desire for private gain and, in fact, is promised, by or on behalf of a Party to the conflict, material compensation substantially in excess of that promised or paid to combatants of similar ranks and functions in the armed forces of that Party; (d) is neither a national of a Party to the conflict nor a resident of territory controlled by a Party to the conflict; (e) is not a member of the armed forces of a Party to the conflict; and (f) has not been sent by a State which is not a Party to the conflict on official duty as a member of its armed forces'. Available at <http://www.unhchr.ch/html/menu3/b/93.htm>. For a detailed analysis from the perspective of international law, see Peter W Singer, 'War, Profits, and the Vacuum of Law: Privatized Military Firms and International Law', *Columbia Journal of Transnational Law*, vol 42 (2004) 521; Emanuela-Chiara Gillard, 'Business Goes to War: Private Military/Security Companies and International Humanitarian Law', *International Review of the Red Cross*, vol 88 (2006) 525. For an analysis of an associated subject—the involvement of private companies in peace operations—see chapter ten of this volume by Chia Lehnardt.

functions are not directly covered by this norm of international law. However, from a broader perspective, this norm should still be understood as a warning against the privatization of military functions in the strict sense.[27]

Right-based analysis

From the perspective of the protection of human rights, the question should be whether privatization initiatives are liable to cause infringements of fundamental rights. Thus, for example, the privatization of enforcement and punishment powers has significant potential to infringe liberty and dignity (because the powers would be wielded by corporations guided by economic incentive vis-à-vis people who are removed from society and often even despised by it). Arguably, this concern can be addressed by effective administrative supervision over the operation of the private prison (or any other privatized activity of this kind).[28] However, it is difficult to conceive of effective modes of control with regard to actions that are conducted on a daily basis vis-à-vis other individuals, and which involve a high degree of discretion and immediacy (such as policing or combat). A noteworthy example in this context is the failure of the American authorities to supervise the administration of the Abu Ghraib prison facility in Iraq, which was operated by a private contractor.[29]

The decision-making process on privatization

The process by which the decision to privatize is made is of great importance. In this context, it is vital to develop legal doctrines that will guarantee that privatization decisions are made in a framework which ensures public debate, broad participation

[27] In fact, the privatization of military actions is sometimes hard to regulate, because hegemonic states may find indirect ways to achieve their goals by affording financial support to the military operations of an ally country. However, when this route of operation is chosen, the financing state does not enjoy full control of the actions, and may therefore not consider this a good enough alternative.

[28] On the aspect of supervision as a condition of the constitutionality of a privatization initiative, see Gillian E Metzger, 'Privatization as Delegation', *Columbia Law Review*, vol 103 (2003) 1367.

[29] See Steven L Schooner, 'Contractor Atrocities at Abu Grhaib: Compromised Accountability in a Streamlined, Outsourced Government', *Stanford Law & Policy Review*, vol 16 (2005) 549. It is worth adding that in other contexts, privatization may have an effect on the realization of social rights. For example, privatization that entails charging fees for certain social services is likely to have ramifications for social rights in systems that recognize such rights. Thus, it will be necessary to examine whether the privatization of services in the area of health or education is conducted in a way that guarantees universal access to those services and prevents discrimination. At the same time, it is clear that not every privatization of a social service will necessarily result in a constitutional violation (as in circumstances in which the service is supplied by a private entity but through state funding or subsidization). There are also 'mixed' examples in which the potential for infringement of rights involves both a civil rights aspect and a social rights aspect. This is the case when the police wish to charge demonstrators for the expenses of policing their demonstration. See *Majority Headquarters v Israeli Police*, HCJ 2557/05 (2006) (Supreme Court of Israel).

and public access to relevant information. In other words, it is necessary to consider whether the decision-making process that led to the decision to privatize took into account the ramifications of the privatization decision on the quality of the services provided to the public and enabled public scrutiny. Traditionally, the discussion of the decision to privatize tended to focus on the facet of competition; that is, on ensuring that the decisions were not aimed at benefiting government cronies. From this perspective, rules of bidding and contracting proved to be important. In contrast, the current discussion calls for scrutiny of the preliminary decision to privatize—not only of the implementation of the decision to privatize in a fair and equal manner vis-à-vis other potential competitors for the privatization initiative. Generally speaking, the procedural concerns that should be addressed include the requirement to ground privatization decisions in a pre-formulated policy, public participation, and freedom of information rights.

To ensure informed decisions regarding privatization, it is necessary to recognize an administrative duty to formulate a policy on privatization in a certain area of activity before promoting a specific privatization initiative in that area. Thus, for example, the agency should be obligated to formulate a policy regarding the idea to transfer public schools to private management before it can enter into a contract with a private education network for the privatization of a specific school. The duty to formulate a policy on privatization shifts the focus from the question of the 'minimum' that the state must do, to a duty to justify the change (even when the state continues to provide the required minimum).

In addition, it is important to ensure public participation in the decision-making process that leads to privatization. This additional requirement is consistent with the general trend towards reinforcing the democratic dimensions of the administrative process. In order to guarantee meaningful participation, privatization initiatives should be publicized well in advance, before their execution, in order to enable the submission of comments and objections. It is important to stress that public participation in the formal stage of rule-making is not enough with regard to privatization conducted by contracting out. In this context, many significant details are not set in the framework of a statute or regulations, but rather in the contract with the private entity (and perhaps even in the tender that precedes it). Therefore, in addition to guaranteeing meaningful participation, the tender and proposed contract must also be publicized properly, because at least some of their terms are likely to include matters of public significance (for example, the terms that define the living conditions of the inmates and the quality of education and professional background of their guards).

Participation in the substantive sense must be based on information. Thus, the democratization of privatization initiatives must be based on full disclosure of the details of the contractual relationship with the private entity (both the terms of the proposed contract and the terms of the contract as finalized), or at least on guaranteed access to them. Revealing the details of the contract to the public is vital to allow for the possibility to assess the exchange equivalence of the transaction, which transfers public assets or public services to private hands, as well as for monitoring of the execution of the contract by the private party (for example, whether the contractor meets the standards set in the contract regarding the services it supplies to the public).

Providing the public with information regarding privatizations must be conducted both actively—through publications initiated by the government—and passively—in response to specific requests for the disclosure of information. In practice, agencies may be reluctant to disclose the details of their contracts with private entities, principally in order to protect the trade secrets of their contracting party or confidential public information (for example, the details of the security system in a private prison). In the majority of cases, however, the details of the contract with the private entity must be open to public scrutiny in order to facilitate public debate and supervision over the privatization initiative. The presumption should always be in favour of disclosure of the contracting details, and therefore when the government seeks to prevent disclosure it should be required to provide a detailed reasoning supporting its position. Indeed, transparency is also the accepted norm in the commercial world with respect to transactions involving a broad public interest, such as those in the stock market. Thus, in a similar vein, transparency should also prevail in the context of privatization.

The regulation of privatized functions and activities

Finally, the regulation and supervision of privatized bodies and functions are of paramount importance as they touch upon the ongoing operation of activities that have undergone privatization. Assuming that notwithstanding the controversy over privatization, considerable areas of public activity will be privatized, their long-term regulation is crucial.[30] This regulation should set the standards for the operation of the privatized activities. The potential for criminal sanctions[31] and tort actions[32] in cases of grave infringements of rights is important, but does not suffice. The regulation of privatized activities should take various forms:[33] direct application of constitutional duties,

[30] For an argument in favour of focusing on the supervision over privatized bodies in the American context, see Minow, 'Partners, Not Rivals', n 14 above.

[31] An interesting question in the context of criminal law is whether employees of private corporations who execute public functions should be considered subject to the special offences that have traditionally applied only to public officials (such as bribery).

[32] For an action for infringement of rights in the context of a privatized prison, see *Richardson v McKnight*, 521 US 399 (1997). In this case, the US Supreme Court declined to apply to employees of a private prison the qualified immunity that would have been applicable in similar circumstances in the context of a government prison.

[33] The discussion here focuses on regulation based on national law, and does not extend to self-regulation by the industry itself. For the potential contribution of self-regulation and other forms of hybrid public-private regulatory regimes, see chapter seven of this volume by Rebecca DeWinter-Schmitt.

statutory regulation and regulation through conditions in the tender and in the contract.

When private actors function as de facto substitutes of the government in the fulfilment of important public functions, they should be subject to duties similar to those that would have applied to the government had it conducted the same action. The doctrinal way to achieve this goal may vary among legal systems, in accordance with their view with respect to the application of constitutional principles to private actors. In the context of the United States, the way to achieve this goal would be to use the state action doctrine, which also applies to private actors that perform traditional functions of the government or work in close connection with it.[34] The problem with using this specific doctrine is its relatively narrow interpretation in the case law, which enables its application only with regard to a relatively small core of governmental activities. This narrow interpretation would not pose a barrier to the application of constitutional standards to private actors performing traditional military functions, but unfortunately this would not be the case (in the United States) with regard to many other privatizations.[35] The conclusion that private actors who act in cooperation with the military should be subject to constitutional duties, as they constitute an integral part of the army apparatus, finds additional support in developments in the area of international law.[36]

Statutes that open the door for privatization should include provisions stating the duties and the supervising mechanisms that would apply to the activities of the private actors. Ensuring the possibility of effective review of the decision-making processes in the privatized bodies has to be one of the factors to be considered when evaluating the constitutionality of the privatization initiative. In addition, the preparation of a detailed statutory regulation with regard to the activity planned for privatization is important for another reason: the efforts invested in drafting the legislative scheme are likely to expose the difficulties in guaranteeing effective supervision, and can even lead to a reconsideration of the decision to privatize. Another factor to be considered here is that in many cases, the privatized activities are operated by large corporations which are not subject to domestic control. It is likely that such corporations will not be mindful of public criticism unless they are obliged to conduct decision-making processes based on disclosure and participation rights.

In addition to establishing supervision mechanisms, the statutory provisions dedicated to privatization initiatives should address the decision-making processes within the privatized bodies with regard to such matters as granting the right to a hearing (to those dependent on the decisions of the privatized body),

[34] Daphne Barak-Erez, 'A State Action Doctrine for an Age of Privatization', *Syracuse Law Review*, vol 45 (1995) 1169.

[35] Daphne Barak-Erez, 'Civil Rights in the Privatized State: A Comparative View', *Anglo-American Law Review*, vol 28 (1999) 503.

[36] See chapter two of this volume by Olivier De Schutter.

and the right to receive information (in order to enable public debate around the operations of the privatized body).[37]

The privatization contract should also play a central role in the regulation of the privatized activity.[38] It is important to define the duties of the private entity (especially with regard to the protection of human rights) in the framework of the contract. A number of examples illustrate this. First, the privatization contract can set the labour terms and wages of the workers employed by the private contractors. The efficiency of the privatization project should not flow from violations of employees' rights; or alternatively, be based on the possibility of hiring employees lacking proper training and skills. Second, the privatization contract should include instructions with regard to equal access to the privatized services. The breach of any one of these conditions would constitute a breach of contract. In the context of social and welfare-related services, the contract should also include detailed provisions regarding the procedural rights of the recipients of the privatized services (such as a right to a hearing). In some cases, the privatization contract should also create a supervision mechanism for the prices charged by the private entity. Indeed, in many instances, the privatization endeavour is intended to release the government from the need to operate in the area of price setting, and to transfer this process to the market. However, there are privatized activities that relate to areas in which there is no market (or at least not a sophisticated market). Furthermore, it is important to guarantee the supply of vital services even for those who cannot afford to pay.

An additional matter that should be regulated by the privatization contract is the compensation to be paid to the private contractor if and when the government decides to terminate the contract. Indeed, there is a danger that the prospect of paying significant compensation in the event of withdrawal from the privatization initiative may prevent the government from taking this action even when it had established that the initiative did not achieve its goals or led to other unwanted consequences.[39]

Toward a public law of privatization

Privatization will continue to be a central phenomenon in the functioning of many governments around the world. This reality necessitates a rethinking of

[37] In other contexts, such as the privatization of utilities, the content of the regulation may have other focuses, for example an emphasis on equal access and universal provision. See Toni Prosser, 'Public Service Law: Privatization's Unexpected Offspring', *Law & Contemporary Problems*, vol 63 (2000) 63.

[38] For an analysis focused on the use of contracts for the regulation of privatized activities, see chapter six of this volume by Mariana Mota Prado.

[39] This consideration places at risk, for example, the possibility of effective supervision of the operation of a private prison. In principle, privatization contracts in this area provide for a step-in right for the state. However, the government may be deterred from relying on this provision if the expected scope of compensation to the private concession holder is excessive.

the basic principles of constitutional and administrative law beyond the mere adjustment of specific rules and doctrines.

The approach proposed by this chapter to contend with this challenge is based on posing three questions, and thus distinguishing among three distinct spheres of discussion: the boundaries of privatization, the privatization process, and the regulation of privatized actions. More specifically, the chapter calls for analysing the challenge posed by the privatization of security as one (important) instance on the continuum of privatization. The problems posed by the privatization of military and security functions are indeed *sui generis*, but at the same time they are also an extreme example of the issues that should be addressed with regard to other privatizations, and which have been part of the public sphere for some time.

5

Private prisons and the democratic deficit

Alfred C Aman, Jr

Outsourcing is a common form of privatization in the United States—calling on the private sector to deliver what were once government-provided services. A key question, centrally confronted in Part III of this volume, is whether certain functions should be regarded as 'inherently governmental' and thus precluded from outsourcing. This chapter examines privatization in the US prison context with a view to mapping out an answer to that question. Is there something 'inherently governmental' in the realm of prisons that should set restrictions on outsourcing? What might prison privatization teach us about other privatized governmental functions, such as those having to do with military matters? At the state level, there is currently a range of legislative initiatives involving specification of conditions under which prisons, specific prison services, and other governmental services may be contracted out. What can these privatization policies and approaches at the state level, particularly those dealing with private prisons, teach us about what activities are 'inherently governmental', as well as their procedural demands?

Prisons are a useful case for considering these questions of inherent governmental functions. On the one hand, they are buildings and workplaces like any other, servicing inmates as if they were clients—with clean laundry, occupations, education, and so forth. On the other hand, they are settings in which responsibility for the care of inmates—nutrition, medical care, basic life conditions—reach the level of human rights concerns. The former functions might easily be outsourced, but the latter—where the fundamental integrity of the body and the basic dignity of the person are at stake—pose more challenging questions. This chapter is primarily concerned with that grey zone, where the vulnerability of the prison population poses challenges to the current standards by which inherent governmental functions are assessed.

Privatization of state and federal prison systems provides a rich example of the selective shift away from traditional government-provided services to a system highly dependent on private providers.[1] In the United States, while there remain

[1] See Paige M Harrison and Allen J Beck, 'Prisoners in 2005', *Bureau of Justice Statistics Bulletin*, US Department of Justice, November 2006, 5, available at <http://www.ojp.usdoj.gov/bjs/pub/pdf/p05.pdf>.

several states that do not currently allow for privatized correctional facilities, at least 33 states house a percentage of inmates in privately owned and operated prisons.[2] Several states have also outsourced to private companies for the provision of services within state-run prisons, such as health care, often with less than desirable, or even disastrous, results.[3]

Since the 1980s, privatization has gained prominence as a tool of governance[4] and, as has been argued elsewhere, is of a piece with a neoliberal conception of globalization that has introduced new ways for states to carry out their duties.[5] This neoliberal approach, as it has been implemented in the United States, tends to treat social services almost exclusively as costs rather than as investments in the state's human infrastructure. When applied to state functions, such as prison administration, it treats privatization through a series of technical questions, which emphasize technical expertise and substantially minimize public participation. A democracy deficit, however, occurs when public functions are carried out by private actors to the extent that requirements of transparency and public participation—the keystones of administrative democracy—are reduced or set aside.[6]

The Federal Activities Inventory Reform Act, which prohibits the privatization of 'inherently governmental' functions, specifies that an 'inherently governmental' function is one that is 'so intimately related to the public interest as to require performance by Federal Government employees,' including the execution of laws that 'significantly affect the life, liberty, or property of private persons.'[7] The phrase 'inherently governmental' (discussed more fully by Simon Chesterman in chapter nine of this volume) has been explicated more fully in the context of the Office of Management and Budget (OMB) Circular A-76, which establishes federal policy and procedures regarding the performance of commercial activities and whether they may be performed by commercial

[2] Ibid. 5–6 (at the end of 2005, '33 States and the Federal system reported a total of 107,447 prisoners held in privately operated prison facilities . . . Private facilities held 6.0% of all State prisoners and 14.4% of Federal prisoners'). In comparison, the percentage of juveniles housed in private facilities is much higher than the percentage of adults in private prisons. As of October 2002, only 40% of juvenile facilities (housing 69% of juvenile offenders) were publicly operated. Melissa Sickmund, 'Juvenile Residential Facility Census, 2002', *Juvenile Offenders and Victims National Report Series*, Office of Juvenile Justice and Delinquency Prevention, US Department of Justice, June 2006, 2, available at <http://www.ncjrs.gov/pdffiles1/ojjdp/211080.pdf>.

[3] See 'Lawsuit over Michigan Death Settled for $3.25m', *Associated Press*, 8 July 2008. See also Michael D LaFaive, 'Privatization for the Health of It', Mackinac Center for Public Policy, Winter 2005, 4, available at <http://www.mackinac.org/article.aspx?ID=6910>.

[4] See Ruth Hoogland DeHoog and Lester Salamon, 'Purchase of Service Contracting in The Tools of Governance', in Lester Salamon (ed), *The Tools of Government: A Guide to the New Governance* (New York: Oxford University Press, 2002) 319–39.

[5] See Alfred C Aman, Jr, *Privacy and Democracy: Resources in Administrative Law in Government by Design* (Harvard University Press, forthcoming).

[6] See Alfred C Aman, Jr, *The Democracy Deficit: Taming Globalization Through Law Reform* (New York: NYU Press, 2004).

[7] US Congress, Federal Activities Inventory Reform Act of 1998, PL 105–270, codified at 31 USC § 501 (1998), s 5.

sources or if government employees must perform them.[8] The 'inherently governmental' test has not been significantly restrictive when it comes to privatization at the federal level.[9] Much of the federal government's contracting is not subject to the restrictions of the OMB Circular A-76, and there is a lack of concern about outsourcing involving 'inherently governmental' functions.[10] The OMB has liberally granted outsourcing requests made by federal agencies. State legislation also provides for a variety of approaches to privatization in general and the privatization of prisons in particular.

The criteria set forth in these various state approaches to privatization can be read with a view toward understanding some of the key factors that are currently in play as criteria for outsourcing decisions. As we will see, these seldom yield bright lines that would clearly delineate what activity is or is not considered 'inherently governmental'. In the end, these decisions are largely political and, as this chapter will also argue, this is as it should be. As we shall see through a reading of these statutes, the question of inherent governmental function is closely tied to procedural values with respect to participation, transparency, oversight and accountability. Administrative law reforms will thus feature prominently in this discussion.

The primary management tool for outsourcing prisons to the private sector is the contract. Government agencies remain responsible for the outcomes reached by these private providers under these contracts, but they are no longer involved in the day-to-day regulation or management of the enterprise. Under these arrangements, private actors become the dominant players by virtue of their contract with the state. And unlike public agencies, these private actors are unlikely to be subject to statutes such as the Administrative Procedure Act or the Freedom of Information Act at either the state or federal levels. Privatization tends to imply that oversight and accountability will remain as they would under the government, but this is not always explicit nor is it consistently the case. Those who operate private prisons may be considered state actors for purposes of the Due Process Clause of the US Constitution, but the application of this body

[8] 'Performance of Commercial Activities', OMB Circular No A-76 (Revised), White House Office of Management and Budget, 29 May 2003 available at <http://www.whitehouse.gov/omb/circulars/a076/a76_incl_tech_correction.pdf>. See generally Paul Verkuil, *Outsourcing Sovereignty: Why Privatization of Government Functions Threatens Democracy and What We Can Do About It* (New York: Cambridge University Press, 2007).

[9] See generally Dan Guttman, 'Inherently Governmental Functions and the New Millennium', in Thomas H Stanton and Benjamin Ginsberg (eds), *Making Government Manageable* (Baltimore: Johns Hopkins University Press, 2004) 40 (citing *Flagg Bros. v Brooks*, 436 US 149 (1978)). In *Flagg Bros. v Brooks*, the Supreme Court found that in the history of the United States the only two activities that could be termed 'exclusive public functions' are elections and police activities of company towns.

[10] Paul R Verkuil, 'Public Law Limitations on Privatization of Government Functions', *North Carolina Law Review*, vol 84 (2006) 441. Verkuil observes that if an agency erroneously classifies an activity as non-inherently governmental, that designation is not subject to administrative review. The designation may only be challenged by 'an agency official who is competing against a private contractor to save her job'.

of law to prisons generally does not provide much protection for prisoners. Moreover, the contracting process itself is often some form of a least-bid contract procedure, one that tends to focus predominantly on cost.[11] Reducing everything to cost considerations would imply that any private provider capable of making a profit on the activity can, and perhaps should, provide this service—the assumption being that profitability will be passed onto taxpayers as savings.

The discussion in this chapter follows the framework proposed by Daphne Barak-Erez in chapter four of this volume, but its main focus is on the first two prongs of the inquiry Barak-Erez proposes: the boundaries of privatization and the administrative process of privatization. The next section of this chapter will discuss how legislatures have sought to deal with the issues of privatization in general and prisons in particular. The chapter then examines the reaction of courts to various privatization issues, especially those involving prison disciplinary proceedings. The reaction of both legislative and judicial public bodies suggests some criteria for considering whether and how to outsource prison management functions. Accordingly, we shall explore the outer boundaries of the use of privatization as a governance tool as well as the need for processes that can accommodate a broad spectrum of political views in making these decisions.

The chapter thus argues for a new administrative law that ensures participation, transparency and accountability when outsourcing decisions are made. The comprehensive marketizing of government services artificially restricts the realm of 'inherently governmental', which ordinarily involves the test of whether the service is inherently viable. Factors other than cost must also be involved in assessing what is and is not 'inherently governmental'. Are there other aspects of running a prison that limit outsourcing and what are the implications of these limits in other privatization contexts? Can the government outsource the adjudication of disciplinary disputes arising from prisoners' behaviour? Could the government outsource executions of prisoners already sentenced to death? Are cost and efficiency factors alone the only considerations in delegating such tasks?

Drawing on the discussion of prisons, the conclusion is that certain democracy considerations should be important limitations on privatization. There are some issues that require a collective response at the time they arise. Issues involving life or death or the loss of liberty are 'inherently governmental' because those decisions speak for us all in a fundamental way. Considering how private prisons should operate to mitigate the democracy deficit raises the more general question of when a democratic, collective response requires a public decision-maker. It is at this level that the legislation affecting private prisons is more broadly relevant to the privatization of military services, especially in the detention context. The outcry over Abu Ghraib focused primarily on

[11] See generally Alfred C Aman, Jr, 'An Administrative Law Perspective on Government Social Service Contracts: Outsourcing Prison Health Care in New York City', *Indiana Journal of Global Legal Studies*, vol 14 (2007) 301.

interrogation methods, but the situation there also revealed fundamental problems regarding the integration of military and private contractors from the standpoint of chain of command, oversight and accountability.[12]

Regulating private prisons: Legislative responses

There are various examples of state legislatures attempting to regulate privatization processes and their effects, especially in the prison context. The legislatures have treated these issues largely in economic terms, with little regard for the more fundamental question of what can or cannot be outsourced. The processes have tended not to allow direct public participation outside of legislators themselves.

Statutes involving the privatization of prisons vary widely from state to state in the protections they afford to the human rights of prisoners. They also vary in the extent to which they involve the public at large in a timely way.[13] As a result of cost-saving concerns dominating the decision-making process for privatization of prisons, state privatization legislation rarely, if ever, mentions prisoners' human rights. Even where the rights are mentioned in the legislation, there is little or no guidance on how the rights should be respected and enforced as a matter of process. The fact that decisions to privatize are often made hastily, usually in the face of budget pressures or court orders to relieve overcrowding at public facilities, further exacerbates the problem.

This section begins the discussion of legislative reactions to privatization with a review of the cost assumptions underlying the privatization of prisons. This is followed by a consideration of which prison services can be privatized in ways that involve the public generally and retain the government's accountability for the human rights of prison inmates. Finally, criteria that should signal the outer limits of privatization in the context of prisons are proposed.

Privatization, cost, democracy, and inequality

Much of the pressure to privatize prisons is driven by cost. Even when prisons remain state-operated, many have turned to privatizing certain financially draining services, such as inmate health care. Take prison health services, for

[12] Two reports recently released by independent commissions note various concerns and problems with the structuring of direction and command with respect to Abu Ghraib. See generally James R Schlesinger, 'Final Report of the Independent Panel to Review Department of Defense Detention Operations', August 2004, available at <http://news.findlaw.com/hdocs/docs/dod/abughraibrpt.pdf>; MG George R Fay, 'Investigation of the Abu Ghraib Detention Facility and 205th Military Intelligence Bridge', AR 15–6, pp 109–20, available at <http://news.findlaw.com/hdocs/docs/dod/fay82504rpt.pdf>.

[13] For a list of state statutes and regulations governing private prisons, see <http://www.afscme.org/docs/stateppregsakfl.pdf>.

instance, the 'biggest for-profit company providing medical care in jails and prisons' which '[d]espite a tarnished record . . . has sold its promise of lower costs and better care, and . . . amassed 86 contracts in 28 states, and now cares for 237,000 inmates, or about one in every 10 people behind bars'.[14]

In the United States, individual states take varied approaches to privatization, subjecting private service providers to differing degrees of public accountability. Many states have statutes regarding the privatization of prisons, some allowing and encouraging them, some banning their use altogether.[15] A number of states also have general privatization statutes covering the privatization of services more generally. These general statutes reflect a variety of views towards privatization. On the one end of the spectrum is Colorado's privatization statute, which provides that 'it is . . . the policy of this state to encourage the use of private contractors for personal services to achieve increased efficiency in the delivery of government services.'[16] In contrast, the Massachusetts legislature 'finds and declares that using private contractors to provide public services formerly provided by public employees does not always promote the public interest.'[17] The danger of statutes like Colorado's is that they state as fact the debatable claim that private providers are more efficient; the statute assumes that private companies would more efficiently provide *any* service. This statute operates as a presumption that privatization is in the public interest, which may stifle debate on the actual merits of any individual privatization decision.

There is a continuing debate about whether private prisons offer any real cost benefit. It is common, however, for some privatization statutes to require a minimum-percentage cost savings from private prison operators.[18] Some states set a bar to outsourcing at a certain level of cost savings. While there would be little point in privatizing if some savings were not anticipated, the risks to prisoners' rights would seem to increase directly with the scale of the cost-savings requirement. Contrary to popular wisdom, many states operate their own prison systems with great frugality even without outsourcing. Alabama's public prisons, for example, spend \$1.08 to feed each prisoner each day. It is hard to imagine how private companies could best such a low level expenditure without compromising the nutritional status of the inmates—a fundamental human rights concern. In addition, in Alabama prisons, much of the work required to run the

[14] Paul von Zielbauer, 'As Health Care in Jails Goes Private, 10 Days Can Be a Death Sentence', *New York Times*, 27 February 2005.

[15] See, eg, NY Corrections Law § 72(1) (McKinney 2003) (requiring the department to house and care for all inmates); Ark Code Ann § 12-50-106(a) (Michie 2002) (authorizing contracts for construction, financing, and operating facilities).

[16] Colo Rev Stat Ann § 24-50-501 (West 2003).

[17] Mass Gen Laws Ann ch 7, § 52 (West 2003).

[18] See, eg, Ky Rev Stat Ann § 197.510(13) (Banks-Baldwin 1998) (requiring at least 10% savings); Tenn Code Ann § 41-24-104(C)(2)(B) (2002 Supp) (requiring at least 5% savings); Ohio Rev Code Ann 9.06(A)(4) (West 2002) (requiring at least 5% savings); Fla Stat Ann § 957.07 (West 2003 Supp.) (requiring at least 7% savings).

facility—maintenance work such as painting, weeding, lawn mowing, staffing the kitchen, unloading supplies, and even growing vegetables—is performed by prisoners, further reducing the costs of operation.[19]

Privatization of prison services is not a monolith. In some areas, prisons involve the basic living conditions of inmates and their human rights status. In others, they do not—and are much like institutions outside the criminal justice context. Thus, it is necessary to ask what costs the legislators have specified in their statutes as ones that would or should be lowered by the private entities and what gains they anticipate as a result of the freedom given private companies in making those provisions.

The Colorado privatization statute explicitly allows private providers to adjust worker wages and benefits: 'The general assembly recognizes that such contracting may result in variances from legislatively mandated pay scales and other employment practices that apply to the state personnel system.'[20] In contrast, Washington DC requires a private provider to offer displaced workers a right of first refusal for jobs with the private company and further requires that the private company comply with the government pay-scale for six months.[21] The DC statute restricts a private provider's ability to meet cost targets by hiring more efficient workers or changing incentive structures; any required efficiency gains must, therefore, come from the reduction of other costs. The Colorado statute, like many others, requires that 'privatization of government services not result in diminished quality in order to save money.'[22]

In addition to addressing cost-saving concerns, privatization statutes need to address the questions of quality benchmarks: how should quality be assessed and from whose perspective? Unless prison contracts entered into under the statute contain verifiable measures of quality, such statutory terms are, in all likelihood, unenforceable in practice. With a few exceptions, states in the United States do a poor job of specifying what the state desires (besides low cost) to get for their agreement to employ a private prison provider. Michigan, in its statute allowing the privatization of juvenile-correction facilities, mandates that private providers of prisons require prisoners without high school degrees to receive a general education certificate (GED).[23] Colorado requires that private providers guarantee education services (and other services including dental, medical, psychological, diet, and work programmes) of at least as high quality as public prisons.[24] The problem with Colorado's provision is that it does not provide any specific, concrete standards by which a comparison of quality can be judged.

[19] Carla Crowder, 'Alabama Feeds Prisoners on $1.08 a Day', *Birmingham News*, 26 November 2003.
[20] Colo Rev Stat Ann § 24-50-501 (West 2003).
[21] DC Code Ann § 2-301.05(d)(2)-(4) (West 2003).
[22] Colo Rev Stat Ann § 24-50-501 (West 2003).
[23] Mich Comp Laws Ann § 791.220g (West 2001).
[24] Colo Rev Stat Ann § 17-1-202(f) (West 2003).

Part of the reason for concern about the potential for human rights abuses in private prisons is that private prisons are unlikely to be able to sustain the conditions that would support a 'relatively strong relationship between democratic forms of government and the protection of human rights'.[25] Even in the case of activities that would not require government retention of responsibility in other settings (such as the provision of food services in government buildings) the prison context might call for such attention. Furthermore, the axiom to the effect that 'the civil liberties usually associated with democracies . . . enable citizens and opposition groups to publicize abuses'[26] loses its force in the prison context. In prisons, where a defined population has lost some of its civil liberties (including, often, the right to vote after release from prison), prisoners are therefore excluded from the bargaining necessary to prevent oppression, and, especially in a privatized context, the general public usually is excluded from regular information about the treatment of inmates. Even if adequate democratic checks exist for prison privatization decisions, most states do not subject providers to oversight sufficient to ensure accountability with respect to those issues.

As discussed above, privatization of prison services by definition involves shifts in cost allocations and direct or indirect subsidies—for example, on the part of prisoners whose conditions of confinement will be affected so as to meet the cost savings threshold. But it should not alter basic democratic processes. For example, the question of how costs are to be shifted (for example, to workers) should be subject to the same procedural checks (participation, oversight, accountability) as any 'inherently governmental' service would be. This is why the procedures recommended below take on special importance in contexts such as these. But the point also has wider relevance—for example, in issues of wages and other cost savings that directly affect workers or the quality of services. Privatization of prisons sidesteps important statutory public law protections such as the Freedom of Information Act. Even when the due process clause of the Fourteenth Amendment is brought to bear, courts are most reluctant to intervene, except in the most extreme situations.

More broadly, a major criterion for determining what is (or is not) 'inherently governmental' should be guided by procedures in which those directly affected by the decisions participate—even if indirectly through representation. In the prison context, this might refer to workers or to inmates; indeed, democracy concerns should not be suspended for the inmate population as if their exclusion from the management of their own affairs were a normal condition of their confinement.

[25] Wesley T Miller, 'Economic Globalization and Rights: An Empirical Analysis', in Alison Brysk (ed), *Globalization and Human Rights* (Berkeley, CA: University of California Press, 2002) 83.

[26] Ibid.

Determining what is 'inherently governmental' is a political process involving basic questions of democracy. Administrative procedures are thus key to our concerns in this chapter. The need for public participation is stressed including, but not limited to, those directly affected by the service area in question. Without public input, there is no real check on the powers of the providers. Cost is a check, too, but only superficially at best, since without other safeguards, costs can easily be shifted to segments in the population that cannot participate in or defend their own interests.

Private prisons, transparency, and accountability

A major limiting factor on privatization is the need for the government to 'step back in' and take over the functions from the private company, for example, if the private providers involved go bankrupt or if the provider is incompetent or for various reasons cannot perform the contract agreed upon. Prisons are integral to a state's criminal law—so continuity of service and 'step-in' ability are needed.

In order for a government to retain legitimate accountability for private prisons '[t]he state must retain and be able actually to exercise "step-in" rights—that is, to reclaim any privatized portion of its prison system—and to do this it needs to have ongoing capacity and skill levels of its own. This can only be done if it remains a direct service provider in relation to at least some part of its prisoner population.'[27] For some services, such as janitorial services, the ability to 'step-in' would not require the retention of a pool of state workers, even if such services were deemed to be a high human rights priority. For positions such as prison guards, in contrast, the state would have to retain a pool of public guards. Otherwise, if human rights problems developed at a private facility because of inadequate training, the state could not 'step-in' with workers to take over security provision, and the state would likely have also lost the institutional ability even to train workers to perform the duties of a prison guard. In both 1982 and 1997 the Tennessee legislature considered, and rejected, proposals to privatize the state's entire prison system.[28] The Correctional Corporation of America promised the state that it would be able to save $100 million per year with a completely privatized system. Not only would a state lose the ability to 'step-in' if it accepted such a proposal, but if the private provider was really able to save such a large sum of money, it would be difficult to see how a state would be able to quickly take back a prison system. States have shown a propensity to spend or return in tax-cuts any surplus money, and Tennessee, as a mid-sized state, would be hard-pressed to come up with the money necessary to pay for the re-establishment of a public prison system in the event the private provider was

[27] Richard Harding, 'Private Prisons', *Crime & Justice*, vol 28 (2002) 282.
[28] Ibid. at 281.

unsatisfactory. The ability of a state to 'step-in' can be ensured, at least in part, through a 'contestability' process where public providers are able to bid against private providers for contracts. Such a procedure, however, risks the removal of a governmental check on the dominance of economic concerns over human rights issues, insofar as the public providers are subjected to the same dominance of economic issues over non-economic values in the provision of services.

While there are over one hundred privately run prisons in the United States, their performance is often not compared with those of public prisons because most government agencies 'have been satisfied with monitoring compliance with the terms of the contracts'.[29] The fact that most government oversight of private prisons concerns the monitoring of contract terms necessitates the inclusion of human rights provisions in privatization contracts.[30] This is especially true given the increasing judicial indifference in the United States to prisoner suits,[31] though the Supreme Court has recognized that private prisons and their employees are less immune from suits than their public sector counterparts.[32]

One way to increase the accountability of private prison operators to the state, and thereby ensure that the state retains ultimate responsibility for prisons, is to limit the length of the privatization contract. The Supreme Court recognized this form of accountability in *Richardson v McKnight*, where a Tennessee statute limited a contract's term to three years. The majority stated that the firm's 'performance is disciplined . . . by pressure from potentially competing firms who can try to take its place.'[33] Many states, however, do not specify a maximum contract length; some statutes explicitly allow for long-term contracts. Arkansas, for example, states that contracts with private prisons 'may be entered into for a period of up to twenty (20) years.'[34] On the other end of the spectrum, Ohio provides that a contract 'shall be for an initial term of not more than two years, with an option to renew for additional periods of two years.'[35] Shorter contracts increase the potential frequency of public input into the process, which ideally would be encouraged before contract renewal takes place.

One criterion of a service's status as an 'inherently governmental' function that emerges from the statutes is the degree of competition involved in the market. If privatization only means the replacement of a public monopoly with a

[29] Douglas C McDonald, 'Private Prisons in the United States: An Assessment of Current Practice', Abt Associates Inc, 16 July 1998, available at <http://www.abtassoc.com/reports/priv-report.pdf>.

[30] In general, accountability provides 'a management standard that can work even where fundamental values are in dispute'. See Sarah Armstrong, 'Bureaucracy, Private Prisons, and the Future of Penal Reform', *Buffalo Criminal Law Review*, vol 7 (2003) 300. In the prison context, however, accountability is reduced to 'reaffirming the functionalist role of prisons' by making sure the private contractor meets certain contractual benchmarks that may have nothing to do with the humane treatment of the prisoners. Ibid. 302.

[31] Harding, 'Private Prisons', n 27 above, 320.

[32] See *Richardson v McNight*, 117 S Ct 2100 (1997) (holding that private prison guards do not enjoy the qualified immunity, in 42 USC § 1983 cases that public prison guards do).

[33] Ibid. at 2106.

[34] Ark. Code Ann. § 12-50-106(d) (Michie 2002).

[35] Ohio Rev Code Ann 9.06(A)(1) (West 2002).

private monopoly, the absence of market competition would call for procedural checks parallel to those applicable to inherent governmental functions. We must consider the court's praise for short term contracts in this light. A problem with the Court's praise of the short term provided by Tennessee law is that the Court assumed that there would be a number of firms available if the private provider should fall short in its performance. Whether there is any real competitiveness in the privatized prison industry, however, is questionable because of its oligopolistic nature. By the end of 1998, over 76 percent of the private prison capacity in the United States was controlled by just two companies: Wackenhut Corrections Corporation (WCC) and Corrections Corporation of America (CCA),[36] and CCA is a former subsidiary of WCC.[37] When states privatize they must realize that the benefits of any market-like effects are concentrated in the period before a contract is entered, 'The distinctive feature of contracting out is the element of *ex ante* competition—competition *for* the market as opposed to *in* it.'[38] The imposition of long-term contracts between states and prison providers is likely to further concentrate the industry, by providing fewer opportunities for new companies to enter a market with a very limited number of potential customers.

In addition to the provision for a short contract period, Tennessee also provides that any private prison 'must agree that the state may cancel the contract at any time after the first year of operation, without penalty to the state, upon giving ninety (90) days' written notice.'[39] This provision encourages the state to oversee the running of any private prison more closely, because the delegation can easily be reconsidered. Private groups that are interested in the privatization of prisons also have an incentive to monitor the private provider more closely, because at any time after the first year they can lobby the state to rescind the contract if it becomes apparent that a different provider (either public or private) would be preferable. All privatization contracts that represent the possibility of significant infringements upon human rights should contain a provision allowing the state to cancel the contract if it believes that human rights abuses may be occurring at a facility without fearing that the private provider might be able to hold the state liable for breach of contract. Clearly, prison guards have an important enough role to qualify; and it can be argued that medical providers do, as well. By contrast, janitorial and secretarial services would fit within the category of services that may be fully privatized.

[36] James Austin and Garry Coventry, *Emerging Issues on Privatized Prisons* (Washington, DC: Bureau of Justice Assistance, 2001) 4.

[37] Stephen Pounds, 'Florida-Based Prison Operator Wackenhut Corrections Makes Changes to Expand', *Palm Beach Post*, 24 August 2003, A3.

[38] Simon Domberger and Paul Jensen, 'Contracting Out by the Public Sector: Theory, Evidence, Prospects', *Oxford Review of Economic Policy*, Winter 1997, 67–8.

[39] Tenn. Code Ann. § 41-24-104 (2002 Supp).

Another important factor in retaining government responsibility for human rights abuses is the political accountability of the entity that actually makes the contract to privatize, and what involvement other actors have in this process. To the extent that contracts become immutable, often even to later legislatures, and to the extent that, as mentioned above, states for the most part stick to contractual issues when policing private prisons, it is important that the participation of the public and the public's representatives be maximized as early in the process as possible. Tennessee's statute provides a complex contract approval procedure involving several individuals and entities, but makes no provisions for the input of the general public. Any contract must be approved by the state building commission, the attorney general, and the commissioner of correction. Additionally, all proposals are reviewed by two congressional committees, which can make comments to those responsible for approving contracts before such approval takes place. All approved and proposed contracts are sent to the state and local government committees of both the senate and the house.[40] While this procedure involves various members of the legislative and executive branches, it does not provide direct opportunities for the public in general to affect these officials' decisions. Nevertheless, at least the privatization procedure involves members of both the executive and legislative branches, and includes legislators themselves, which are often very accessible to public input. In Idaho, the decision to enter into a contract with a private prison provider is left solely to the state board of correction;[41] most of the public would not know whom to contact to affect privatization contracts, or whom to hold accountable for the decisions of the board.

While several privatization statutes, such as Tennessee's, provide for some participation from the legislative branch in the contracting phase, few suggest any method for direct involvement from the public. Montana, one of the only states to call specifically for a public hearing, does so in a statute covering all forms of government privatization. Montana requires an agency to form a privatization plan before any programme can be privatized. Additionally, the state provides that:

> The privatization plan must be released to the public and any affected employee organizations and must be submitted to the legislative audit committee at least 90 days prior to the proposed implementation date. At least 60 days prior to the proposed implementation date, the legislative audit committee shall conduct a public hearing on the proposed privatization plan at which public comments and testimony must be received. At least 15 days prior to the proposed implementation date, the legislative audit committee shall release to the public a summary of the results of the hearing, including any recommendations of the committee relating to the proposed privatization plan.[42]

[40] Ibid. [41] Idaho Code § 20-241A (Michie 1997).
[42] Mont Stat Ann § 2-8-302 (2002).

Florida requires 'public sessions of the Correctional Privatization Commission to be held at which contract variations are [not only] discussed [they are also] explained.'[43] Public hearings produce little benefit, however, if the public is not provided with adequate information with which to make informed suggestions. Kentucky law requires the production of information necessary for the public to make informed decisions about the quality and value of privatized services:

> The private provider shall develop and implement a plan for the dissemination of information about the adult correctional facility to the public, government agencies, and the media. The plan shall be made available to all persons. All documents and records, except financial records, maintained by the private provider shall be deemed public records.[44]

Kentucky does not rely solely on voluntary disclosure by the provider to amass information on the functioning of privatized prisons. The legislature has also required that:

> [t]he department shall annually conduct a performance evaluation of any adult correctional facility for which a private provider has contracted to operate. The department shall make a written report of its findings and submit this report along with any recommendations to the private provider and the Legislative Research Commission.[45]

The prison privatization provisions create a large amount of data, and attempt to transmit most of the data to the public. However, they do not provide any mechanism for the public to participate in the privatization decision, they do not limit the length of any contract, and they do not contain many concrete requirements for the actual running of the prisons, all of which would be necessary for meaningful accountability.

Most US prison privatization statutes require certification by the American Correctional Association (ACA). As Richard Harding notes, however, '[i]mportant as [ACA] standards are in maintaining a level of accountability in US corrections, they are primarily processual . . . and formulaic. Practical, on-the-ground compliance or breach is seldom clear-cut, yet clarity and predictability are crucial for accountability.'[46] Requiring certification, therefore, cannot absolve a state from responsibility for prison services touching on basic human rights such as prisoner safety.[47] Britain and Australia do not require accreditation; the British system instead relies upon government prison inspections:

[43] Harding, 'Private Prisons', n 27 above, 308.
[44] Ky Rev Stat Ann § 197.510(7) (Banks-Baldwin 1998).
[45] Ibid. § 197.515 (Banks-Baldwin 1998).
[46] Harding, 'Private Prisons', n 27 above, 301.
[47] Privatization is not lawless; it is pluralistic and polycentric, involving many sources and kinds of law as well as other norms. Democratic safeguards should be set throughout the process, but so far this is not consistently done.

[t]he primary source of information, in contrast to ACA accreditation processes [where the ACA spends most of its time during announced visits reviewing a prison's written procedures], is direct observation, discussions with prisoners and staff, participation in some programs, follow-up interrogation of management. All this is fortified with detailed scrutiny of documentation and records.[48]

By using government inspectors, Britain also maintains direct public oversight of prisoner conditions, a necessary element in preserving prisoner rights. Additionally, as Angelina Fisher notes in chapter three of this volume, Britain—as well as Australia, Canada, and New Zealand—grant prisoners access to an ombudsman to whom prisoners can complain about violations of human rights by private prison providers; no such system is found in most US systems.[49]

Statutes that clearly specify the required elements of any prison privatization contract are preferable to those that establish few (or no) concrete requirements of the private entity in such contracts. In contrast to contract provisions, statutory language is readily accessible to the public; almost all of a state's statutory law can be located free-of-charge through the state's homepage.[50] Additionally, even if the public cannot comment, legislative sessions are often open for the attendance of interested individuals (the Colorado General Assembly website allows the public to listen to the proceedings in the state house and senate, even including committee meetings).[51] Furthermore, incorporating contract terms into a statute allows interested groups to focus their efforts on the design of every privatization contract in the state. Trying to influence each contract individually (even where a group is notified before the finalization of a contract) might often prove to be too taxing on an interested group's or individual's resources. Finally, legislatures are directly accountable to the public through elections, while entities such as state corrections boards are not.

In short, there are several factors involved in assessing the 'inherently governmental' nature of an activity. Some differentiating factors are the monopolistic or oligopolistic character of the private market, the level of government or private subsidy, and the extent to which there is a need for the government to retain the ability to step in. The more monopolistic the market, and the greater the other factors, the more likely it is that we are dealing with a public function that has the quality inherent to government. In such cases, the conventions of legitimacy demand direct participation or at least a clearly defined democratic process open to all affected parties or their representatives. The next section explores this aspect more fully.

48 Harding, 'Private Prisons', n 27 above, 318. 49 Ibid at 319.

50 See, eg, Colorado General Assembly Homepage, available at <http://www.leg.state.co.us> and Arizona @ Your Service, available at <http://az.gov/webapp/portal>.

51 See <http://www.leg.state.co.us/>.

The limits of privatization: Scope for a new administrative law?

The previous section considered legislative checks on privatization, providing us with at least some implicit tests of inherent government functions. We reviewed legislative approaches to the cost criteria normally associated with privatization as a basis for suggesting some specific democracy and human rights checks on privatization in the prison context. In this section we will first look at the way courts have responded to these issues. A review of judicial attempts to sustain democracy considerations in privatized government functions is also productive, yielding a number of specific considerations for the question of inherent government functions. We will then turn consideration to the kinds of procedural reforms that are necessary to ensure both that these various criteria for determining what is and what is not 'inherently governmental' are considered and that key stakeholders in the outcomes have a chance to participate.

Judicial responses: The outer limits of privatization and prisons

One of the inherent human rights problems created by the privatization of prisons is the blurred line between inmate discipline and the administering of additional prisoner punishment. Obviously, in order to run a prison effectively, the private provider must be able to assert some form of authority without clearance from a public supervisor. There is a point, however, where the discipline exacted by a private prison crosses over into punishment and constitutional due process concerns require public oversight.

In the United States, many 'disciplinary functions for breach of prison rules are carried out directly by the private operator.'[52] For example, in most US jurisdictions inmates can receive time off their prison sentences for 'good time' served; in other words a prisoner's sentence is reduced for behaving well behind bars. To maintain discipline, these good time credits can also be revoked, which increases the length of incarceration. This revocation of 'good time' amounts to a deprivation of liberty significant enough to require an action by the state. As a result, prisoners are entitled to a disciplinary hearing when they lose good time credits.

When disciplinary hearings occur, public prisons often have an incentive to credit prisoners for 'good time' because of prison overcrowding. Private prisons, however, can have the opposite incentive, as they are usually paid according to their daily occupancy. In addition, guards at CCA facilities can have a personal financial interest in maintaining high occupancy, because they are sometimes stockholders of the company. Such incentives have produced obvious results. 'The New Mexico Corrections Department found that inmates at the [state's]

[52] Harding, 'Private Prisons', n 27 above, 275.

CCA facility lost "good time" eight times more frequently than prisoners at the state institution.' Furthermore, in Tennessee, 'CCA guards say privately that they are encouraged to send balky inmates to administrative segregation; by placing prisoners in the "hole",' which increases the prisoner's sentence by 30 days, earning the company an extra $1,000.[53]

In private prison settings, when private parties with a financial interest in the outcome conduct the hearings, there is an increased danger of an unconstitutional deprivation of due process rights.[54] As a result, the private contractor should not be able to adjudicate the prisoners' liberty rights when its profits are directly impacted by the decisions made during these disciplinary hearings.[55] To address this problem, '[s]tate courts generally invalidate statutes and administrative regulations that delegate adjudicative power to private parties when there is no provision for judicial review of the private adjudications.'[56]

In the federal prison system, for example, Congress has entrusted the power to supervise the discipline of federal prisoners to the Bureau of Prisons ('BOP') under the Attorney General's Discretion.[57] The BOP often contracts with private corporations to provide incarceration for federal inmates. The courts have upheld the BOP's delegation of authority to discipline inmates to the private contractors, including the disallowance of good time credit, because the BOP provides a final layer of *de novo* review of any disciplinary actions. Similarly, Britain retains state control over disciplinary matters, and in private prisons, 'disciplinary charges laid by custodial officers are adjudicated by . . . public sector officials . . . who work on-site'.[58]

In the United States, it is now common for inmates to be shipped to private prisons in other states, in an effort to find the lowest cost provider. As Harding points out, this situation 'stretch[es] the chain of accountability beyond the breaking point' since the prisoner's state of origin has no oversight within the private prisons of another state.[59] These transfers are often to distant states, increasing the 'accountability deficit' created by these arrangements, distancing prisoners from their community representatives and (as Harding also points out) from their families.[60] For example, two of the largest prisoner-exporting states are the only two not within the contiguous forty-eight: Hawaii sends prisoners to Minnesota and Alaska sends prisoners to Arizona.[61] Furthermore, such

[53] Michael Welch, *Punishment in America: Social Control and the Ironies of Imprisonment* (Thousand Oaks, CA: Sage Publications 1999) 291.

[54] See Kenneth L Avio, 'On Private Prisons: An Economic Analysis of the Model Contract and Model Statute for Private Incarceration', *New England Journal on Criminal and Civil Confinement*, vol 17 (1992) 282.

[55] See Warren L Ratliff, 'The Due Process Failure of America's Prison Privatization Statutes', *Seton Hall Legislative Journal*, vol 21(1997) 402 (noting that 'prisoner's liberty interests . . . conflict directly with private prison contractors' profit motives').

[56] See Ira P Robbins, 'The Legal Dimensions of Private Incarceration', 38 *American University Law Review*, vol 38 (1989) 569.

[57] See 18 USC § 4042(a).

[58] Harding, 'Private Prisons', n 27 above, 276.

[59] Ibid. at 280.

[60] Ibid. at 290.

[61] Ibid. at 280.

exporting of inmates may deter inmate rehabilitation efforts, as '[s]everal recidivism studies have found that convicts who keep in touch with family members through visits and phone privileges are less likely to violate their parole or commit new offenses.'[62] States often fail to consider all of the possible scenarios in which the switch to private prisons affects the status of the prisoners. For instance, when Oregon sex offenders housed in a Texas prison escaped in 1998 (Texas officials were not even informed that they were housing these prisoners), Texas officials 'could not charge them with escape because in Texas it was not yet a crime to flee a private corporation'. CCA stated that it 'had no legal obligation to inform city or county officials' of the transportation of sex offenders to their jurisdiction.[63] This lack of information on the part of host states arguably violates a right to information on the part of citizens of the host state, who deserve to know potential risks they might be exposed to because of private inmates. While such a lack of information might occur in prisons housing in-state offenders, the risks are greatly reduced.

While every state has seen a dramatic increase in incarceration levels, Arizona's prison population has had increases of almost 1,000 percent in the last 25 years.[64] The state is also facing a $1.3 billion budget shortfall, leading to massive jail overcrowding.[65] In the face of budget shortfalls, legislators are reluctant to spend money on prison construction, and this reluctance translates into a *de facto* ceding of ever-greater proportions of inmate housing to private facilities. One issue of growing national concern—but of greater effect in Arizona—is the housing of increasing numbers of foreign national prisoners. About 10 percent of Arizona's prisoners are Mexican nationals, and state officials have estimated that housing all prisoners in Mexico could possibly save over $8,000 per inmate each year.[66] Arizona's Senate last year rejected a bill that 'would have required the state to seek proposals from private prison operators to build and operate a prison . . . within the neighboring Mexican state of Sonora.'[67] This issue has been discussed in Arizona for several years, however, and it is likely that it or another state with high numbers of Mexican nationals (such as New Mexico) will experiment with a cross-border facility in the future.

Even more worrying, from the standpoint of accountability, is the emerging trend in the United States of 'bed brokering' where private companies (such as Inmate Placement Services) find a prison bed in another state to house prisoners who the home state cannot place.[68] With private prisons responsible for small

[62] Solomon Moore, 'States Export Their Inmates as Prisons Fill', *New York Times*, 31 July 2007, available at <http://www.nytimes.com/2007/07/31/us/31prisons.html?pagewanted=print>.

[63] Welch, *Punishment in America*, n 53 above, 289.

[64] Robert Nelson, 'Big House Inc.', *Phoenix New Times*, 3 April 2003.

[65] Robert Nelson, 'Clink!', *Phoenix New Times*, 23 October 2003.

[66] Howard LaFranchi, 'Arizona Plans to Export Mexican Inmates', Christian Science Monitor, 17 June 1997, 8.

[67] Paul Davenport, 'Senate Panel Rejects Proposal to House Prisoners in Mexico', *Associated Press*, 7 March 2003.

[68] Harding, 'Private Prisons', n 27 above, 281.

numbers of inmates from numerous states, there is a danger that no individual state will have enough incentive to properly oversee human rights compliance, especially where the housing state does not send any of its own prisoners to the facility. Consequently, states should be required to house, and therefore retain responsibility for, their own prisoners.

This observation may point to yet another criterion of 'inherently governmental' functions: ethical limitations on lobbying. A state should prohibit private providers who either house inmates in the state or accept inmates from the state within facilities found in other states to lobby the state on criminal sentencing laws. It is true that private corporations can be more cost-sensitive than public entities because of their accountability to shareholders. There is no evidence that private providers attempt to either influence sentencing decisions or statute drafting in order to increase the number of prisoners, thereby increasing their potential 'clients'. However, as private prisons begin to saturate markets and deepen their relationships with state legislators, prudent drafting should require that all prison privatization statutes make clear that contracting prisons are prohibited from lobbying the legislature on criminal-sentencing matters. Richard Harding has correctly stated the danger that 'regulatory mechanisms in relation to private prisons are more susceptible to capture—that is, a situation where "regulators come to be more concerned to serve the interests of the industry with which they are in regular contact than the more remote and abstract public interest"—than in relation to other, more strictly commercial activities'.[69] It is consequently more important for the legislature to circumscribe the administering agency's discretion than in other privatization contexts.

A need for new approaches to administrative law

There are seldom any clearly defined lines separating activities that are or are not 'inherently governmental'. It is with the actual contract and contracting process that the most important reforms are most urgently needed. It is here that a new conception of administrative law is important, one that is not solely state-centric in its application to decisions with broad policy effects, but relevant to the public/private decision making that occurs in various privatized settings. Once an agency decides to contract out its primary functions, the proposed contract should be noticed to the public on the agency web site as if it were a rule promulgated for public comment. The public should have a chance to comment on the goals of the contract, its mode of enforcement, the monitoring of its implementation (including what shall constitute monitoring), and all other issues deemed relevant. As with a rule in a regulatory proceeding, the agency need not adopt all or any of the suggestions made, but it should provide its own reasons for accepting the ultimate contract.

[69] Harding, 'Private Prisons', n 27 above, 306.

An important role for administrative procedure is to accommodate most if not all of these interests with a process that allows them to speak to one another as well as the ultimate decision-maker. Once a contract is entered into, it is also important that these discussions occur with some frequency. The nature of the enterprise requires ongoing monitoring of the contract terms, as well as opportunities to comment on implementation, and provision for amendments regarding the duties of the private actor. Procedurally speaking, the privatizing agency should be willing to treat the proposed contract more like a rule than a contract negotiated between two parties. It could be put up on the prison authority's web site, calling for public comments, suggestions, alternative language and ways to achieve its substantive reform goals from whoever wishes to comment. In our extended example, this would include prisoners and their representatives as well. The agency should also provide extensive information on the track records of firms competing for the contract. Finally, government regulators should ensure fair competition among the bidders. All of them should agree that if they are chosen, they will be subject to regular reporting requirements and a modified Freedom of Information Act allowing interested members of the public to make relevant inquiries about their operation while the contract is in place. That contract should be no more than three years in length, subject to renewal but only after another round of competitive bidding occurs.

The simplicity of notice and comment procedures when it comes to public service contracts makes transparency reasonably efficient, and transparency need not impose undue impediments to the bargaining process. A presumption in favour of the bargains struck in such contracts can be written into the governing statutes. Courts need not be involved unless there is corruption or an unconstitutional exercise of discretion. Indeed, the purpose of these citizen-oriented procedures is to ensure that the many views and voices involved in such public-regarding private arrangements are heard. It is not just that there is a public dimension involved; it is that there are genuine public values at stake that necessitate debate and contest. The various positions are different formulations of democracy—as inherent in the operations of the market, or external to the market as a larger framework of critique and reform.[70]

Conclusion

Now we are in a position to consider whether privatization—as illuminated by the prison context—should have limits, and, if so, how they might best be

[70] This article does not address global administrative law as such, but issues including the lack of an independent judge in disciplinary proceedings, the export of prisoners based on cost and not on social factors, and the use of private interrogators such as those used at Abu Ghraib, raise human rights concerns that may have an international significance.

enforced through administrative law. There certainly appear to be constitutional limits on the ability of private providers to adjudicate disputes involving prisoners without involvement of courts; however, as we have seen, even these limits are relatively easily met, constitutionally speaking, with a judicial review of these private decisions. This is not an insignificant check on private decision-making power, but it does not go far enough in terms of meeting the democracy and human rights concerns raised in the prison context. The ability to engage in processes that enable important stakeholders to have a say in the contracting process is also of great importance. In the end, these are almost always political decisions that do not usually lend themselves to a yes or no answer. Still, there are some outer limits to the ability of government to outsource. Judicial review, for example, would be an insufficient basis for an account as to why we should resist a public prison's effort to outsource the execution of an inmate sentenced to death.[71] Though a hypothetical scenario, it points to a line that may not be legitimately crossed in reality—confirming the existence of limiting conditions in relation to privatization in the prison context and beyond, in addition to those set forth by courts and legislatures.

In the hypothetical scenario of outsourcing executions, even if there were—by some stretch of the imagination—a competitive market involving legitimate firms able to provide the so-called service, by definition those firms would have been created wholly as an extension of the government's monopoly on legal executions. Let us leave aside—if we can—the moral reprehensibility of creating an industry licensed to kill. More relevant for our purposes would be the reservation that it separates the execution from the collective judgment claimed at sentencing. This reservation sheds light on the question of limits under more ordinary circumstances—in that while it may be possible to separate the management of prisons from government to the extent that they involve institutions, buildings, workplaces, and residences like others outside the prison context, they also entail elements that are unique to the function of prisons and the consequent vulnerability of prisoners in their physical status and in relation to their fundamental human dignity. If only the state can take a life legally, then it follows that *any* function in which the physical body of the prisoner is directly at stake—in nutrition, medical care, and the basic living conditions inside the prison—are also 'inherently governmental' functions.

In practice, the question of what is and is not 'inherently governmental' is a decision that must be made democratically, through an open political process that meets the standards of transparency and accountability set in place by legislatures and courts. For that reason, it is suggested that a new kind of administrative law can, and should, be created to respond to the new forms of democracy deficit associated with privatization. Since prisons involve such a wide range of services, the prison context is useful for thinking through the

[71] I wish to acknowledge and thank Simon Chesterman for raising this important question.

promise and limits of privatization in relation to 'inherent governmental' functions. The pragmatics of privatization have emerged as an important terrain where a new administrative law might emerge, assuring public forums for input and debate and a flow of information that can help create meaningful politics around private actors doing the public's business. The democracy problem is, and should be, one of the primary concerns of a new administrative law as we face the costs and benefits of the privatization trend in contemporary governance.

6

Regulatory choices in the privatization of infrastructure

*Mariana Mota Prado**

Many of the benefits of privatization depend on the existence of an appropriate regulatory framework that defines the conditions for the provision of the services, sets up a system of incentives to improve efficiency and quality in their delivery, and establishes mechanisms of control and accountability of private providers.[1] This chapter discusses the circumstances under which such a regulatory framework is established, designed, or enforced by developing a comparative analysis of the privatization processes in infrastructure sectors (such as water, electricity, roads) with the process in military and security services.

The circumstances under which governments decide to privatize may create incentives to adopt regulation or not. As a consequence, the reasons to privatize may influence what kind of regulation (if any) is feasible or likely to be implemented by the government. Circumstances that could potentially affect the enforcement of an adequate regulatory framework can also influence the choice of certain regulatory arrangements over others. Moreover, the benefits of privatization might not be achieved if there is an appropriate regulatory framework, but it is not properly or effectively enforced. Thus, a state that lacks an independent and efficient judiciary may adopt alternative regulatory arrangements to deal with the enforcement problem. The circumstances under which a regulatory framework is established, designed or enforced might also affect the calculation of potential benefits and costs of privatization.

* I am grateful to Marcio Grandchamp, Michael Trebilcock and the participants of the conference 'Private Security, Public Order: Governance & Limits', organized by the Institute for International Law and Justice of the New York University School of Law, for comments to an earlier version of this chapter. Many thanks to Javier Gonzales for the excellent research assistance.

[1] David Parker and Colin Kirkpatrick, 'Privatisation in Developing Countries: A Review of the Evidence and the Policy Lessons', *Journal of Development Studies*, vol 41, no 4 (May 2005), 513–41 (showing that in infrastructure sectors a regulatory framework establishing competition is more relevant than private ownership); D Andrew Smith and Michael Trebilcock, 'State-Owned Enterprises in Less Developed Countries: Privatization and Alternative Reform Strategies', *European Journal of Law and Economics*, vol 12 (2001) 217–52.

There are a number of regulatory instruments that could be potentially relevant for private military and security companies (PMSCs).[2] These include international law, national statutes of the state where the service is being delivered (host state), statutes and regulations in the state in which PMSCs are headquartered (home state), and contracts. This chapter will focus on contracts, home state regulations and, more specifically, on contractual arrangements between governments and PMSCs and the regulatory framework that is embedded in these contracts. There are numerous similarities between these regulations and contractual instruments in infrastructure sectors, which allows for interesting comparisons and a few lessons.

Why do governments privatize?

The word privatization usually refers to a shift from public to private provision of goods and services. But what exactly are we referring to when we say that private parties are providing a certain service? As John Donahue explains,

> [T]he choice between public and private has two basic dimensions. The first dimension concerns *financing*: Should we pay for our goods and services individually, out of our own resources, or should we pay for it collectively with funds raised through one form or another of taxation? The second dimension concerns *performance*: Should the good be produced or the service delivered by a governmental organization or by a non-governmental organization?[3]

Privatization of military and security services does not refer to the financing dimension. After privatization, the provision of these services continues to be financed by the state. In contrast, consumers generally pay for infrastructure services. Even when a state-owned company provides the service (performance is public), consumers pay individually for its consumption. In other words, the financing of infrastructure services is normally private (although there might be exceptions where subsidies are provided). The only thing that these two sectors have in common regarding this first dimension is that the existing financing scheme does not change when privatization takes place.

Privatization of military and security services often refers to the second dimension, performance. Privatization means that a private entity, a PMSC, provides a service that would otherwise be provided by a governmental entity,

[2] Despite being referred jointly in the remainder of the chapter, private military companies and security companies are different. The main difference is that military companies engage in combat operations, whereas security companies stop short of combat by offering support services in the battlefield, such as logistics and training. For a more detailed explanation of the differences, see International Institute for Strategic Studies, 'Complex Irregular Warfare: The Privatisation of Force', *The Military Balance*, vol 106, no 1 (June 2006) 411.

[3] John D Donahue, *The Privatization Decision: Public Ends, Private Means* (New York: Basic Books, 1991) 7–8.

the army. This also applies to infrastructure sectors. Privatization often refers to private investors delivering utility services, either after acquiring a state-owned company that previously provided these services, or via 'greenfield' projects, such as commencing the provision of services where none existed before (for example mobile telephony in many developing countries).

There is yet another important similarity between privatization of military and security services and many (but not all) infrastructure services: these sectors are natural monopolies; as a consequence, one company is likely to be the sole provider of the privatized service. Due to the possibility of abuse of market power, natural monopolies have often been regulated by the state. In the case of goods and services financed by the state, such as military and security services and social services, a great deal of this regulatory framework is embedded in contractual arrangements. Contractual arrangements and regulations are designed to provide incentives for providers and consumers to achieve relevant public policy goals, such as efficiency or equity, or something else, and accountability for outcomes.[4]

Accumulated experience has shown that some regulatory arrangements work better than others, and certain regulatory frameworks provide better incentives than others. This helps regulators and experts define best practices and advise governments on the best regulatory options. However, these best practices and recommended frameworks are not always implemented because they are not chosen in a vacuum. Circumstances under which a regulatory framework is designed and implemented can significantly affect its content.[5] These circumstances include, for instance, the reasons why a government decides to privatize: there is a connection between reasons to privatize and the arrangements between governments and service providers set up in contracts or regulatory frameworks. This section will explore this idea by identifying possible reasons for governments to privatize, and analysing how they can potentially affect the incentives for governments to adopt regulation or not, and to choose certain regulatory arrangements over others. The section will then discuss when a government's regulatory choices might be justifiable and when they might be questionable.

Four reasons to privatize

If the government is publicly financing provision of services with fiscal resources (instead of charging individual consumers directly), transferring the provision of services from public to private hands can be advantageous for the government for at least four reasons. First, it may be cheaper. In the case of military and

[4] Ronald Daniels and Michael Trebilcock, *Rethinking the Welfare State: The Prospects for Government by Voucher* (London and New York: Routledge, 2005) 17.

[5] This argument is developed at greater length in Mariana Mota Prado, 'Policy and Politics: The Privatization of the Electricity Sector in Brazil', doctoral dissertation, Yale Law School, October 2008.

security services, costs of private provision may be lower because PMSCs have more flexibility than the military forces and can deliver the same service with fewer people or less equipment.[6] Alternatively, it might be the case that '[PMSCs] have cheaper running costs because they hire already trained personnel and because they do not provide the extensive range of personnel support and benefits that the state provides for its soldiers'.[7] In any event, a state facing fiscal or financial constrains might transfer the provision of some services to the private sector to save money.

Secondly, privatization may be more efficient. Hiring private military contractors can be a better use of state resources if the relationship between quality and cost is superior with private provision. For instance, PMSCs may provide a better service at the same cost or the same service at a lower cost. In these cases, privatization frees up financial resources for governmental projects of higher value. Also, there could be a more efficient allocation of human capital: if financial costs for private and public provision are the same, privatization may free up soldiers to perform more valuable duties.[8] In all these cases, privatization would be motivated by a concern for better allocation of state resources.

Thirdly, transferring the provision of services to private hands may be less troublesome. In this case, the government may want to avoid burdensome bureaucratic or procedural requirements in providing the service publicly. Privatization may eliminate these obstacles and increase the government's flexibility. Privatization of security and military services, for instance, allows governments to deploy forces 'without the lead time required for mobilizing military forces . . . As quickly as these forces can appear, they can disappear; once dangers pass or local forces are trained and deployed, contracts can lapse and these personnel can be quickly de-mobilized.'[9] This increased flexibility might be useful in some circumstances.

Fourthly, governments may privatize for lack of choice if the state does not have the technical or material capacities to provide the service and is not capable of obtaining these resources in a timely fashion. For instance, the government may lack troops to engage enemies. In the middle of a war where more deployments are needed privatization might be the only option available. Another example of lack of choice is the privatization of specialized services, which can only be delivered by contractors when 'military personnel no longer have the basic skills or equipment to perform the tasks'.[10] This might happen

[6] Deborah Avant, 'Contracting for Services in US Military Operations', *PS Online*, July 2007, 458. See also Deborah Avant, 'Mercenaries', *Foreign Policy* (July/August 2004) 22 (indicating that in addition to flexibility, reduced costs depend on a competitive market).

[7] International Institute for Strategic Studies, 'Complex Irregular Warfare', n 2 above, 412–13.

[8] Ibid. ('Using [PMSCs] in certain roles frees military personnel for other duties. Accordingly, fewer soldiers are needed (. . .) and these soldiers will be doing the jobs for which they are specifically trained'.)

[9] Avant, 'Contracting for Services', n 6 above, 457.

[10] Peter W Singer, *Corporate Warriors: The Rise of the Privatized Military Industry* (Ithaca and London: Cornell University Press, 2003) 162.

because 'these companies recruit from databases of mostly retired military and police personnel. This makes it easier for them to find people with particular experience. . . . It is much harder for military organizations to find those kinds of specific skills and experience and deploy them to a particular arena.'[11]

Certainly, the line that distinguishes these four reasons is more blurred than my description suggests,[12] but exploring these intricacies is beyond the scope of this chapter. Also, some of these reasons may be more important for some states than for others. Lack of choice, for instance, might apply to failed states and countries embroiled in civil wars, such as Sierra Leone. The other reasons, in contrast, might be more prevalent in stable polities, such as the United States. Some of the implications that follow from this will be explored further in this chapter.

The decision to regulate and the choice of regulatory framework

Reasons to privatize may affect the arrangements between the state and the private contractors in at least two ways. One is creating (or eliminating) incentives to adopt regulation. The other is favouring one type of regulation over another.

Incentives to adopt regulatory arrangements exist if regulation can foster the government's privatization goals. In cases in which regulation undermines privatization goals, the government may not adopt it even if it is necessary for other public policy reasons. Imagine, for instance, that a state is privatizing because it is cheaper than providing the services publicly. In this case, if the government pays for private provision with fiscal resources, it will have reduced incentives to establish regulation that will increase the costs of these services, even if this regulation could be important for safety reasons.

For instance, the US Government Accountability Office suggested, in a report published in July 2005,[13] that contracts with PMSCs should have a training requirement to ensure that those providing the privatized services are properly qualified, prepared, and equipped to perform their functions. However, governments might be less willing to require such training, or to impose any other

[11] Avant, 'Contracting for Services', n 6 above, 458. One question that Singer raises is whether the lack of choice is the cause or the consequence of privatization. He suggests that in a number of instances, the army lost capacity to perform certain functions due to privatization. He then concludes that other arguments, such as efficiency, need to be analysed more critically if they will generate this as a consequence. Lack of choice can be a high cost during war time. See Singer, *Corporate Warriors*, n 10 above, 163.

[12] For instance, the decision of the US government to hire Brown & Root to provide humanitarian assistance in the war in Kosovo was in part due to lack of choice, because the government could not send army personnel, and in part a strategy to avoid the politically burdensome process of deploying reserve forces or the National Guard. See Singer, *Corporate Warriors*, n 10 above, 6.

[13] United States Government Accountability Office, 'Rebuilding Iraq: Actions Needed to Improve Use of Private Security Providers', GAO-05-737, July 2005, available at <http://www.gao.gov/new.items/d05737.pdf>.

costly requirement on PMSCs, if the main goal of privatization is to save money. Incentives to require training are reduced if private contractors include the cost of stricter training in the final price of the service, thus increasing the cost for the government. If the requirement is imposed on all companies via regulation, and there is competition among PMSCs, the government might be able to force contractors to internalize these costs by using a competitive bidding process to grant these contracts. However, even under vigorous competition, costs may be passed on to the government (even if partially) if this is necessary to guarantee a margin of profit to private companies.

A second example related to military and security services is harmonized regulation and agency coordination. For instance, standards for use of force in the United States vary from agency to agency.[14] To avoid having contracts that apply different standards, there should be harmonization, which requires major regulatory reform. Such reform, however, can be very costly and time consuming. Under these circumstances, there would be fewer incentives for governments to harmonize use of force standards if they were privatizing to save money or to free up financial resources for more valuable activities.

A third example is accountability, discussed in Part I of this book. Much of the debate over PMSCs concerns the lack of transparency and the powers effectively granted to the executive branch, with a diminished role for the legislature.[15] This increases governments' flexibility. In the United States, for instance, Congress approves the military budget but has very limited access to information about contracts with PMSCs.[16] There are very few incentives for the government to increase accountability if such measures will create burdensome processes and reduce its flexibility. Otherwise, the government would be avoiding procedural and bureaucratic obstacles for military action by privatization and then allowing these obstacles to come back through the back door via strict measures to secure accountability.

A fourth example is enhancing competition among PMSCs. Generally, many of the benefits of privatization, such as reducing costs and increasing efficiency in the delivery of services, are only guaranteed if there is competition among private companies. If the government is privatizing because it has no choice, however, it might have reduced incentives to adopt measures that will increase competition, such as selecting PMSCs through a competitive bidding process. This could happen, for instance, if there are security-related concerns. As Avant notes, 'governments often curtail competition to preserve reliability and continuity'.[17]

[14] Laura Dickinson, 'Private Security Companies: the US Experience', presentation at the conference 'Private Security, Public Order: Governance & Limits', organized by the Institute for International Law and Justice of the New York University School of Law, 3–4 April 2008.
[15] Avant, 'Contracting for Services', n 6 above, 458–9.
[16] Avant, 'Mercenaries', n 6 above, 23–4.
[17] Avant, 'Mercenaries', n 6 above, 22.

In conclusion, the reasons for privatizing affect the incentives that governments have to adopt certain regulatory arrangements. Therefore, a discussion of regulatory frameworks should be informed by a reality check: that is, in addition to determining the best regulatory practices, we need to assess whether governments have the incentives to adopt them. The reasons why governments are privatizing may provide some important information in this assessment.

Principal-agent problems in the decision to privatize

Reasons to privatize similarly affect the incentives that governments have to adopt certain regulatory arrangements in the infrastructure sectors. A clear example is governments that privatize companies as monopolies to reduce their fiscal deficits. A monopoly tends to increase the sale price and therefore allows the state to obtain more revenues from the sale. In this case, governments have an incentive to sell companies as monopolies rather than to set up a regulatory framework that could foster competition (assuming that it is feasible, which is not the case in all infrastructure sectors). The problem with this arrangement is that consumers end up paying more for services. Thus, although the government might have chosen this type of regulation for one public policy reason (reducing the fiscal deficit), it is ignoring other public policy concerns that could justify the opposite decision (equity and distributive concerns, for example). This is particularly troublesome when the groups negatively affected by the regulatory framework (consumers) did not participate in the decision-making process.

By regulating, the government is acting as an agent for its principal, the citizens of the state (who are also consumers). This can raise two types of problems,[18] as the example above illustrates. First, the government might be assuming that it is informed about its principal's preferences when it is not. Another version of the same problem is when the government thinks it knows better than the citizens what is good for them. For instance, the government may decide that distributive and equity concerns are of lesser importance, imposing a significant burden on consumers, because it assumes that the priority should be to control the deficit and achieve macroeconomic stability. Alternatively, there might be a conflict of interest—in its most extreme form, government officials might have been bribed to sell companies as monopolies, acting on their own interest to the detriment of consumers.

The financing structure of military and security services is public, so the financial costs of service provisions cannot be directly passed on to consumers as they can be in infrastructure sectors. However, there are other costs that can be imposed on citizens and groups. In the first example described above, the government may hire a PMSC for reasons of efficiency but might not impose training requirements to avoid increases in the price of the service. In doing so,

[18] Daniels and Trebilcock, *Rethinking the Welfare State*, n 4 above, 19.

the government is considering the goal of saving fiscal resources to be of greater importance than the goal of hiring personnel prepared to perform their functions. It might be that citizens of the state will pay the cost by not being as protected as they would have been by properly trained personnel. If troops are deployed abroad, costs might be imposed on groups in other states, who might be subjected to abuses and inappropriate behaviour by PMSC personnel. Thus, these savings come at a cost that needs to be balanced against any possible fiscal benefits of privatization.

The same problem arises when the executive branch privatizes military and security services to increase flexibility and avoid burdensome procedures. The US Constitution, for example, requires that Congress authorize any deployment of military forces—this is intended to provide accountability for the actions of the executive branch. Under certain circumstances, specific military actions might justify valuing flexibility higher than accountability, but accountability schemes also serve an important purpose: they reduce the risk of potential abuses. Thus, when the government decides to favour flexibility over accountability, it is making a decision that may impose costs on citizens.

The conflict between flexibility and accountability can also occur due to a conflict of interests. Those who drafted the Constitution might have required Congressional authorization before military forces could be deployed in order to ensure that the United States would only go to war with the polity's approval. If private provision of services is used to avoid the need to seek this approval, there is a clear conflict of interest between the government and the citizenry as represented in Congress. An example is the use of private military forces as a strategy to circumvent congressional restrictions to fight the 'war on drugs' in Colombia.[19] Politically burdensome processes can also include cases in which there is national opposition to the deployment of the armed forces, or there is a high political cost associated with the death of soldiers. People are less likely to resist the deployment of contractors, or to react as negatively to their deaths, as they do in the case of soldiers. It is questionable whether privatization can be justified in these situations.

Finally, there is the conflict between enhancing competition among private contractors (to obtain cheaper or more efficient services) and privatizing without competition because there are underlying security concerns. In this case, again, the government might consider security more important than saving resources, but citizens' priorities may be different. A lack of competition among private contractors (with a bidding process in a public auction, for instance) can also result from a pure conflict of interests. Privatization can be designed to provide lucrative contracts to political allies and supporters. In this case, it is clear that members of the government are acting in their own interests to the detriment of citizens' interests. Like the case in which the government is trying to circumvent

[19] Singer, *Corporate Warriors*, n 10 above, 207.

political opposition, under these circumstances, privatization becomes highly questionable.

Regulatory schemes for privatization of military and security services should avoid blatant conflicts of interests while guaranteeing that different values are properly weighed when relevant. For instance, it is necessary to avoid privatizations that are used only to bypass political opposition to wars, while at the same time allowing for privatization when the specific circumstances justify prioritizing flexibility over congressional control.

How governments privatize

Even if we could design and implement a regulatory framework adequate in theory to overcome the concerns identified above, it might not be enforced in practice. Compliance with contractual provisions needs to be monitored, sanctions need to be imposed when breaches occur, and contractual disputes need to be settled. The content of the regulatory framework embedded in contractual agreements is important, but so is the institutional environment that guarantees that this framework will be implemented, monitored, enforced, and modified when necessary. A state's institutional environment comprises a series of institutions, such as the legislature and the bureaucracy, but this analysis will primarily be centred on the courts.

If not effectively and properly enforced, a regulatory framework does not perform its functions. For instance, provisions that require disclosure of information (accountability), demand training of military personnel, or set up strict and harmonized standards for the use of force by contractors are valuable if they can be effectively enforced. If these provisions are embedded in contracts and bilateral agreements, their enforcement requires institutions that are able to effectively monitor compliance with the contract and to sanction non-compliance accordingly. If such institutions do not exist or are not effective, it is unlikely that any of these provisions will influence the behaviour of PMSCs.[20]

In addition to monitoring and enforcement, there needs to be an effective dispute resolution mechanism. In contractual arrangements, disputes are likely to arise between parties (which can be private contractors and the government or the governments of the home and the host state). Dispute resolution mechanisms are important in resolving issues related to interpretation of contractual provisions. These mechanisms can also help parties make the necessary

[20] Martha Minow, 'Outsourcing Power: Private Military Efforts and the Risks to Accountability, Professionalism, and Democracy', in Jody Freeman and Martha Minow (eds), *Government by Contract: Outsourcing and American Democracy* (Cambridge, Massachusetts, and London, England: Harvard University Press, 2009) 114–17.

contractual adjustments due to changing circumstances. Finally, they also deal with breaches and non-performance in contracts.

The judiciary

One key determinant of the success of privatization is an effective and efficient dispute resolution mechanism. Contracts cannot possibly predict all situations that the parties will face, or might not deal with changing circumstances, and sometimes there could be divergent interpretations of contractual and regulatory provisions. A dispute resolution mechanism is needed to deal with such situations.

In addition to disputes arising out of incompleteness, uncertainty and vagueness, there is also the risk of breach. The service provider might not deliver the service and the beneficiary might not pay. Certainly, the two can be connected: the provider might refuse to perform when it becomes aware that the beneficiary might refuse to pay for the service. The situation is no different when services have been privatized. In the case of both infrastructure and military and security services, both parties to the contract face the risk of the other party's default. In the case of military and security services, private contractors might be afraid of delivering services and not being paid by governments. In the case of infrastructure services, the risk of payment default is diffused among consumers. But private companies might still be concerned about the government breaching what is called the 'regulatory contract', which are the rules under which private companies agree to provide the service. The government might reduce the price paid by consumers for the services, therefore reducing the provider's rate of return.

To deal with situations like these, parties normally rely on an institution that is able to enforce the original agreement or the terms of the contract. This institution will then determine if a company that delivered a service is entitled to payment, or if a private utility company was expropriated by an arbitrary and unjustified change in regulation. If the answer is yes, the institution will enforce the contract or original agreement. A court of law can resolve disputes and enforce contractual arrangements. Thus, the judiciary is an institution that can perform the functions required for a regulatory framework to work.

If parties decide to use the judiciary to resolve disputes, however, there are a number of possible problems. In most cases, the parties will need to choose a jurisdiction. In the case of PMSCs, possible jurisdictions are generally the home state or the host state. In some cases, however, judicial institutions are not stable in the host state due to war or conflict. According to Avant, the states that are less likely to have strong institutional capacities to monitor compliance, deal with disputes, and impose sanctions are often the ones that have the most potential to benefit from PMSCs.[21] In these cases, courts of law in the home

[21] Deborah Avant, *The Market for Force: The Consequences of Privatizing Security* (Cambridge: Cambridge University Press, 2005), 57–8.

state will be the best (and maybe the only) judicial option available. However, choosing the courts of the PMSC home state can undermine the effectiveness of some regulatory provisions. If the contracting party is the host state, it might be too costly and burdensome to bring a lawsuit in the PMSC home state. In these cases, the party may resort to non-legal strategies to guarantee compliance, as discussed below.

An unreliable judiciary in the host state also affects bilateral agreements between the host and home states. The clearest example is the US Status of Forces Agreement with Iraq, which states that foreign contractors cannot be prosecuted in Iraqi courts. Their prosecution, as a consequence, depends on the initiative of American prosecutors, who might not be as responsive as the host state citizens would expect. As the *Economist* reported, 'American prosecutors are loath to wade into such murky legal waters. Some Iraqis who were apparently mistreated in the American-run prison of Abu Ghraib have given up trying to seek redress through the criminal law and have instead lodged a civil suit in American courts against CACI, a company allegedly involved in the Abu Ghraib abuses.'[22]

Secondly, even if the judiciary in the host state exists, is stable, and has institutional guarantees of independence, it still might not perform its function with the efficiency and effectiveness that is required to protect the interests of the parties involved. In many developing countries, for instance, judges can take years to render judicial decisions. These delays seriously undermine the protection of private investors in infrastructure sectors.[23]

In the case of military and security services, decisions may need to be swift. This is illustrated by recent Canadian military experience:

> In July 2000, the GST Katie, a contracted military transport ship was carrying back from Bosnia a unit of Canadian Army soldiers, more than 550 vehicles, including tanks and armoured personnel carriers, and 350 containers of ammunition and other sensitive military gear. Due to a financial dispute between two subcontracting agents, the ship began sailing in circles outside Canadian waters. Until the matter was resolved, the ship refused to make the delivery, essentially holding about one-third of the Canadian army's entire equipment and soldiers hostage. The standoff lasted for almost two weeks.[24]

Matters could have been much worse if the ship had been carrying troops and equipment intended for deployment in a conflict zone.[25] This example shows how an efficient dispute resolution system is essential for the successful privatization of military and security services.

[22] 'Whose Law Must Mercenaries Obey?', *The Economist*, 21 August 2008.
[23] See Prado, 'Policy and Politics', n 5 above, chap 1 (discussing the case of Brazil).
[24] Singer, *Corporate Warriors*, n 10 above, 160. [25] Ibid.

Alternative dispute resolution and enforcement mechanisms

There are circumstances in which an independent, functional, and efficient judiciary is not available. The lack of a judiciary is often combined with an increased risk of expropriation of public utilities or payment default by governments hiring military contractors.[26] In the military and security services, for instance, effective judiciaries are absent in the states of some contracting parties, for example many African states facing insurgencies. While the judiciary of the host state (contracting party) is dysfunctional or non-existent, the judiciary of the home state (where the company is based) may not be attractive to the contracting party.

In these cases, private companies might make alternative arrangements to reduce their vulnerability or compensate for the increased risk. In the case of infrastructure sectors, private investors might pay less for the shares of privatized companies, or they might require higher rates of return for a faster recovery of sunk investments. Alternatively, as was the case in Brazil, the government can provide loans through state-owned banks, allowing companies to default on the payment of these loans if the government expropriates their returns.[27] Under this arrangement, the private companies' interests (having their assets and rate of returns protected) are aligned with the government's interest in having the loans paid back.

PMSCs often use a similar mechanism. Companies related to or affiliated with PMSCs buy mineral and oil rights through veiled privatization programmes.[28] The pressing need for military services might reduce the government's ability or willingness to charge a fair price for these mineral and oil concessions or require it offer a discount in royalties. Thus, even if there is a default in payment, PMSCs are compensated with profits from these businesses. Interestingly, this arrangement also increases the incentives for PMSCs to succeed in their missions, because they need to protect the deposits of natural resources to guarantee the expected stream of revenues from their exploitation.

However, such oil and mineral rights arrangements can be detrimental to the host governments. In 1995 in Sierra Leone, contractors turned to local militias to protect the mines, given that mines were key to their payment, strengthening a parallel force that compromised peace negotiations.[29] Such arrangements can also reduce governmental revenues in the long term. In Sierra Leone, 'the government traded roughly $200 million worth of long-term diamond concessions, in exchange for military bailout from the Sandline firm that

[26] Singer, *Corporate Warriors*, n 10 above, 166.
[27] Prado, 'Policy and Politics', n 5 above, chap 4.
[28] Singer, *Corporate Warriors*, n 10 above, 166.
[29] Avant, 'Mercenaries', n 6 above, 24.

was valued at $10 million.'[30] These events in Sierra Leone suggest that alternative arrangements can come at a high cost for privatizing governments. The same is true for public utilities. Companies can be sold for a reduced price, or private investors can secure higher rates of return by imposing higher prices on consumers. Similarly, the Brazilian arrangement (public financing of privatization) has led to renegotiation of debts that can be considered detrimental to the government.[31] Thus, these alternative arrangements should not be considered perfect substitutes for effective enforcement mechanisms. In fact, depending on the costs they impose, they might not be advisable alternatives at all.

Other alternatives to dysfunctional judiciaries include arbitration clauses and tribunals, but these solutions also have problems: they can hamper government flexibility, distort incentives for efficiency, or expose consumers and taxpayers to unnecessary costs or liabilities.[32]

Peculiarities of military and security services contracts

The discussion of contract enforcement in the previous section assumes that it is easy to identify a contractual breach. In some contracts with PMSCs, however, it is hard to measure outputs, making it difficult to claim that there was a breach. For instance, losing a battle is a breach only if one could ascribe the failure to lack of willingness to perform, but this is rather difficult for PMSCs as 'military failures depend on the opponent as well'.[33] As a result, private companies might not fulfil their contractual or regulatory obligations if they perceive that they will not be penalized for non-compliance. Any attempt to mitigate this by establishing clear proxies for measuring both contract effort and success is likely to provide an incomplete picture and may lead to problems, as 'an agent may be motivated to direct its efforts toward those representative goals rather than toward true success'.[34] In these cases, contracts are not an appropriate regulatory instrument. They would be an appropriate instrument if there was a clear and measurable definition of the service to be delivered, but in the absence of this, governmental provision of services may be preferable.[35] Perhaps the problem could be overcome by sophisticated mechanisms of monitoring and oversight of companies' behaviour for the duration of the contract.[36] However, it is not clear what these mechanisms would look like and whether they exist for PMSCs. In this case, even the existence of a healthy institutional environment might not be sufficient for effective oversight and monitoring to occur.

[30] Singer, *Corporate Warriors*, n 10 above, 167.
[31] Prado, 'Policy and Politics', n 5 above, chaps 4 and 8.
[32] Warrick Smith, 'Covering Political and Regulatory Risks: Issues and Options for Private Infrastructure Arrangements', in Timothy Irwin and Guillermo Perry (eds), *Dealing with Public Risk in Private Infrastructure* (Washington: World Bank Publications, 1997) 53.
[33] Singer, *Corporate Warriors*, n 10 above, 157. [34] Ibid.
[35] Avant, *The Market for Force*, n 6 above, 46.
[36] Singer, *Corporate Warriors*, n 10 above, 152.

There are also further obstacles to effective monitoring of contracts with PMSCs. One of these obstacles is that the government has reduced incentives to monitor these contracts, as compared to those regulating infrastructure services. Consumers pay for infrastructure services and it is in their own interest to oversee and control increases in rates and reductions in quality and reliability. As a consequence, the government's decisions are more likely to be monitored by consumers, who can pressure the government not to enter into bad deals.

The same incentive is not present in the case of PMSCs. Citizens of PMSC home and host states have different incentives to demand effective regulation and control from the state. In the case of infrastructure services, citizens can benefit from effective monitoring and enforcement because they are also consumers of these services. In contrast, in the case of PMSCs, citizens of PMSC home states are less likely to be consumers, and will probably not be the direct victims of abuses. They have a different kind of incentive: to monitor whether fiscal resources are being well-spent or whether the procurement regime is faulty and potentially contributing to budget deficits. These incentives might be weaker because they have an indirect and often low-visibility impact on citizens, unlike utility services bills. Certainly there might be demands from home state citizens that are concerned with human rights violations and governmental accountability, but they are likely to be a much smaller group than the group of citizens that monitor companies in infrastructure sectors for self-interested reasons. As a result, it is less likely that the PMSC home states will be under significant popular pressure to monitor contractors effectively, as is the case for public utilities. This makes monitoring PMSC contracts more difficult than monitoring infrastructure services contracts.

Citizens of the host state in which a PMSC operates are more directly affected than those of the home state, and may have stronger incentives to influence their governments. In this sense, they are similar to consumers of infrastructure services except for the fact that they are not paying the bills. The problem in these cases is that citizens of the PMSC host state may not have the means to pressure the contracting party. In the case of democratic governments, citizens might be able to use political pressure, but they may lack mechanisms to monitor and control PMSCs if the jurisdiction chosen to deal with contractual and regulatory disputes is not the host state. In these cases, it is unlikely that contractual arrangements or national regulations will be adopted to control the behaviour of PMSCs. A possible solution to this problem is for the states where these companies are headquartered to impose regulations that apply to their contracts abroad.[37]

The incentive to monitor and oversee PMSC contracts can be reduced even further if the consumer is different from the contracting party. Governments

[37] See chapter two of this volume by Olivier De Schutter and chapter seven by Rebecca DeWinter-Schmitt.

may contract with PMSCs to provide services to international organizations on their behalf. In this case, 'the party paying for the service is not the recipient and does not see the actual delivery. Thus, the service agent/supplier may give less to the actual consumer than it was paid for.'[38] Perhaps this problem can be mitigated with a voucher system. Instead of contracting with PMSCs directly, governments could provide international institutions with vouchers, which could be used by these institutions to hire the PMSCs of their choosing. Such vouchers could be a tied demand-side subsidy—that is, a subsidy provided directly to consumers (demand-side) to fund the consumption of a pre-defined good or service (tied subsidy). They could be used either as a complement or a substitute for public provision of goods and services, such as housing, food, health care and education.[39] The expectation is that vouchers create incentives for providers to improve the efficiency and quality of their goods and services by giving consumers an exit option. The expected outcome is that 'decisions regarding consumption and production of goods and services will be made more efficiently'.[40] In a private security context, vouchers can create incentives for PMSCs to provide what was paid for, especially if they foresee the possibility of being hired in the future.

All this suggests that even in a healthy institutional environment, there might be further obstacles for the proper monitoring and enforcement of regulatory provisions applicable to PMSCs.

Whether governments should privatize

The privatization of certain functions and services, such as infrastructure and military and security services, generates complex and heated debates. These debates often revolve around the question of whether there is a category of services that are 'essentially public' and should never be delegated to private providers.[41] Normally, there are four types of arguments to support the idea of 'essentially public services': historical, symbolic, political or utilitarian.[42] Martha Minow explains the first three:

> Collecting taxes may seem fundamentally public because historically it has been conducted by agents employed by governments, whether monarchs or democratic officials. Criminal prosecution may carry special symbolism as a public rather than private action. Although some historical traditions permitted prosecutions initiated by private parties,

[38] Singer, *Corporate Warriors*, n 10 above, 153.

[39] For a discussion of the voucher system in these sectors, see Daniels and Trebilcock, *Rethinking the Welfare State*, n 4 above.

[40] Ibid. at 2.

[41] In the United States context this is the 'inherently governmental' question, discussed in chapter five of this volume by Alfred Aman and chapter nine by Simon Chesterman.

[42] Martha Minow, 'Public and Private Partnerships: Accounting for the New Religion', *Harvard Law Review*, vol 116 (2003) 1234.

contemporary US practice consolidates prosecutorial power in the government, with the symbolic message that the government stands in for the community and private victims. Some may view the task of running prisons as importantly public because the political system currently assigns a monopoly over the legitimate use of force to the government, although historical practices included private prisons.[43]

The political argument is very influential in the debate about privatization of infrastructure services. For instance, the wave of privatization around the world in the 1990s raised a debate about whether we were moving away from the welfare state, or from the interventionist state, which controls the commanding heights of the economy, and towards a new model, called the regulatory state.[44] The concept of the regulatory state shows how political theories can end up determining what we consider essentially public or essentially private. Resistance to privatization of security and military services can also be influenced by political arguments. As with certain arguments against the privatization of prisons, one could argue that the functions of the armed forces cannot be privatized because in our political system the state has a monopoly over the legitimate use of force. The resistance to privatization of military and security services can also be informed by the symbolic argument that only the government can assume the responsibility of protecting its citizens (or the citizens of other states). This is the argument used against the privatization of prosecutorial powers, for instance.

The utilitarian argument, in turn, is consequentialist. In contrast to the symbolic or political argument, the question here is not 'what is our conception of the state?' Instead, the question is: 'if I want to provide a certain service or perform a certain function, what kind of provision is better?' The choice between public and private, in this context, will not be determined by a concept of what is 'essentially public', but instead by a complicated analysis of costs and benefits of public versus private provision vis-à-vis the main objectives or the main purpose for the delivery of that particular service. The consequentialist considerations that might guide the decision of whether to privatize will form the focus of this section.[45] In this perspective, many issues related to the 'whether question' are intrinsically connected to the 'why' and the 'how' questions, discussed earlier in this chapter.

Should governments privatize military and security services?

From a consequentialist perspective, there are at least two main arguments against privatization of military and security services. One is against private financing and the other is against private performance. The argument against

[43] Ibid.

[44] Giandomenico Majone, 'From the Positive to the Regulatory State: Causes and Consequences of Changes in the Mode of Governance', *Journal of Public Policy*, vol 17(2) (1997) 139–67.

[45] But see Minow, 'Public and Private Partnerships', n 42 above, 1234 (suggesting that the historical, symbolic, and political dimensions may tacitly influence utilitarian debates).

private financing of military and security services is based on the fact that these services may be public goods.[46] Public goods are those whose enjoyment is non-rivalrous and non-excludable: all citizens can simultaneously benefit from the same level of protection of the state's army. However, if citizens were asked to pay private providers for such goods, a free rider problem emerges: some citizens could enjoy them without paying for it, for as long as some are paying, everyone enjoys the benefit. This problem may be an obstacle that prevents private providers from collecting from consumers, and which may ultimately compromise provision of the service.[47]

The non-rivalrous and non-excludable nature of military services explains why we do not require citizens to pay for them individually as we do with infrastructure services. Individuals in a market are unlikely to properly finance the provision of these goods. However, as discussed earlier, public financing does not necessarily need to be coupled with public performance. Indeed, the fact that military and security services are public goods does not explain why the government must provide them. As long as the financing function is centralized in the state, private provision should be feasible.

The second consequentialist argument is contrary to private performance of military and security services. It focuses on the fact that these services are generally not provided in a competitive fashion. Duplicating the provision of these services—two armies, for instance—might generate inefficiencies. In infrastructure sectors, for instance, it would be inefficient to duplicate the electricity grid to distribute electricity within a city. And even if such duplication happened, it is unlikely that both electricity distribution companies would be able to survive in the market. In other words, these are natural monopolies. Lack of competition is problematic because a great deal of the benefits that result from the private provision of services emerges from the competition between private companies.[48]

Private provision of services in case of natural monopolies not only lacks competition, but also creates opportunities for abuse. Private companies seek profits, and monopolists try to maximize their gains by decreasing output and increasing prices. Public provision of these monopolized services is one possible way of avoiding these costs to consumers. Public provision of utility services such as telephone, water, and electricity is often justified on these grounds.[49]

There is, however, another way of addressing the problem of natural monopolies: a competitive bidding process. By creating competition for the market, public bids are supposed to create a structure of incentives that do not allow

[46] Michael Trebilcock and Edward Iacobucci, 'Privatization and Accountability', *Harvard Law Review*, vol 116 (March 2003) 1433.

[47] Ibid.

[48] Clive Harris, 'Private Participation in Infrastructure in Developing Countries—Trends, Impacts, and Policy Lessons', World Bank Working Paper no 5, 2003, 24.

[49] Trebilcock and Iacobucci, 'Privatization and Accountability', n 46 above, 1435.

these companies to charge abusive prices or require contractual provisions that are too beneficial for the companies and costly for society.[50] However, certain reasons to privatize, such as security concerns or the need for an expedited and uncomplicated process, might reduce the government's incentives to use a competitive bidding process. Without these bids, privatization is less likely to generate benefits. On the other hand, legitimate public policy concerns can be jeopardized if there is a general rule requiring competitive bidding. Thus, exceptions to the bidding rules may be necessary, but legislators should limit and control the circumstances under which these exceptions can be used.[51]

Even if bidding is used, it might not generate benefits if there is not effective competition for the market because the industry is too concentrated and there is collusion between the players. In these cases, private companies can distribute bids among themselves, according to their interests, minimizing the potentially beneficial effects of competition. Concentration and collusion seem to occur frequently in the case of PMSCs.[52] Under these circumstances, a competitive bidding process will not produce the expected outcomes. Properly designing the auction for the bidding process might mitigate these risks, but it is hard to determine upfront which form of auction would be the best:

> Auctions are very sensitive to context; that is, the best form of an auction when regulated firms are involved depends on the market environment, for example, what information participants have, how this information is generated, how many participants there are, whether there are concerns of collusion in the auction, and so on. Different types of auctions perform well in different circumstances, and the consequences of choosing the wrong form can be dramatic.[53]

Thus, the form of auction for the bidding process would have to be determined on a case-by-case basis.

Competitive public bids are not a panacea for natural monopolies. Companies face competition to enter the market, but once they have successfully done that, they became monopolists. Thus, after an auction, there is still a need for effective regulation of natural monopolies. This suggests that public provision should not be compared simply with private provision. Instead, it should be compared with private provision with regulation but on what grounds can this comparison be made? Edward Iacobucci and Michael Trebilcock argue that the

[50] Harold Demsetz, 'Why Regulate Utilities?' *Journal of Law and Economics*, vol 11, no 1 (April 1968) 55–65. But see Oliver E Williamson, 'Franchise Bidding for Natural Monopolies—In General and with Respect to CATV', *Bell Journal of Economics*, vol 7, no 1 (1976) 73–104.

[51] Minow, 'Outsourcing Power', n 20 above, 117 (indicating that the United States passed legislation to that effect, but whether it will be effective remains to be seen).

[52] Singer, *Corporate Warriors*, n 10 above, 152.

[53] Flavio M Menezes, Rohan Pitchford, Andrew Wait, 'Tendering and Bidding for Access: A Regulator's Guide to Auctions', *Australian Journal of Management*, vol 28 (2003) 345.

privatization decision must be based on a cost-benefit analysis that compares public provision with:

(1) the advantages of private markets (better able to motivate agents with profit motive and other incentive structures);

(2) the costs of private markets (such as those generated by externalities, public goods, and natural monopolies); and

(3) the flaws in public oversight of private actors.[54]

It is beyond the scope of this chapter to assess all the costs and benefits of private provision of military and security services. Instead, the next section will identify a few of the costs of private provision and discuss the extent to which regulation can mitigate or reduce these costs.

Should governments regulate PMSCs?

The main advantage of private markets, according to Iacobucci and Trebilcock, is that 'the pursuit of self-interest by competitive, profit-maximizing firms drives prices down to marginal cost, which in turn maximizes society's gain from trade'.[55] In this context, 'to draw a general distinction between private values and public values is inappropriate; private, self-interested actions often serve the public interest well'.[56] However, the profit maximization mindset may be a reason for concern because it can set up a system of incentives that will influence private companies' behaviour in a way that is incompatible with other public policy goals, or because it can generate social costs. Regulation may arise in response to these costs.[57]

In infrastructure sectors, there generally have been benefits from private provision:

> The most thorough studies of the impacts of privatization have shown that well designed schemes can bring about substantial increases in overall welfare. . . . Six cases of private participation studied in detail in the telecoms, power and ports sectors . . . have found that the main sources of benefits were increased investment to bring service to new consumers, lower prices, and improved productivity and efficiency.[58]

However, in the particular case of new consumers and expansion of the infrastructure network, the profit maximization mindset cuts both ways. Private provision is aligned with public values when companies can expand the network by reaching consumers that were not previously reached by the existing network for lack of investments in expansion. However, universal services (provision of utilities services to all citizens in a state) could be non-profitable if companies

[54] Trebilcock and Iacobucci, 'Privatization and Accountability', n 45 above.
[55] Ibid, at 1430. [56] Ibid. [57] Ibid, at 1431 and fns.
[58] Harris, 'Private Participation in Infrastructure', n 47 above, 17.

were obliged to expand the network to remote rural areas. In such a context, regulation has played an important role. In the case of La Paz-El Alto in Bolivia, for instance, new connections to water and sanitation services increased by two thirds after privatization, due to binding obligations to expand the service and targets to increase access that were included in concession contracts.[59] Of course, prices charged by utility companies will reflect the costs of expansion, and the government needs to plan on cross-subsidies or direct subsidy schemes to finance service delivery in areas where there is no return or negative returns in the provision of these services.

This example shows that regulation can be used to protect public policy goals, such as distributive goals, when these will not naturally result from profit-maximization motives. In contrast to infrastructure sectors, there is no distributive concern in military and security services at the individual level because it is fiscal resources, not private parties, that fund them. However, there may be a distributive concern at the global level because less wealthy states may be unable to afford proper military protection and may find themselves forced to rely on PMSCs. Lack of choices and money could potentially lead some states to accept clauses and provisions that are highly disadvantageous to them. This can affect a state's ability to adopt regulation to protect legitimate public policy goals. Some form of regulation by home states that imposes restrictions and requirements on the behaviour of PMSCs abroad could possibly address this problem.[60]

If a government has sufficient bargaining power to establish regulation, it can address conflicts between profit motives and other public policy goals. One example is imposing standard training requirements for all PMSCs. Companies operating under a profit maximization motive have incentives to reduce costs and may fail to provide the necessary training to their personnel. A proper regulatory framework requiring standard training requirements could solve this problem. However, the government might not have incentives to adopt such regulation, as discussed earlier.

Unfortunately, regulation has limitations: some conflicts between profit maximizing motives and other public policy goals are not easily solved with regulation. There may be an inherent tension between the government's security goals and a company's quest for profit maximization.[61] Profit maximization might not maximize a state's security. The state places its security in the hand of an army and its individual soldiers based on the assumption that they are loyal to the state, committed to its citizens, and generally trustworthy. A profit-making company or a rent-seeking individual tends to compare costs and benefits. The profit motive puts things in perspective: it is no longer a matter of defending the state at all costs (due to goodwill or honour), but instead it becomes a matter of

[59] Trebilcock and Iacobucci, 'Privatization and Accountability', n 45 above, at 18–19.

[60] See chapter two of this volume by Olivier De Schutter and chapter seven of this volume by Rebecca DeWinter-Schmitt.

[61] Singer, *Corporate Warriors*, n 10 above, 151.

defending the state as long as it is profitable. In other words, 'the locus of judgements about military action has changed, as well has the underlying motives'.[62]

The tension between security and profit maximization is particularly delicate if we consider that these are armed forces, which can turn against their employers. Of course, this is less likely to happen in cases in which there is a strong government that is unlikely to be overturned and the percentage of the army that is privatized is not considerable. In these cases, companies will prefer to honour their contracts and avoid damaging their reputation and losing the opportunity to be hired again in the future. The problem is that in weak or failed states, 'military provider firms are typically the most effective local force, even with their small numbers'. In these circumstances, a PMSC might revolt against its employer:

> 1) when the employer decides that it no longer needs the troops' services, and makes no guarantees about his future behaviour towards them, 2) when the hired troops calculate that they can profit more by being taken onto the payroll of their employer's rival, or 3) when hired troops or their leaders decide that an opportunity to seize power exists and they can take over the employer's place.[63]

These are not trivial risks and, as Singer notes, even if a firm is loyal there is no guarantee that its employees will be.[64]

Even in those cases in which there are regulations to deal with conflict there may be obstacles to the implementation or proper enforcement of such regulations. This creates flaws in the public oversight of private provision, increasing the costs of privatization. Some causes of these flaws were discussed earlier in this chapter: even a perfectly designed regulatory framework can be ineffective if embedded in a dysfunctional institutional environment. Moreover, military and security services have a series of peculiarities that impair effective monitoring of contracts with PMSCs.

A dysfunctional institutional environment lacks an effective or efficient judiciary, as discussed earlier. Another important institutional feature is a competent bureaucracy that is able to manage and monitor contracts, and decides what should be privatized and under which conditions.[65] In the privatization of infrastructure sectors, independent regulatory agencies have performed these functions. These agencies were designed to be insulated from political pressures and make decisions based on expertise, but the attempts to make them independent have not always succeeded.[66] An independent body could also play a role in the privatization of military and security services if successfully insulated

[62] Ibid. [63] Ibid, at 164. [64] Ibid, at 165.

[65] Minow, 'Outsourcing Power', n 19 above, 117.

[66] Mariana Mota Prado, 'The Challenges and Risks of Creating Independent Regulatory Agencies: A Cautionary Tale from Brazil', *Vanderbilt Journal of Transnational Law*, vol 41, no 2 (March 2008).

from political pressure and interest groups. Some suggestions in this regard will be presented in the conclusion to this chapter.

If an appropriate regulatory framework cannot be implemented or will not be effective, the costs of privatization certainly increase. However, this is not necessarily an argument against it. According to Iacobucci and Trebilcock, the 'whether' question cannot be answered because there are flaws in the public oversight of private provision of services. Instead, public provision of services is appropriate if the costs of market provision exceed those of governmental failures.[67] In other words, the advantages of private provision minus its costs should be compared to the costs of governmental failures overall. This is certainly a complicated cost-benefit analysis, and it is beyond the scope of this paper to determine which costs are higher. Instead, this last section will consider other potential costs of private markets.

Similarities between infrastructure and military and security services contracts

There are at least three types of problems that are common to infrastructure sectors and military and security services contracts. First, there could be regulatory problems *ex ante*, caused by a captured government that does not impose strict requirements and adequate limits on private monopolies. If there is capture, private companies make the government their puppet. In this case, the regulatory framework will not seek to protect the public interest, but will instead protect the interests of private investors. The problem of capture was originally identified in a case study of infrastructure sectors,[68] but it is also a risk in the regulation of PMSCs.

Secondly, there can be regulatory problems *ex post*, which are caused by opportunistic renegotiations. Once the regulatory contract is signed, one party might force the other to renegotiate the terms of the contract under unfavourable conditions. The idea is that private companies might try to influence changes in the regulatory framework once it is established, *ex post*. This can happen with renegotiation of contracts after public bids. In the case of infrastructure sectors, renegotiations of the terms of concession contracts initiated by companies have often proven to be favourable to them and detrimental to consumers.[69] The same has been reported in the case of PMSCs. For instance, 'in the case of "Train and Equip" program in Bosnia, it is believed that the military consultant firm used its position of trusted expertise continuously to identify additional contract needs for the client. In effect, it pushed the goalposts

[67] Trebilcock and Iacobucci, 'Privatization and Accountability', n 45 above.

[68] George Stigler, 'The Theory of Economic Regulation', *Bell Journal of Economics and Management Science*, vol 2, no 3 (1971) 21.

[69] Jose Luis Guash, Jean-Jacques Laffont and Stephane Straub, 'Renegotiation of concession contracts in Latin America', World Bank Policy Research Working Paper 3011, 2003.

back as the game progressed, to help it gain more contracts.'[70] There is, however, one important difference between these sectors. In contrast to renegotiations in infrastructure sectors, war can largely undermine any attempt to monitor these renegotiations in the case of PMSCs. In 'a highly complex and uncertain environment', it is harder to verify and assess when changes of the terms of the contract are actually justifiable.[71]

There are a number of circumstances that make opportunistic renegotiation easier. In some markets, once one company wins a competitive bid, it effectively becomes a monopoly in the delivery of services, and it uses this position to its own benefit.[72] This is more likely to happen when the company becomes the sole provider of the service and it cannot be quickly or easily replaced. In these cases, the costs of renegotiation may be lower than the costs generated by the disruption of replacing that company via competitive bids.

Jose Luis Guash, Jean-Jacques Laffont and Stephane Straub show that such renegotiations happened quite often in concession contracts for infrastructure sectors in Latin America from 1985 to 2000 and identified two possible reasons for renegotiations:

> First of all, there are renegotiations initiated by operators. These might be shock related, when a devaluation or a recession make the operation of a given concession unsustainable. In a region that has proved very volatile over the last 20 years, this is a major concern for policy makers. They might also be opportunistic, when a firm uses its bargaining power in bilateral negotiation with the government or the regulatory agency to strike a better deal than the initially agreed one. This affects one of the central benefits of the concession model, namely the competitive pressure introduced by the ex ante auction procedure. To the extent that firms are aware of the potential gains due to their bargaining power in a subsequent bilateral negotiation with sometimes inexperienced government officials, they may be tempted to strategically undercut rivals at the bidding stage.[73]

In contracts with PMSCs, the circumstances that favour renegotiations are present in lifetime support contracts for highly technical weapons systems. 'These contracts create an essential monopoly once signed, even if competitively bid. This can distort the original bidding, as firms have an incentive to low-ball initial bids, knowing they can negotiate add-ons later.'[74] Another possible circumstance involves information asymmetries. In certain contracts, the government cannot assess whether the demands are justifiable, and thus accepts the private companies' proposal due to its lack of expertise in the area. There are reports of abuses by PMSCs in a number of cases.[75] In infrastructure sectors, some states adopted mechanisms to review the principal terms of contracts such

[70] Singer, *Corporate Warriors*, n 10 above, 153. [71] Ibid.

[72] Donahue, *Privatization Decision*, n 3 above, 105.

[73] Jose Luis Guasch and Stéphane Straub, 'Renegotiation of Infrastructure Concessions: An Overview', *Annals of Public and Cooperative Economics*, vol 77, no 4 (December 2006) 484.

[74] Singer, *Corporate Warriors*, n 10 above, 155. [75] Ibid, at 156.

as tariffs and regulation every three to five years, reducing the government's discretion to renegotiate contracts due to unforeseen circumstances.[76] For long-term contracts with PMSCs, such mechanisms could also be adopted. Moreover, infrastructure sectors also minimized the risk of private investors' opportunism by creating independent regulatory agencies. Due to their expertise, independent agencies can minimize information asymmetry problems. Indeed, they significantly reduced the incidence of renegotiation in infrastructure sectors.[77] An independent body to assess contracts with PMSCs could perform the same function.

The third problem is an accountability problem, or 'accountability mismatches'. Such mismatches happen when the government opportunistically claims credit for successful initiatives and denies responsibility for unsuccessful ones.[78] This problem is not connected to the profit maximization mindset of private companies. Instead, it is linked with governmental rent seeking. Privatization creates a unique opportunity for governments to claim responsibility in a selective fashion. In infrastructure sectors, independent regulators allow governments to shape public perception of its responsibility for the actual results of certain regulatory decisions. It has been shown that the Brazilian federal government has claimed responsibility for regulatory decisions that were very popular, while shifting the blame to independent regulatory agencies when decisions were not well-received by the consumers (who happen to be also the government's electoral constituency), causing an 'accountability mismatch'.[79]

The 'accountability mismatch' problem can also happen in the case of military and security services. As Singer describes,

> the extensive PMF [privatized military firm] involvement in the war in Colombia and its neighboring states by US-based firms has been entirely without Congressional notification, oversight, or approval. PMF activities provide a new option for outside parties to reset a local environment, while officially staying uninvolved and not bearing risks. A similar rationale appears to have been used in Sierra Leone in 1997, where both the United States and Britain originally supported Sandline's activities to overthrow the Koroma regime, but then claimed no association once it was publicized as being in violation of UN arms embargos. Hiring private military firms as a substitute for official action gives a cover of plausible deniability that official forces now lack.[80]

It is important to note that governments may privatize to avoid political opposition. If this is coupled with the potential risk of an 'accountability mismatch', privatization will generate not only direct but also indirect political

[76] Harris, 'Private Participation in Infrastructure', n 48 above, 9.
[77] Harris, 'Private Participation in Infrastructure', n 48 above, 9.
[78] Mariana Mota Prado, 'Accountability Mismatch: Agências Reguladoras Independentes e o Governo Lula' [Accountability Mismatch: Independent Regulatory Agencies and the Lula Administration], in Gustavo Binenbojm (ed), *Agências Reguladoras e Democracia* (Rio de Janeiro: Lumen Juris, 2006) 225–51.
[79] Ibid.
[80] Singer, *Corporate Warriors*, n 10 above, 209.

costs. The problem of 'accountability mismatch' shows that there is a cost for democracy and the system of checks and balances that might be too high to justify privatization.[81] Transparency requirements could reduce some of these risks, as discussed in more detail below.

Conclusion: Some policy implications

Throughout this chapter, examples of how regulation can deal with problems in private provision of services that are common to infrastructure sectors and military and security services have been mentioned. This conclusion highlights concrete policy implications that might address some of the problems identified earlier.

First, the government contracting with PMSCs should be forced to justify why privatization is necessary. For instance, the government might claim that it is more efficient to privatize. An independent body should assess whether that is the case, and the government will then be authorized to proceed with privatization (similar to the cost-benefit analysis of regulation performed by the Office of Management and Budget in the United States). This independent body should also oversee contracts and monitor compliance. This will help ensure that public policy goals such as increasing efficiency will be achieved and will also reduce the risk of conflicts of interests and corruption.

Secondly, a competitive bidding process should be the default rule for contracting with PMSCs, allowing for limited exceptions. The best form of auction should be determined on a case-by-case basis, but there should be clear and predetermined exceptions to the default requirement for competitive bids. For example, the government may be authorized to hire PMSCs without a competitive bidding process if there is an emergency or if security reasons do not allow for that. The government would need permission from an independent body to claim such an exception. In order to determine whether an exception applies, the body should evaluate the reasons presented by the government and the terms of the contract, and determine whether they justify departing from the default rule. Thus, the government would only be able to contract PMSCs without a competitive bidding process if it were able to show that this is necessary for other public policy reasons. This would avoid blatant conflicts of interest, such as using privatization to overcome political resistance or to favour political allies. Privatization should happen only when justified by public policy reasons.

Thirdly, the contracting government needs to assess some of the broader national public policy concerns that are connected to privatization of military and security services and impose across-the-board regulations to address them. There could be statutory provisions imposing training requirements, so that the

[81] Ibid. at 215.

government lacks the discretion to decide whether or not to include these requirements in contracts. These requirements would not only reduce the risk of principal-agent problems, but could also reduce the risk of bad bargains when the executive branch has no choice other than to privatize. In addition, they can guarantee that public policy goals that are not achieved by private markets will be properly protected.

Fourthly, home states need to address some of the broader international public policy concerns that are connected to privatization of military and security services and impose regulations that apply to the activities of their PMSCs abroad. This could mitigate problems that exist when citizens of host states are not able to press their governments to adopt regulation to control abuses, and it could also address the wealth inequality problem that leaves poor states with no option but to enter into abusive contracts with PMSCs.

Fifthly, governments should be allowed to contract PMSCs to provide services to international organizations only through vouchers. International organizations would then be allowed to hire the company of their choosing.

Finally, the privatization of private military and security services should be informed by transparency. Citizens should have access to all the information related to the competitive bidding process and to contractual provisions, so as to avoid capture of the government by private interests. Transparency would also minimize the risks of 'accountability mismatches' and reduce the political costs of privatization. When confidentiality issues do not allow for full disclosure of the documents, they should be made available to the independent body that approved the privatization in the first place. This body would have an obligation to investigate and publicly expose possible irregularities.

These policy implications should not be considered outside the broader regulatory context of different states. This chapter discussed the circumstances under which a regulatory framework is established, designed, or enforced in cases of privatization of public services. These circumstances are relevant because they can affect the content of such a framework and its effectiveness. Thus, they can have an impact on the success or failure of a privatization process which is largely dependent on the existence and enforcement of adequate regulation.

The chapter did not seek to answer the question of whether to privatize or to determine when privatization is preferable to public provision, but it did indicate that—as in the case of infrastructure sectors—a discussion about the costs of private provision of military and security services should consider how regulation can mitigate these costs and whether this regulation could be adopted and properly enforced. To answer the question of whether governments should privatize, we need to consider *how* they will privatize. If properly designed, regulation can significantly reduce the costs of private provision and (from a consequentialist perspective) help determine whether private provision is desirable or not.

7

Human rights and self-regulation in the apparel industry

Rebecca DeWinter-Schmitt

It may seem curious that an edited volume which addresses the possible need to limit the outsourcing of 'public functions', in particular security provision, would contain a chapter on lessons learned from the apparel industry. However, this is only the case if we are misled by the word 'public' to believe that a clear dichotomy exists between the public and private sectors and that traditionally the public sector has, or should, deliver essential goods and services. Historically, their provision—including security (discussed in chapter one of this volume), prisons (discussed in chapter five in this volume), infrastructure (discussed in chapter six of this volume), fire fighting, education, and so on—has been assured at different times by the public sector, the private sector, or a combination of both. In contrast, the production and distribution of apparel has always been a private activity: it was initially produced in homes through familial labour for personal consumption, and later in factories through wage labour, distributed at market prices for mass consumption.

The public concerns with the apparel industry, however, have been guaranteeing respect for labour rights and the enforcement of national labour laws and international human rights standards. The organizations in charge of addressing these obligations have been public entities, like labour departments; private, non-governmental organizations (NGOs), like the Worker Rights Consortium (WRC) (a monitoring group discussed below); or a mixture of both, as with efforts under US Secretary of Labor Robert Reich's 'No Sweat, Eradicating Sweatshops' programme against sweatshops, also addressed below, which encouraged manufacturers to sign voluntary agreements with brands and retailers. Bearing in mind that certain essential goods and services are themselves basic rights[1] and that their delivery can impact the overall human rights situation of a state, one can approach the issue through a human rights lens by asking

[1] See, eg, Universal Declaration of Human Rights, 1948, Resolution 217 A (III); UN Doc A/801 91, UN General Assembly (UDHR), art 25(1): 'Everyone has the right to a standard of living adequate for the health and well-being of himself and of his family, including food, clothing, housing and medical care and necessary social services'.

if it matters whether a person's rights, like security[2] and labour rights,[3] are ensured publicly or privately. The human rights perspective is especially relevant to the provision of security as a basic right since, ironically, its assurance potentially entails the use of lethal force, which can negatively impact the attainment of that right as well as others. Hence the decision as to who provides security and controls the legitimate use of means of violence is an important one within any political system.

The human rights group Amnesty International (AI) has taken the position that it matters not whether public or private actors provide essential services as long as the fundamental rights to those services are upheld and their private delivery does not worsen the overall human rights situation.[4] In addition, AI notes that while corporations as non-state actors have human rights obligations under the Universal Declaration of Human Rights (UDHR),[5] the state has the ultimate obligation to 'respect, protect, fulfill, and promote' human rights and thus must act as the final guarantor of rights, stepping in if the private sector fails in its delivery.

AI has outlined seven principles concerning the delivery of essential services, four of which are particularly relevant to security provision.

(1) The first principle, *protect rights*, indicates that in light of a state's human rights obligations, its primary commitment must be to improve the current human rights condition. Any decision to shift from public to private service provision or vice-versa must be made with an eye towards ensuring that the condition does not worsen.

(2) The second principle, *regulate*, maintains that even if the state does not own the means of delivering an essential service, it still has an obligation to oversee private providers through an adequate regulatory framework and legal system of accountability to ensure that human rights are not denied.

(3) The third principle, *assess impact*, captures the idea that the state must conduct an assessment of the human rights impact of either public or private provision of an essential service and ensure that whatever path is chosen, it

[2] UDHR, art 3: 'Everyone has the right to life, liberty and security of person'.

[3] UDHR, art 23: '(1) Everyone has the right to work, to free choice of employment, to just and favorable conditions of work and to protection against unemployment. (2) Everyone, without any discrimination, has the right to equal pay for equal work. (3) Everyone who works has the right to just and favorable remuneration ensuring for himself and his family an existence worthy of human dignity, and supplemented, if necessary, by other means of social protection. (4) Everyone has the right to form and to join trade unions for the protection of his interests.' UDHR, art 24: 'Everyone has the right to rest and leisure, including reasonable limitation of working hours and periodic holidays with pay'.

[4] See 'Human Rights and Privatisation,' Amnesty International, POL 34/003/2005, 17 March 2005.

[5] The preamble to the UDHR states that 'every organ of society', which AI interprets as including private economic actors, 'shall strive . . . to promote respect for these rights and freedoms and . . . secure their universal and effective recognition and observance'.

contributes to furthering human rights. The state must set benchmarks to measure a private provider's human rights performance within contracts.

(4) The fourth principle relevant for the provision of security, *be transparent*, calls for any privatization process to be carried out in a transparent, open, and fair manner, free from corruption, and in consultation with all affected stakeholders. Private providers must report publicly on service delivery and disclose the terms of contracts with the state.

AI's neutrality on the acceptability of privatization is useful for a number of reasons. First, it is a very pragmatic position that recognizes the fact that outsourcing is not likely to abate any time in the near future as long as the majority of governments believe markets are more efficient than bureaucracies at delivering goods and services and that smaller government is better. Secondly, since AI claims that human rights standards apply to corporate actors, even if state actors must guarantee them in the final instance, outsourcing done right—in keeping with the above principles—should not negatively affect human rights. Thirdly, these principles are also very practical, offering a convenient metric for assessing the human rights impact of a decision to deliver a basic right 'publicly' or 'privately' and determining if there should be a reversal. Thus, it would be entirely in keeping with these principles for a government to decide not to outsource certain activities, and to designate them 'inherently governmental functions', if the evidence suggests that their private provision would likely lead to human rights violations and a worsening of the human rights climate.[6]

The next section examines the current situation in the global apparel and security industries. In the apparel industry, the state has largely forfeited its regulatory role and outsourced labour standard-setting, surveillance, and enforcement to civil society groups and apparel brands, retailers, and manufacturers. Singularly, in collaboration with each other, and at times with the support of government actors, they have developed various alternative regulatory regimes, including forms of voluntary corporate self-regulation through multi-stakeholder initiatives (MSIs). In the security industry, states have utilized private security forces within major contingency operations, such as those in Iraq and Afghanistan, but have failed to set up a regulatory framework to ensure adequate oversight and accountability for companies accused of human rights violations—ranging from workers rights abuses to excessive, even lethal, use of force and torture. Corporate self-regulation has potential, but is at an early stage of development. This section also examines how the present state of affairs came about, drawing parallels between the two industries, and highlights some of the human rights challenges.

The second section describes alternative regulatory regimes that have been developed in the wake of privatization of labour standards assurances and

[6] See chapter nine of this volume by Simon Chesterman for an elaboration of this point.

security provision. In the apparel industry, the focus will be on the two most advanced MSIs based in the United States—the Fair Labor Association (FLA) and the WRC—which were the outcome of nearly two decades of public pressure generated by the advocacy of the anti-sweatshop movement and sustained media attention to the sweatshop issue. Their strengths and weaknesses are analysed, as well as their overall effectiveness in upholding human rights as required by the four principles described above. In the final section of the chapter, the argument is made that while these two initiatives have a mixed record of promoting labour rights and ensuring corporate social responsibility (CSR), there are important lessons learned that can be applied to nascent efforts at corporate self-regulation within the security industry. In the US context, the International Peace Operations Association, an industry trade association for private military and security companies (PMSCs), has come the farthest in developing a code of conduct mechanism. This effort is analysed and suggestions for improving it are made based upon lessons derived from the experience of the apparel industry. Recognizing that states are unlikely to reverse their decision to privatize the provision of essential services in the near future, the conclusion argues that there need not be a stark dichotomy between mandatory and voluntary forms of regulation and makes recommendations on using hybrid public-private initiatives to ensure that human rights are respected.

The global apparel industry and security industry

AI and other advocacy groups argue that the state must be the final guarantor of human rights. In practice, however, many states have not met their responsibilities. Economic globalization has made it challenging for states to regulate corporations, as Olivier De Schutter has shown in chapter two of this volume. This is true for the apparel industry and private military and security industry, which display remarkable parallels in regards to their global structures, inadequate regulatory frameworks, human rights challenges, and drive towards voluntary self-regulation.

The nature of production and regulation in the apparel industry

The apparel industry has been described as geographically 'footloose' because of its highly mobile nature.[7] Production requires little more than a relatively low-skill workforce and limited capital investments in the form of machines for cutting, sewing, and pressing. Combined with advances in information, communication, and transportation technologies, nearly the whole world is open as a

[7] Michael Piore, 'The Economics of the Sweatshop', in Andrew Ross (ed), *No Sweat: Fashion, Free Trade, and the Rights of Workers* (New York: Verso, 1997) 135–42.

potential production location. Big brands and retailers in the global North, rather than directly owning factories, have outsourced production to manufacturing facilities mostly in the global South that can produce their labels at the lowest price possible to satisfy consumer demand for inexpensive apparel.[8] Host governments in the global South have made conditions especially conducive to foreign direct investment (FDI) by establishing export processing zones offering low wages, tax exemptions, and other subsidies; providing infrastructure; eliminating tariffs and duties; and removing, or intentionally not enforcing, labour laws. Even if attempts were made to enforce labour laws—and ironically on paper many workers in developing states enjoy better protections of their workplace rights than do workers in the United States—manufacturers, brands, and retailers could avoid regulation by moving production elsewhere or sourcing goods less expensively from factories that glean a premium from lax labour standards. Anti-sweatshop activists complain that the result has been a global 'race to the bottom' in labour standards as governments, manufacturers, and workers all compete with their counterparts in other states to attract FDI.[9] While host governments in the South are complicit in failing to enforce their labour laws, they are also hamstrung by heavy debt burdens and the demands of international financial institutions.

The most frequent labour rights violations experienced by the predominantly female workforce include refusal to pay minimum wages and overtime, unreasonably long work days, failure to respect rights to freedom of association and collective bargaining, gender discrimination, and, in extreme instances, child labour, forced labour, and physical and verbal abuse. Since they do not own the production facilities or directly employ apparel workers, big brands and retailers have sought to use complex contracting chains as a means to distance their 'clean' brand images from the 'dirty side' of production and sweatshop accusations.[10] However, beginning in the early 1990s, the anti-sweatshop movement emerged and successfully framed the sweatshop as a legitimate social problem in need of remediation, bringing widespread public attention to the issue of poor conditions in apparel factories in the United States and around the world.[11] Activists claimed that brands and retailers contributed to human rights violations through the terms of their sourcing contracts, which stipulate low prices

[8] Inexpensive is meant to imply not only cheap, low-end apparel products, but also prices that do not reflect the full costs of providing workers with a living wage and producing apparel in conformity with internationally recognized labour rights.

[9] For an activist perspective on the origins of modern day sweatshops, see the Frequently Asked Questions website for Global Exchange's Sweatfree Communities campaign, available at <http://www.globalexchange.org/campaigns/sweatshops/sweatshopsfaq.html>

[10] Naomi Klein, *No Logo: Taking Aim at the Brand Bullies* (New York: Picador USA, 1999).

[11] For a discussion of the formation of the anti-sweatshop movement and the framing of the sweatshop problem, see Rebecca DeWinter-Schmitt, 'Business as Usual? The Mobilization of the Anti-Sweatshop Movement and the Social Construction of Corporate Identity,' unpublished dissertation, American University, 2007, chaps 2 and 3.

and short delivery times, leading manufacturers to commit workers rights abuses to meet their contractual obligations. Even though apparel brands and retailers did not directly commit the abuses, by highlighting the structure of economic ties between workers in the South and companies and consumers in the North, activists were able to establish the complicity of companies and consumers in the exploitation of workers convincingly enough to move company and government officials to respond to the allegations.[12]

The globalization of the apparel industry and the outsourcing of production occurred with a concomitant outsourcing of the regulation of the industry by the US government, which supported the proliferation of voluntary forms of corporate self-regulation and civil society oversight over binding government regulation at both the domestic and international levels. The privatization of labour standard-setting, surveillance, and enforcement happened with little forethought to the implications for the protection of labour rights. By the time anti-sweatshop activism peaked during the 'year of the sweatshop',[13] the Clinton administration, some major brands, and a number of mainstream anti-sweatshop groups seeking to change corporate behaviour through engagement and market pressures had arrived at a consensus position on the state of affairs in the apparel industry.[14] All three acknowledged there was indeed a problem with sweatshops abroad and their 're-emergence' in the United States, and that efforts to eliminate them should focus on improving working conditions rather than brands and retailers simply 'cutting and running' from contracted factories.

However, corporate and government actors repeatedly pointed to the limits of binding regulatory approaches for a global industry, and some advocacy groups, such as human rights and consumer groups and those within the faith-based and socially responsible investment communities, seemed to largely accept their argument. Increasingly they viewed the pyramid structure embedded in global apparel commodity chains—and the neo-liberal economic theory that underpinned outsourcing as a business model—as unalterable. They conceded that voluntarism was the most feasible means to oversee the global activities of the industry and consented to cooperating with corporate and government actors in MSIs to develop standards and compliance mechanisms, setting the stage for the creation of the Fair Labor Association, discussed next. The possibility of conducting an earnest discussion and exploration of mandatory public regulation of apparel corporations had been foreclosed.

[12] Iris Young, 'From Guilt to Solidarity: Political Responsibility and Sweatshops', *Dissent*, vol 50 (2003).

[13] See Andrew Ross (ed), *No Sweat: Fashion, Free Trade, and the Rights of Workers* (New York: Verso, 1997) 291.

[14] See David Bobrowsky, 'Creating a Global Public Policy Network in the Apparel Industry: The Apparel Industry Partnership', Global Public Policy Institute, United Nations Vision Project on Global Public Policy Networks, 1999.

A similar process is now underway in the private military and security industry. Although the industry has always been global in nature, the US government's reliance on PMSCs increasingly grew after the end of the Cold War and is peaking at an all time high with the contingency operations in Iraq and Afghanistan. These developments took place with virtually no public debate, which tended to focus on specific scandals rather than the larger questions of what, if any, services are 'inherently governmental' and the potential human rights implications of privatization. At this point, it is conventional wisdom that PMSCs are an essential part of the US military's Total Force[15] and cannot be eliminated without significantly increasing the size of US armed forces, which most agree is not politically viable.

This would be less of a concern if it were not for the fact that, as with the apparel industry, the globalization of the private military and security industry makes regulation challenging. National laws and regulations and international legal regimes were not promulgated quickly enough to keep pace with its growth. As Deborah Avant argues, 'its transnational nature, low capitalization, fluid structures, and lack of commitment to territory all decrease the usefulness (or raise the costs) of traditional style state regulation'.[16] PMSCs, like apparel corporations, are geographically mobile and they can relocate if they are unhappy with a state's regulatory environment or they can reconstitute themselves into different corporate forms to avoid regulation and liability for their actions. Furthermore, in their areas of operation host governments may be incapable of exercising any type of effective oversight capacity because they are weak or corrupt, face internal strife, may not have control over their territory and population, have inadequate laws and judicial systems, and essentially are incapable of governing—much like governments in the global South have problems enforcing their labour laws in contracted apparel factories. Arguably, this places a greater responsibility on governments in the North that are home to PMSCs or hire them to regulate their activities.

However, for a number of reasons, the home governments of PMSCs have largely forfeited their responsibility to oversee the industry and hold contractors accountable when they abuse human rights. First, with both state and non-state actors hiring PMSCs, the 'multiple principals problem' arises, whereby there is a diffusion of control over PMSCs as the number of clients of their services increases. This poses a hurdle to efficient regulation since, among other things, it may encourage state actors to free-ride on the costs associated with overseeing

[15] The 2006 Quadrennial Defense Review defines the Total Force as including contractors along with active and reserve military components and civil servants. 'Quadrennial Defense Review Report', United States Department of Defense, 6 February 2006, available at <http://www.defenselink.mil/pubs/pdfs/QDR20060203.pdf>, 75.

[16] Deborah Avant, 'The Emerging Market for Private Military Services and the Problem of Regulation', in Simon Chesterman and Chia Lehnardt (eds), *From Mercenaries to Market: The Rise and Regulation of Private Military Companies* (Oxford: Oxford University Press, 2007) 185.

and sanctioning PMSCs and shirk the collective responsibility to develop and enforce national and international standards, thus potentially resulting in a 'race to the bottom' as individual clients may have an interest in PMSCs breaching human rights and humanitarian law if it serves their purposes.[17] Not only are there numerous clients, but contractors often in turn subcontract out to numerous other companies. Complex contracting chains, akin to those found in the apparel industry, make it difficult for the US government, when it is one of the principal clients, to have adequate oversight over all the companies ultimately providing it with services. This allows both the government and the prime contractor a certain degree of plausible deniability when subcontractors engage in human rights violations or unlawful activities, much as apparel brands use complex apparel commodity chains to distance themselves from poor production conditions.[18] Secondly, there are limitations on the ability of home governments to apply their laws extra-territorially: the laws may not be in place, and in any event investigating and prosecuting crimes committed overseas is practically challenging and prohibitively expensive. Finally, there appears to be a deliberate failure on the part of governments to ensure oversight and accountability.[19]

As is the case with the apparel industry and the neo-liberal ideology fostering global trade, outsourcing of military and security functions is grounded in a belief in the superiority of markets over public provision of security and military services. The decision to outsource is justified through alleged cost savings, efficiencies, and flexibility that only the private sector can provide, although few studies support this claim. Despite the failure to regulate, there is also recognition that security is a different kind of good that, since it involves the use of violence, should be regulated.[20] Unlike failed efforts to regulate the apparel industry, this has led to wider political support—at least in the United States—for regulation of the industry, though the current legal and regulatory regime is patchy at best.[21]

A number of human rights concerns persist as a result of this inadequate regulatory framework. According to AI, the three main types of human rights violations perpetrated by PMSCs in Iraq include torture and abuse of detainees; sexual harassment and assault; and excessive use of force resulting in injuries

[17] See James Cockayne, 'Make or Buy? Principal-Agent Theory and Regulation of Private Military Companies', in Chesterman and Lehnardt, *From Mercenaries to Market*, n 16 above, 209, and Avant, 'Emerging Market', n 16 above, 186.

[18] Cockayne refers to this as a 'chain configuration' of multiple principals, which can allow principals to work with PMSCs to increase their 'agency slack', claim plausible deniability for the agents' actions, and 'shift blame' to agents. See Cockayne, 'Make or Buy?', ibid. at 212.

[19] 'Private Security Contractors at War: Ending the Culture of Impunity', Human Rights First, 2008, available at <http://www.humanrightsfirst.info/pdf/08115-usls-psc-final.pdf>; Deborah Avant, 'The Real Blackwater Controversy', *San Diego Union-Tribune*, 20 June 2008.

[20] See chapter one of this volume by Michael Likosky.

[21] See 'Private Security Contractors at War', n 19 above, 27–36.

and lethal shootings of innocent civilians.[22] Labour rights violations have also been identified as a problem. Much as apparel companies can source from anywhere in the world—usually wherever workers' wages are the lowest—security providers can be recruited from around the world resulting in a 'race to the bottom' in pay scales and work conditions.[23] Finally, 'third country nationals' can also be difficult to vet due to inadequate public records in their home states, which poses the danger of PMSCs hiring personnel with a history of human rights violations.[24] Should they commit human rights abuses on foreign soil, neither their home state laws, nor those of their employer or host state, may apply.

As occurred in the apparel industry, when governments are incapable or unwilling to exercise their regulatory responsibilities, the industry, especially if faced with bad press, finds means to self-regulate. Andrew Bearpark and Sabrina Schulz, from the British Association for Private Security Companies (BAPSC), support this view, stating that as 'there are no adequate legal frameworks that fully address the activities of [PMSCs] on either a national or international level,' a 'matrix of international codes of conduct, national regulation, and industry self-regulation' is needed.[25] To date, within the US context, the most thorough effort to self-regulate, beyond the individual codes of conduct, ethics policies, and mission statements developed by a handful of companies, is the International Peace Operations Association (IPOA) Code of Conduct.[26] As the IPOA Code is a voluntary trade association effort that has experienced only limited development since the standards were first adopted in 2001, much can be learned from the two advanced self-regulation initiatives in the apparel industry, discussed in the next section of this chapter. The section thereafter provides a brief background and analysis of the IPOA Code process before applying lessons learned from the apparel industry to the security industry.

Alternative forms of regulation in the apparel industry

When US Secretary of Labor Robert Reich made fighting sweatshops one of his main goals during his tenure under the Clinton administration, he faced a

[22] See AI's campaign to ensure corporate accountability in the 'Global War on Terror' at <http://www.amnestyusa.org/our-priorities/military-contractors/page.do?id=1101665&n1=3&n2=157>.

[23] See, eg, Eric Stoner, 'Outsourcing the Iraq War: Mercenary Recruiters Turn to Latin America', *Upside Down World*, 2 July 2008, available at <http://upsidedownworld.org/main/content/view/1360/68>; Craig Kielburger, Marc Kielburger, and Chris Mallinos, 'Cheated into Working in a War Zone', *The Epoch Times*, 4 July 2008.

[24] Sean McFate, 'The Art and Aggravation of Vetting in Post-Conflict Environments', *Military Review*, vol 87 (2007) 79–87.

[25] Andrew Bearpark and Sabrina Schulz, 'The Future of the Market', in Chesterman and Lehnardt, *From Mercenaries to Market*, n 16 above, 246.

[26] See IPOA Code of Conduct, available at <http://ipoaworld.org/eng/codeofconduct.html>.

political climate that made regulation of apparel workplaces challenging. As a result, Reich relied increasingly on voluntary agreements between brands, retailers, and manufacturers to monitor workplace conditions and ensure that labour laws were being upheld. As Reich put it, the private sector was going to have to do more, if the public sector was going to do less.[27] His 'No Sweat' programme also relied on civil society groups to act as watchdogs over the industry. Yet the initiative did not merely respond to exigent circumstances; instead, it served to reinforce the idea that corporations were not to be interfered with through regulatory channels, but rather more indirectly guided through voluntary mechanisms, preferably launched in conjunction with civil society groups.

The Fair Labor Association

A central component of Reich's program to address sweatshops overseas was the FLA. The FLA sought to tap into market incentives to encourage compliance with labour standards, including consumer demand for 'sweat-free' goods; companies' desire to boost sales by meeting that demand and to protect their bottom-line by maintaining the integrity of their brand images; and contractors' attempts to attract FDI by demonstrating their ability to comply with the CSR standards embodied in companies' codes of conduct. In addition, both brands and contractors sought to avoid the possibility of binding government regulation by demonstrating their ability to self-regulate. As the FLA became increasingly institutionalized and received the recognition of the Department of Labor (DOL) and the buy-in of big brands and mainstream media, any alternative developed had to justify itself vis-à-vis the FLA. Thus, instead of completely shunning mechanisms of private oversight, the more 'radical' anti-sweatshop groups opposed to the FLA responded with their own voluntary, civil society-based solution: the WRC. These groups created a legitimate space for the WRC by demonstrating how, unlike the FLA, it was an extension of the precepts of a solidarity model[28] for protecting labour rights, and was exemplary of 'truly independent' third-party oversight that would create the space for worker empowerment through unionization.[29]

The formation of the FLA began in July 1996 when Secretary Reich used the media coverage around the Kathie Lee Gifford scandal as an opportunity to

[27] Robert Reich, *Locked in the Cabinet.* (New York: Knopf, 1997) 292–3. For details about Reich's programmes, see '"Standard" and "Advanced" Practices in the North American Garment Industry', Commission for Labor Cooperation, 2000.

[28] For a comparison of the solidarity versus market-based strategic model of anti-sweatshop mobilization, see DeWinter-Schmitt, 'Business as Usual', n 11 above, 229–42.

[29] DeWinter-Schmitt, 'Business as Usual', n 11 above, 281–324; Jill Esbenshade, *Monitoring Sweatshops: Workers, Consumers, and the Global Apparel Industry* (Philadelphia: Temple University Press, 2004) 177–89.

bring together apparel brands and NGOs at a Fashion Industry Forum to discuss the creation of a sweat-free apparel label. Out of this emerged a presidential task force, and on 2 August 1996, the first anniversary of the El Monte, California sweatshop raid, President Clinton announced the formation of the Apparel Industry Partnership (AIP) at a Rose Garden ceremony. By April of the following year, the AIP participants[30] reached agreement on a Workplace Code of Conduct and Principles of Monitoring[31] and the creation of an association to develop a 'reliable, independent means to provide for public confidence' that companies were in compliance with code standards, as indicated through a 'seal of approval'.[32] The negotiations had taken eight, instead of the allotted six, months because participants disagreed about standards for wages, hours of work, and monitoring.[33] Not only was the AIP plagued by internal disagreements between NGO and corporate participants, its announcement also elicited a negative response from anti-sweatshop groups outside the process.[34] The FLA was finally launched in November 1998, long after the six month timeframe allotted for its formation.[35] The Charter Document contained the code, monitoring guidelines, and plans for overseeing compliance and accrediting monitors. Over the course of the negotiations, it had become clear to the unions (UNITE and RWDSU) and the Interfaith Center for Corporate Responsibility that they were not going to be able to shape the standards and monitoring protocols as hoped, and all three withdrew from the process.[36]

The groups that left joined other key NGOs in the movement in issuing a stinging critique of the FLA agreement. The opposition of this faction of the

[30] The company participants at the outset were LL Bean, Nike, Phillips-Van Heusen, Liz Claiborne, Nicole Miller, Patagonia, Hanover Direct, Tweeds, Reebok, Karen Kane and Warnaco. NGO participants were selected by the DOL based on their past records of engaging with corporate and government actors and included UNITE (now UNITE-HERE); the Retail, Wholesale, and Department Store Union (RWDSU) of the AFL-CIO; National Consumers League; Interfaith Center for Corporate Responsibility (ICCR); International Labor Rights Fund; the Lawyers Committee for Human Rights (now Human Rights First); the Robert F Kennedy Memorial Center for Human Rights; and Business for Social Responsibility.

[31] For the current code of conduct, see <http://www.fairlabor.org/about_us_code_conduct_e1.html>. For monitoring principles, see <http://www.fairlabor.org/images/AboutUs/fla%20principles%20of%20monitoring.pdf>.

[32] See Joanna Ramsey, 'Clinton Urges Industry to Enlist in the War Against Sweatshops', *Women's Wear Daily*, 15 April, 1997.

[33] See Steven Greenhouse, 'Apparel Industry Group Moves to End Sweatshops', *New York Times*, 9 April, 1997. The NGOs wanted inclusion of living wage language rather than a reference to 'basic needs', work hours capped at 60 per week with no exceptions for 'extraordinary circumstances', and local groups, rather than large accounting firms, utilized for monitoring contractors.

[34] Tim Shorrock, 'Workplace Agreement Gets White House Nod', *Journal of Commerce*, 15 April, 1997.

[35] The FLA was formally incorporated in May 1999 and received start up funds from the Department of State and the US Agency for International Development.

[36] Steven Greenhouse, 'Groups Reach Agreement for Curtailing Sweatshops', *New York Times*, 5 November 1998.

movement was at one level about the most appropriate set of labour standards for corporations to uphold and what constituted 'independent' monitoring.[37] At another level, the faction critiqued groups who stayed in the FLA process for not having the 'true interests' of workers at heart. At a deeper level, the disagreements were about the very nature of the global apparel contracting system and the appropriate roles for corporate and government actors, workers, and NGOs in remediating sub-par workplace conditions.[38] Those who stayed in the process depicted the FLA as a pragmatic outcome in light of the constraints of a system in which neither the home governments of the brands and retailers, nor the governments hosting manufacturing facilities, were going to take steps to regulate the workplace and enforce labour rights. The anti-sweatshop movement split between those supporting the FLA as a voluntary, market-based strategy to reform production conditions versus those pursuing a solidarity-based strategy and viewing corporate engagement as co-option.

The Worker Rights Consortium

Although the FLA was experiencing a 'legitimacy crisis',[39] those opposed to the FLA were not sure how to gain a more credible enforcement of workers rights in the face of a divided anti-sweatshop movement and waning media coverage after two years of headline grabbing exposés. At that moment, activism surged again with students mobilizing across the country to bring their schools to adopt codes of conduct for goods carrying their logos.[40] University administrators, searching for a way to ensure compliance with the newly adopted code standards, were encouraged by the DOL to join the FLA. Students, viewing the organization as 'FLAwed', demanded that schools either drop out or refuse to join. In need of a credible alternative, students, NGOs and academics created the WRC.[41] They saw the WRC as marrying a voluntary strategy leveraging the collective market power of universities with a solidarity approach to mobilization. Rather than

[37] Specifically, their main complaints were that companies selected and paid monitors and suggested factories for inspection; audits were announced; local groups merely had to be 'consulted' during audits; companies retained control of audit results and reporting of companies' performance was limited to an annual basis with no public disclosure of factory locations; external factory audits were required only in 30% of facilities in the initial three year period and in 5–15% thereafter, yet companies could potentially gain a sweat-free certification for all their products; production could occur in countries, like China, that did not respect associational rights; and the composition of the governing board gave corporations a good deal of control and required a supra-majority to change code provisions and expel non-compliant companies. See Esbenshade, *Monitoring Sweatshops*, n 28 above, 179–81.

[38] Ibid, at 245, fn 66.

[39] Kevin Danaher and Jason Mark, *Insurrection: Citizen Challenges to Corporate Power* (New York: Routledge, 2003) 94.

[40] See Liza Featherstone and USAS, *Students Against Sweatshops* (New York: Verso, 2002).

[41] The main creators of the WRC were United Students Against Sweatshops, UNITE, Campaign for Labor Rights, National Labor Committee, People of Faith Network, Sweatshop Watch, US/Labor Education in the Americas Project, and various academics, including Edna Bonacich, Jill Esbenshade, and Dara O'Rourke.

seeking to monitor as many factories as possible in companies' supply chains, the WRC was based on the idea that it is more effective to respond to and verify worker complaints with the intention of empowering workers by supporting unionization drives. Hence, the WRC became known as the 'verification model', in contradistinction to the FLA's 'monitoring model', and reflected an 'inversion of private monitoring', since it concentrated on workers rights rather than workplace conditions and created a system triggered by the worker rather than the company.[42] Furthermore, to avoid the pitfalls of the FLA's model of private monitoring[43] and to foster a 'race to the top' in labour standards, the WRC did not include companies in its governance structures, since this would amount to 'the fox guarding the hen house'; its model code of conduct[44] was more stringent than the FLA's, containing stipulations for a living wage, women's rights, country sourcing guidelines, and full public disclosure of factory locations; it viewed university licensing agreements as a form of leverage, establishing a system of penalties for non-compliant licensees; and it sought to remediate attempts to thwart organizing efforts rather than certifying brands as sweat-free.

Although there had been a bitter intra-movement dispute over the FLA and WRC, the two organizations cooperated increasingly over time. This rapprochement was portrayed as a pragmatic outcome of the challenges that both confronted as they sought to rectify poor workplace conditions. Each organization had access to and contributed different resources—the WRC had the strength of its direct contacts to workers and their representatives and the ability to respond rapidly to labour rights complaints, while the FLA was able to work with brands to gain access to factories and use their leverage over contractors to push for remediation. In addition, when labour rights advocate Auret van Heerden was appointed as the FLA's Executive Director in December 2001, he began, with the support of university members, to implement changes in line with the original demands for improving transparency, monitoring, and disclosure made by the NGOs that had withdrawn and created the WRC. With Van Heerden and Scott Nova, Executive Director of the WRC, each agreeing not to disparage the other's organization, the growing collaboration became less controversial. The disagreements that nearly split the movement now seemed forgotten.

Assessment

The rapprochement between the FLA and WRC is important because it demonstrates that a general consensus has emerged on the best practices for

[42] Esbenshade, *Monitoring Sweatshops*, n 28 above, 165. While the WRC primarily responds to complaints, proactive investigations are conducted in areas with patterns of labour rights abuses.

[43] Ibid. at 198–200.

[44] The Worker Rights Consortium Model Code of Conduct is available at <http://www.workersrights.org/university/coc.asp>.

privatized regulation, including multi-stakeholder participation, strong, operational code standards, independent verification of their implementation, enforcement provisions, and public reporting. These will be discussed in more detail in the next section. Unfortunately, even with this knowledge, the record of labour rights advocates and the apparel industry in eradicating sweatshops is mixed. If we return to the four principles outlined in the introduction to determine if privatization of labour standards regulation has resulted in an improvement in the overall human rights situation, the answer is, no. There is no evidence that the general lot of workers has improved, and almost nowhere are they earning living wages, although the most extreme violations—physical and verbal abuse and forced and child labour—occur far less frequently. The few victories that have been won at specific factories are being rolled back as efforts to sustain unions and sign collective bargaining agreements continue to be thwarted. This is in large part because monitoring does not change the dictates of how global markets function and the competitive pressures on manufacturers to reduce prices by lowering wages and workplace standards.[45] The vastness and complexity of supply chains makes it impossible for any monitoring organization to ever inspect more than a small percentage of factories.

If monitoring cannot ensure full compliance, the danger lurks that companies engaging in even minimal monitoring can use it as a public relations tool to challenge legitimate complaints of workers rights abuses. More generally, monitoring is not geared towards long term sustainable improvement in workplace conditions because it puts monitoring organizations, brands, and NGOs in the role of policemen, instead of building the capacities of contractors to improve labour standards and empowering workers to help themselves.[46] Finally, some activists fear that when consumer, media, and advocacy group attention on a company dies down, it may return to business as usual.[47] In general, it is questionable if public pressure is enough to change business practices, despite surveys that suggest people prefer to shop in a socially conscientious manner.[48]

While the US government provided the initial impetus for creating the FLA and at various times funded the FLA and WRC, it left these organizations to their own devices and forfeited its responsibility to provide ongoing protection of workers' rights and an adequate regulatory framework to oversee the global

[45] See, eg, 'Memorandum from WRC Executive Director Scott Nova to Universities', 11 October 2005, available at <http://www.workersrights.org/dsp/WRCExecMemo_10-11-05.doc>.

[46] Esbenshade, *Monitoring Sweatshops*, n 28 above, 9.

[47] My research revealed that for Nike and Gap this was not the case, as the two continued to implement CSR best practices after they were no longer targeted by the movement. See DeWinter-Schmitt, 'Business as Usual?', n 11 above, chaps 4 and 5.

[48] See, eg, 'The Consumer and Sweatshops', Survey Commissioned by Marymount University Center for Ethical Concerns, Conducted by International Communications Research, November 1999, available at <http://www.marymount.edu/news/garmentstudy/overview.html>.

activities of US apparel corporations. Based on the above principles, the state must be the final guarantor of rights and cannot leave their respect up to the goodwill or 'enlightened self-interest' of companies. The fact that outsourcing and privatized regulation are treated as a *fait accompli* indicates that the US government has chosen to put faith in neo-liberal economic doctrine rather than actually conducting an assessment of the impact of this choice on workers' rights protections. On a positive note, both the FLA and WRC have come a long way in increasing transparency in the industry through the public disclosure of factory locations and audit results, countering the legitimacy of corporate claims that disclosure could reveal trade secrets and undermine competitive advantages. However, overall the predominance of voluntary solutions serves to reinforce the marginalization of the state in labour standards surveillance and enforcement, and to reaffirm the shift in boundaries between state and corporate actors, as well as between civil society and corporate actors, as the distinctions between for-profit and not-for-profit and between the dictates of the market and the goal of furthering public purposes meld together in hybrid organizations.

Yet even with this relatively negative assessment, until civil society advocacy brings governments to take on the responsibility of protecting labour rights and holding corporations accountable, it must be acknowledged that the WRC and FLA represent an important step and two of the best models of self-regulation available at the moment.[49] Monitoring can shine a light on human rights abuses inherent to the global contracting system, pushing governments to ensure that labour laws are respected and forcing brands and retailers to become familiar with, and address, poor conditions in their contractors, including finding long term solutions and building the capacities of contractors. The WRC and FLA may also inadvertently foster advocacy since when companies commit themselves to the codes of conduct and standards of the WRC and FLA, it allows activists to 'rhetorically entrap'[50] companies, forcing them to bring 'word' and 'deed' into alignment. In addition, independent monitoring can open up a space for workers to organize, providing them with influence in commodity chains that have rendered them largely powerless—although means must be found to sustain initial victories after public attention dies down. Involving local groups in remediation efforts can also foster local civil society structures. Finally, strong codes and monitoring systems can serve as models for weaker ones. The rapprochement between the FLA and WRC provides an indication of what legitimate self-regulation looks like. These lessons can be applied to the IPOA code mechanism.

[49] As the FLA's CEO and President Auret van Heerden aptly remarked, 'We are an ad hoc response to a regulatory vacuum.' Esbenshade, *Monitoring Sweatshops*, n 28 above, 207.

[50] Frank Schimmelpfennig, 'The Community Trap: Liberal Norms, Rhetorical Action, and the Eastern Enlargement of the European Union' *International Organization*, vol 55 (2001) 47–80.

Self-regulation in the private security industry

The IPOA Code of Conduct was the first and most extensive initiative in the private military and security industry to set standards for companies. Headquartered in Washington, DC, its international membership includes companies that provide services beyond just security. Unlike the FLA code, which was developed in response to grassroots pressure and negative publicity, the first version of the IPOA code was penned in 2000 as the brainchild of its current president Doug Brooks.[51] At that point, PMSCs were not yet the subject of intense public scrutiny as would occur in the wake of infamous incidents, such as the involvement of Titan and CACI contractors in detainee abuse at Abu Ghraib in 2004 and Blackwater's alleged shooting of 17 civilians in Nisour Square in September 2007. Brooks, at the time an academic fellow doing research in Sierra Leone, began to conceptualize the appropriate role for private contractors in supporting peace and stability operations. Consulting with an array of stakeholders, including human rights and humanitarian NGOs, policy-makers, academics, and legal experts, he formulated a set of basic principles on the ethical use of the private sector in conflict zones, which eventually evolved into the IPOA code. Brooks describes the code as a 'working document', the 12th iteration of which was publicly released in March 2009.

The frequent revision of the code is due in large part to the fact that IPOA has not made a concerted effort to extract lessons from other industries that have had extensive experience in developing self-regulatory initiatives.[52] The disputes between the FLA and WRC over such issues as membership make-up, code content, independent monitoring, and public reporting, and their experiences in putting the code into practice, can serve as a guide to the IPOA for creating a truly exemplary MSI—one which would not only serve to minimize human rights violations and boost the business of its members, but would also be perceived widely as legitimate. Legitimacy is essential since ultimately civil society is the arbiter of what constitutes appropriate corporate behaviour and public perception matters for an industry that relies heavily on taxpayers' dollars and has visible operations in conflict environments. Based on the experiences of the FLA and WRC a set of 'ideal type' best practices can be extrapolated that are likely to result in a code of conduct mechanism that is not only effective, but also viewed as legitimate by civil society groups. If companies earnestly pursue these

[51] Doug Brooks, 'From Humble Beginnings in Freetown: The Origins of the IPOA Code of Conduct and Its Importance for the Industry', *Journal of Peace Operations*, vol 3 (2008) 9–10.

[52] Codes of conduct were first formulated in the 1970s, and there is no need to reinvent the wheel. Oliver Willliams (ed), *Global Codes of Conduct: An Idea Whose Time Has Come* (Notre Dame: University of Notre Dame Press, 2000).

practices, advocacy groups will be more willing to engage with, rather than attack, them. A strong self-regulatory mechanism would ensure that:

(1) there is inclusive multi-stakeholder involvement;

(2) the code contains widely recognized, well-defined, and stringent standards;

(3) standards are operationalized so companies can readily implement them;

(4) implementation is regularly monitored both internally and externally, as verified through an independent third party;

(5) an enforcement mechanism is in place to address breaches of code standards; and

(6) protocols for public reporting and transparency exist so that claims made by companies about compliance can be proofed.

Assessed vis-à-vis these best practices, the IPOA code process has its strengths and weaknesses. Although 12 versions is a bit excessive, the fact that the document is open to revisions in light of the changing circumstances facing the industry displays foresight. Impetus for revision is more likely to come from stakeholders impacted by the industry's operations, or those representing the interests of affected communities, than the member companies. Therefore, a legitimate code process must be *multi-stakeholder* in nature, from code formulation through to its implementation and enforcement. As the FLA's experience demonstrated, while it was initially criticized for its corporate membership, the practicalities of ensuring compliance in factories evidenced that corporations had to be part of any remediation effort. Yet, without the involvement of labour rights advocates and local groups, something which the WRC offered, the FLA was lacking the voice of workers and lost credibility. Thus, all relevant stakeholders must be represented. For the past three years IPOA has brought together a shifting cast of member companies, NGOs, policymakers, and other experts for an annual 'standards simulation exercise', during which scenarios of code violations are gamed through the complaint process. Nevertheless, this ad hoc inclusion of stakeholders, all of whom are headquartered in the North, does not represent a sustained multi-stakeholder process. A similar ad hoc process was utilized in September 2008 when the IPOA held a Code of Conduct Convention to elicit input on substantive changes to the standards of the 11th version of the code and the enforcement mechanism.[53] In the end, the IPOA code mechanism remains a corporate-led effort, which will likely lead civil society groups to lob accusations of the 'fox guarding the hen house' against it.

[53] Disclosure: I attended both the standards simulation exercises and the convention representing Amnesty International.

On a positive note, international humanitarian law and human rights instruments form part of the *code standards* cited in the preamble. By drawing on widely recognized international standards, the IPOA can avoid the disputes that plagued the FLA and WRC over defining and interpreting standards. However, signatories merely are to be 'guided by' these international instruments, rather than required to explicitly follow them; it is also not clear what elements of these instruments are applicable to them as corporate actors. More specifically, although there are references to the International Labour Organization (ILO) Minimum Age Convention and the Optional Protocol to the UN Convention on the Rights of the Child on the Involvement of Children in Armed Conflict (regarding appropriate minimum ages of employment for armed and unarmed personnel), as well as prohibitions of forced employment and trafficking in persons, explicit inclusion of the ILO Declaration on Fundamental Principles and Rights to Work would incorporate additional core labour standards, in particular associational rights and elimination of discrimination. These are especially important in light of the labour rights issues that have plagued the industry. The code does stipulate the adequate training and vetting of personnel, yet there is limited elaboration of what this entails. Weeding out personnel who may have engaged in past human rights violations is of utmost importance since PMSCs operate in conflict ridden areas with limited or no rule of law that may encourage rights abuses. It is essential in such a context that signatories' personnel, partner companies, and subcontractors also be explicitly trained on, not merely 'informed' about, international humanitarian and international human rights law and the IPOA code standards. In addition, the 12th version, unfortunately, removed the requirement that personnel be instructed on the 'regional sensitivities' of areas of operation. Furthermore, while the code states that signatories agree to 'provide their personnel with the appropriate training, equipment, and materials necessary to perform their duties', it does not require signatories to ensure the safety of their personnel to the greatest extent possible within their dangerous operating environments.

In addition, the code requires signatories to 'minimize the loss of life and destruction of property', but has no requirements that civilians, who may have been unduly harmed or whose property may have been destroyed, be paid reparations. On a positive note, the pledge signatories made to cooperate with investigations into allegations of abuse was strengthened to require member companies to report to relevant authorities grave breaches of international humanitarian and human rights law by their personnel. Whistleblower protection for personnel reporting violations was also added. However, given past experiences and challenges with investigating allegations of abuse, stipulations are missing that companies do not potentially hamper investigations by destroying evidence; facilitating the alleged perpetrators' evasion of the jurisdiction of authorities; or allowing them to continue to operate in an environment fraught with a high-risk of reoccurrence of abuse. Companies are also not encouraged to make public the outcome of their own internal investigations. More generally, companies have no obligation to disclose the human rights related provisions of their contracts. Finally, as evidenced by the changes to the code over the course of past iterations, it has become clear that for every effort to strengthen standards, there seems to be concomitant changes that weaken them. For example, while the code now requires signatories to refrain from obtaining weapons through illegal channels and from violating UN arms embargos, the clause that force be used only when necessary and proportionate to the threat was removed, and instances when signatories are not required to disclose information were added and elaborated.

Even if the substantive shortcomings of the code were addressed, it would amount to no more than a paper tiger until adequate *implementation* is ensured. The IPOA has not provided its member companies with any guidance on how these standards are to be translated into protocols for daily operations.[54] Without well-defined, practicable, and consistent standards, there is no means to measure and assess each member's compliance or compare compliance across companies. It is not enough to leave the development of implementation guidelines to each company or to conduct sporadic trainings of senior level management and field staff, as the IPOA has done, although it would be useful for companies to share their experiences with best practices. As the sustained criticism of FLA participating companies demonstrated, until they could show how word and deed were being brought into alignment, they continued to be the subject of grassroots advocacy campaigns.

In addition, while companies should internally assess their compliance efforts as part of a continual improvement process, their assurances will mean little without some form of *independent, third-party oversight* of implementation. The FLA addressed this issue by requiring participating companies not only to audit compliance in house for all factories, but also to hire external monitors to inspect a percentage of factories. The longest standing disagreement over the FLA was whether its monitoring was independent enough that the public could be confident in corporate claims of adherence to code standards. The FLA attempted to deal with this by directly certifying and paying for auditors. However, to have true local buy-in, in line with the WRC's model, efforts should be made to consult with workers and their representatives and local authorities during any monitoring and remediation efforts. Of course, the security industry is different in that there are no static workplace sites that can be monitored. Nevertheless, there are means to verify companies' adherence to code standards. Internal policies and processes can be examined to ensure that a corporate culture is being fostered and practices are being implemented that are

[54] The BAPSC's Self-Assessment Workbook could serve as a starting point for a template for companies to evaluate their compliance with standards, although it would need to have a far greater level of detail and be more industry-specific.

in keeping with the code's provisions. For example, companies could be asked to demonstrate that employees are receiving training on international humanitarian and human rights law; that every effort is being made to solicit background information on new hires to vet out those with criminal records; that a whistleblower hotline has been established to report possible code violations; and so forth. More generally, companies can be expected to translate the spirit of the code into some type of written company policy that officially establishes its commitment to the principles of the code as part of the company's core mission and values. With regard to the field operations of companies, auditing would have to be more mobile in nature. For example, in the wake of the Nisour Square shooting incident, the Department of State's Bureau of Diplomatic Security requires that agents ride along with contractors on their missions. One could imagine an independent auditor hired to accompany a certain percentage of missions to assess the professionalism of security personnel in the field.

Oversight is a necessary part of another best practice, an *enforcement mechanism* that provides a way for an individual or organization to report suspected breaches of the code, and that uses non-affected parties to independently adjudicate those complaints. The WRC's verification model is based on the idea that responding to complaints is the most effective means to address labour rights violations within complex sourcing chains and could serve as a template. To the IPOA's credit, in December 2006 it adopted a detailed third party complaint mechanism—mislabelled an 'enforcement mechanism'—which is open for anyone to use.[55] However, it is doubtful if affected communities or other relevant stakeholders are even aware of its existence.[56] In addition, it does not stipulate any type of regularized process for the IPOA staff to undertake when violations of code standards come to light and no third party files a complaint. More seriously, it is a completely closed and internal decision process, which calls into doubt the independence of any outcome.

Finally, *public reporting* of member companies' efforts to abide by the code is integral for increasing transparency, supplying affected stakeholders with relevant information, and ensuring the credibility of the code process. The ability to compare one's performance to industry peers could also be a financial boon for companies that strive to meet best practices and could be used as a selling point to attract clients, much like the FLA certification is meant to attract conscientious consumers. IPOA could consider a similar seal of approval to draw

[55] See 'Enforcement Mechanism', IPOA, available at <http://ipoaonline.org/php/index.php?option=com_content&task=view&id=135&Itemid=135>. The enforcement mechanism is suspended if there is an ongoing government investigation or formal litigation, which would seem to exempt most serious incidents from ever being subjected to this mechanism. It is also unclear what sanctions might be applied to members, beyond expulsion in extreme instances.

[56] For a discussion of PMSC accountability to affected communities, including various non-legal dispute resolution mechanisms, see chapter three of this volume by Angelina Fisher.

clients seeking security providers who abide by ethical business practices and could negotiate with governments, urging them to prefer PMSCs that demonstrate compliance with such standards.[57] The increased business could level the playing field by offsetting the costs associated with adhering to higher standards.

Conclusion

It is clear that the IPOA code mechanism in its current form, as a set of underspecified aspirational standards with a limited and non-transparent third party complaint process occasionally reviewed by an ad hoc group of stakeholders, cannot ensure that security companies live up to their obligations to protect and promote human rights in their operations. However, the US government is also not living up to its responsibility to act as the final guarantor of the human rights of those affected by PMSC activities. Returning to the four principles outlined in the introduction, it is apparent that the outsourcing of private military and security services occurred without the US government exercising due diligence to ensure that privatization has not worsened the human rights conditions in PMSC areas of operation. Regulation to oversee PMSCs and punish those who commit human rights violations is inconsistent and generally has not been enforced.[58] Also, there has been limited discussion about the privatization of security provision, despite its tremendous impact on the notion that the state should have a monopoly over the control of the use of force. Nor has there been much effort to assess the effects of this decision on human rights, although this may change with the formation of the Commission on Wartime Contracting as foreseen by Senators Webb and McCaskill's amendment to the 2008 National Defense Authorization Act. Finally, all indications are that the Bush administration's decision to rely heavily on PMSCs was made in order to avoid transparency and scrutiny of the level of US presence needed to sustain engagement in Iraq and Afghanistan. Any industry self-regulation effort cannot, nor is it intended to, fill the vacuum left by the US government.

[57] Interestingly, a reference to the IPOA Code has found its way into draft Afghan regulations for PMSCs. The Terms of Reference within the 'Procedure for Regulating Activities of Private Security Companies in Afghanistan' (on file with the author) requires that both foreign and domestic PMSCs commit to abide by IPOA code standards in order to be licensed. However, it is unclear how this requirement will be enforced.

[58] An important exception is the December 2008 indictment of five Blackwater guards on charges of voluntary manslaughter and other offences arising from the Nisour Square incident. A sixth guard has pleaded guilty. 'Five Blackwater Employees Indicted on Manslaughter and Weapons Charges for Fatal Nisur Square Shooting in Iraq', Department of Justice Press Release No 08-1068, 8 December 2008, available at <http://www.usdoj.gov/opa/pr/2008/December/08-nsd-1068.html>.

Returning to the original question, if it matters whether security is provided publicly or privately, currently there seems to be little hope that either delivery method alone could guarantee adequate human rights protections. Of course, it is ironic that the industry appears to be fairly receptive to establishing oversight and accountability through state-sanctioned mechanisms. This could be for any number of reasons, from the professional ethics of contractors, many of whom come from a military background, to profit motives and the fear that bad publicity could damage reputations and ultimately the bottom line. Whatever the reason, the desire of PMSCs to bring regulatory clarity to the industry suggests a possible third way of protecting human rights in the form of hybrid public-private regulatory regimes. Pragmatically speaking, this also may be the only viable alternative as long as the privatization trend continues and 'inherently governmental' security services are not clearly delineated. Hybrid regulation also makes sense considering that the dichotomy between voluntary and mandatory regulation may not always be so stark.[59] The Private Security Company Association of Iraq's involvement in drafting regulations for the security industry in Iraq is an existing example of a hybrid effort.

It is conceivable that the US government could become involved in a sustained fashion in developing a thorough code of conduct mechanism, along the lines of Reich's initial role in forming the FLA. While the FLA and WRC's records in improving labour rights conditions have been mixed, the lessons learned from their efforts can provide a road map for moving forward and creating better hybrid regulation—one containing all the necessary elements of high standards, implementation guidelines, independent monitoring, an enforcement mechanism, and public reporting. The initiative could be incentivized by giving compliant companies some sort of industry seal of approval that would indicate their adherence to ethical business practices, which could be attractive to non-state customers, like NGOs and other companies that need security and are worried about the reputations of their providers. The US government could also award preferential hiring to PMSCs that have received the seal of approval, although requests for proposals would have to be phrased in a way that indicates a general desire for companies who can perform to certain levels, including in accordance with international human rights and humanitarian law standards, so as to avoid potential violations of anti-trust laws.

[59] For example, in the extractives sector, a MSI called the Voluntary Principles on Security and Human Rights has found its way into host government agreements with oil companies, thereby giving them binding legal force since non-compliance can be arbitrated in civil courts. See Bennett Freeman and Genoveva Hernandez Uriz. 'Managing Risk and Building Trust: The Challenge of Implementing the Voluntary Principles on Security and Human Rights;, in Rory Sullivan (ed), *Business and Human Rights: Dilemmas and Solutions* (Sheffield, UK: Greenleaf Publishing, 2002) 243–59. Similar suggestions have been made to include human rights commitments in PMSC contracts. See Laura Dickinson, 'Contract as a Tool for Regulating Private Military Companies', Chesterman and Lehnardt, *From Mercenaries to Market*, n 16 above, 217–38.

As long as neo-liberal doctrine reigns supreme and the US public does not have the desire to increase the number of US troops, security companies are here to stay and will need to be regulated in a way that combines government powers of oversight and enforcement with the industry's self-interest in institutionalizing ethical practices. However, hybrid regulation does not alleviate the US government's responsibility to conduct ongoing assessments of the human rights impact of such an effort, with the primary goal of guaranteeing the protection of the rights of affected communities. This would include examining the global structure and operations of the private military and security industry to address the root causes of human rights violations, including possibly reaching the conclusion that ultimately certain security services should not be provided through the private sector. Until then, if the industry does not preserve its integrity by improving its current efforts at self-regulation, the designation of certain forms of security provision as 'inherently governmental' may not be as far off as one may think.

PART III

LIMITS

8

Police informants

Jacqueline Ross

Introduction: Informants and Outsourcing

Outsourcing of government functions raises a variety of challenges for oversight and accountability of private actors and for aligning private incentives with public interest. When delegated powers include core government prerogatives, like the use of force, critics also worry about policy being made and discretion being exercised by contractors with no public mandate to exercise 'inherently governmental functions'. Michael Likosky raises these concerns for the privatization of violence in chapter one of this volume, while in chapter ten Chia Lehnhardt focuses primarily on the outsourcing of peacekeeping operations. Both chapters, however, develop the implications of increased US reliance on private military and security companies (PMSCs), and both authors pose the question: how do democratic states remain accountable for the way power is exercised in their name, when privatization distances the state from the actions of private actors and strains the state's resources for oversight and control?

These issues are not unique to the privatization of military force. As Simon Chesterman shows in chapter nine of this volume, privatized collection and analysis of foreign intelligence raises concerns when private actors do either what public actors may not—in the case of torture—or what only public actors may do, insofar as private actors exercise some of the core prerogatives of the state. Government regulations, after all, forbid outsourcing 'inherently governmental' functions, which may be performed only by democratically accountable actors, that is to say, by government officials.

Much of the debate about US outsourcing of security centres on private contractors' conduct abroad and their dealings with foreign nationals. Domestically, however, the privatization of core government functions is nothing new, particularly in the domain of security. Private security firms are the most common example. Additionally, law enforcement agencies routinely outsource the investigation of crime to non-state actors who serve as informants. Insofar as informants gather intelligence secretly, one can think of them as performing the domestic analogue to the foreign intelligence functions discussed by Chesterman. Unlike intelligence agencies, however, law enforcement agencies generally seek information that can serve as evidence for criminal prosecutions or that can lead to the discovery of evidence. Whether one thinks of informants as sources of evidence or domestic intelligence, however, they perform investigative functions that may fall under shifting government definitions of 'inherently governmental' functions.[1]

Outsourcing core government functions leads to problems of oversight and accountability in all domains of security. In particular, delegating investigative powers to informants may result in abuses similar to those associated with PMSCs. As with contractors, informants sometimes commit crimes while working for the government. If informants subject their targets to unfair pressures or temptations, they may jeopardize the ensuing prosecution (just as unlawful interrogation tactics may undermine the state's ability to prosecute enemy combatants). Informants may invade protected privacy interests or disrupt personal relationships; and, like PMSCs, they may sow distrust among local communities. Lawbreaking by informants may also be difficult to detect, as their role is usually shrouded in secrecy. Like private contractors, informants may claim immunity for illegal conduct, provided their actions were properly authorized. Even when spurious, claims that 'my government handler told me I could do this' may be hard to disprove—whether they are raised by informants or by PMSCs engaged in covert activity.

Despite these shared concerns, delegations to informants are particularly troubling in one further respect. Informants, unlike other private contractors, are typically criminal insiders (though they may also be private citizens or former criminals who co-operate against organizations to which they do not belong). Once recruited as informants, criminal insiders frequently remain in place in their targeted organizations and continue to participate in crimes in order to provide investigators with inside information about the activities of other members. Like undercover agents, informants may purchase and sell contraband undercover or participate in other offences with their criminal associates. Yet in doing so, they may not be playing a part; they may be playing themselves and doing, for the government's benefit, what they usually do for their criminal organization. Informants who are criminal insiders may be more useful to the state than other private actors, like private intelligence analysts, who, as Chesterman notes, are frequently former CIA agents and are functionally interchangeable with public officials (though considerably more expensive). On the other hand, criminal insiders are more compromised and less reliable—not only because they are criminals, but also because they are insiders. Being insiders skews their perspectives and incentives; it places them at an informational and tactical advantage relative to the police; and it gives them a special ability to manipulate the people, setting, and crimes they investigate. This makes it particularly difficult to legitimate and control informants' participation in criminal

[1] See chapter nine of this volume by Simon Chesterman.

activity—particularly when informants commit crimes undercover for investigative purposes.

Any legal system that uses informants for criminal investigations must wrestle with difficult questions about privatization, and specifically the permissible scope of informants' investigative activity. Whether to permit law-breaking by criminal insiders is one of the more striking dilemmas that outsourcing to interested insiders may pose. If the conduct is legal for undercover agents, is it permissible to delegate the conduct to informants who are criminal insiders? To what extent is it possible to delegate investigative powers to private actors while ensuring that discretionary calls and value judgments about permissible investigative conduct remain the purview of the police? Who can be held accountable if such high-risk informants go astray? Privatization thus entails hard choices about how to instrumentalize interested insiders, as public actors cannot implement security policies without the co-operation of stakeholders in local communities.

Regulatory responses to this challenge differ widely across legal systems. The US approach is among the most permissive, insofar as its legal system affords informants the 'public authority' defence, protecting them from criminal responsibility for all otherwise criminal conduct that was duly authorized by the police during the course of a criminal investigation. By contrast, Germany's approach is, at least formally, among the most restrictive, since its law subjects informants to criminal penalties for all offences committed undercover, regardless of whether the informants acted at the direction and behest of the police. Informally, German police and prosecutors do permit informants to take part in the crimes they investigate, but only under limited conditions, and only certain types of informants receive such permission, among whom criminal insiders are the most sensitive and restricted.

German police and prosecutors craft these compromises through their joint implementation of guidelines that govern confidentiality guarantees to informants.[2] These regulations limit the use of organizational insiders as active participants in undercover investigations, in order to limit informants' involvement in criminal activity. In deciding whether to authorize confidentiality guarantees, prosecutors do not decide whether police may use certain private parties as investigative auxiliaries; instead, prosecutors influence the use of such co-operators indirectly, by determining whether their identity and investigative role may be kept secret.

[2] Gemeinsame Richtlinien der Justizminister/-senatoren und der Innenminister/-senatoren der Laender ueber die Inanspruchnahme von Informanten sowie ueber den Einsatz von Vertrauenspersonen (V-Personen) und Verdeckten Ermittlern im Rahmen der Strafverfolgung, 15 RiStBV Anl. D (first issued in 1985 and amended in 1993 and 1994); Klaus Ellenbogen, 'Die verdeckte Ermittlungstätigkeit der Strafverfolgungsbehörden durch die Zusammenarbeit mit V-Personen und Informanten', *Schriften zum Prozessrecht*, vol 187 (2004) 127–30.

This regulatory approach is unique in addressing the risks and pitfalls of outsourcing investigative tasks to organizational insiders. Germany's application and interpretation of these confidentiality guidelines illustrates the ways in which constraints on secrecy can limit the undercover role of compromised insiders and their direct involvement in crime. Using data from 89 interviews[3] conducted with German police, prosecutors and judges, this chapter will explore the implementation of German confidentiality regulations and examine how effective they have proved in limiting police recourse to tainted insiders and informants' involvement in crime. In so doing, it is hoped to illuminate some of the strengths and weaknesses of German confidentiality regulations in comparison with other existing and proposed approaches in the United States and Europe. Without pretence of exhausting all regulatory alternatives, the US and Italian regulation of informants have been selected as contrast cases to illustrate a wide array of possible constraints and accommodations against whose respective strengths and weaknesses those of the German approach can be judged.

The next section describes German confidentiality regulations and explains how they limit the use of organizational insiders as informants. It suggests the place of these guidelines in the broader system of laws and regulations that govern undercover investigations and compares the leeway given to undercover agents with that given to informants. The section that follows contrasts confidentiality regulations with alternative US and European approaches, including proposed and existing warrant procedures, in order to identify the special promise as well as the limitations of Germany's constraints on criminal insiders. The chapter then develops an analogy to certain social science research (namely 'participant action research') in which outside researchers and organizational insiders do field work in the insiders' home institutions. It is hoped this will reveal some of the ethical and epistemological problems that inhere in assigning active investigative roles to organizational insiders outside the criminal context and suggest why these problems—particularly those of informants committing crimes—might be exacerbated when the relevant insiders are informants who work undercover for the police. The final section again draws on field interviews in examining to what extent German confidentiality regulations really limit the police in their undercover use of informants, in comparison with regulatory alternatives elsewhere.

[3] As part of a comparative study of undercover policing in the United States, Italy, Germany, and France, the author conducted these interviews (in German) between 2002 and 2004 with police, prosecutors and judges who oversee undercover investigations at both the state and federal level in 15 of the 16 German states. For reasons of security, I have not provided the names of my respondents, though I distinguish between police, prosecutors, and judges in quoting from interviews in the text. Through open-ended, semi-structured field interviews, I sought to ascertain how rules, regulations, and a variety of normative constraints influence the design and execution of undercover investigations involving both undercover agents and informants. My interviews focused on the personal experiences of those who participate in, supervise, and evaluate undercover operations.

Confidentiality regulations and law-breaking

In order to recruit and retain informants, police everywhere must be able to protect confidential sources from discovery. In Germany, confidentiality regulations determine when, and to whom, the police may promise such protection.[4] Based on detailed information from the police, prosecutors must review each informant's prior criminal history, disqualifying those who have previously been convicted of perjury or similar crimes of dishonesty. Prosecutors also examine each informant's relationship to the targets and the crime under investigation. Prosecutors can only guarantee the confidentiality of informants who have not made themselves liable for participating in the offences they are being used to investigate. In effect, this means that informants may not be used to investigate their associates in an undercover capacity.

The special regulation of organizational insiders and the apparent ban on their undercover use may appear puzzling to US observers, as it has no counterpart in US regulation of informants. The public authority defence is equally available to all types of informants, regardless of their connection to the targets. The Attorney General's Guidelines Regarding the Use of Confidential Informants (October 2008)[5] distinguish between ordinary informants and 'high level confidential informants', defined as 'part of the senior leadership' of a major enterprise involved in criminal activity, and imposes special approval requirements for such informants, but these are mainly administrative in nature. The Guidelines do not impose any special limitations on the recruitment or use of such informants, other than the requirement, which applies equally to all potential informants, of conducting a 'suitability' review to determine, among other things, the closeness of the informant's links to the investigation's targets and his or her motivations for co-operating. A target who is betrayed by a close associate has no special ability to prevail on a claim of entrapment, nor would a 'warrant to infiltrate', which a number of US commentators have proposed, create special barriers to the use of organizational insiders. Under most such proposals, emphasis would be placed on the evidentiary predicate for the government's use of informants, not on the type of informants used or the ways they are deployed.

Germany's ban on the recruitment of tainted insiders flows partly from the need to make sure that targets will not be able to guess the identity of the source. But limitations on the use of criminal insiders also follow from obligations of

[4] See 38 I VwVfG; See also a German directive (jointly agreed by the federal and state secretaries of Justice and secretaries of the Interior) regulating the employment of informants, at <http://www.recht-niedersachsen.de/21021/p23,23,12332,8.htm>. See also Klaus Ellbogen, *Die verdeckte Ermittlungst ätigkeit der Strafverfolgungsbehörden durch die Zusammenarbeit mit V-Personen und Informanten*, (Duncker & Humblot: Berlin 2004),§ 7 III, pp 127–30.

[5] Available at <http://www.usdoj.gov/olp/dojguidelines.pdf>.

transparency and fairness to the accused. A prosecutor explained, 'If some person is the only person with access to certain information, he cannot be promised confidentiality, and, at any rate, he must be identified in the case file, since his willingness to assist the police might give rise to claims of entrapment. It's exculpatory information that has to be disclosed'.[6]

There are other reasons why German police and prosecutors are wary of insiders. Co-operating members of investigated groups are also more likely to commit crimes while working undercover, or to pursue their own agenda, which may conflict with that of their handlers. Accordingly, confidentiality regulations are also meant to prevent informants from committing crimes undercover, even where such activity promotes investigative goals. The distinction between the pretence and the reality of committing a crime may become fairly intangible when the 'pretender' simply continues under government observation to do what he has always done as a 'real' criminal. By prohibiting promises of confidentiality to criminal insiders, confidentiality regulations discourage ambiguous deployments of this kind, while ensuring that the stratagem will eventually be disclosed and that tainted informants will be required to testify if the police do use them against their associates.

This caution about tainted insiders is not merely a matter of prudence. Confidentiality guidelines also reinforce a German legal principle that prohibits both undercover agents and informants from committing crimes undercover. As discussed below, other legal systems exempt the police and their helpers from criminal liability for buying or transporting contraband or for otherwise participating in crime for investigative purposes. But Germany has rejected proposals to enact such immunities.[7] Accordingly, confidentiality guidelines not only reduce the risk of informants going astray and committing crimes on their own account; such regulations also prohibit the police from using organizational insiders as moles, that is, from licensing informants to participate in crime for purely investigative purposes.

Why is this regulatory ban necessary, if existing legal rules already prohibit both undercover agents and informants from committing crimes undercover? The reason is simple. Police and prosecutors interpret the legal rule flexibly when it comes to undercover agents, as most undercover investigations would otherwise be illegal. As interviews revealed, German police and prosecutors do in fact permit undercover agents to purchase, transport, and warehouse contraband, and to provide other support services that seemingly involve them in criminal activity. Prosecutors protect undercover operatives from criminal liability by reasoning that undercover agents lack criminal intent, prevent criminal harms from reaching fruition, or keep their causal contributions to a permissible

[6] All interview data is on file with the author.

[7] See Jacqueline E Ross, 'The Place of Covert Policing in Democratic Societies: A Comparative Study of the United States and Germany', *American Journal of Comparative Law*, vol 55 (2007) 493–579.

minimum. But the logic of these arguments can be applied equally well to the undercover activities of informants, leaving it open to question whether informants may engage in similar conduct when they co-operate with the police in an undercover capacity. If it is legal for undercover agents to offer logistical assistance, why would the same actions be criminal when an informant performs them, at least when the informant serves the same investigative purposes and operates under police supervision?

Affording outside infiltrators and organizational insiders the same investigative flexibility would create a strong temptation to use non-governmental actors as functional substitutes for undercover agents, whose deployment requires a warrant and a showing that the investigated offences were sufficiently serious to merit the use of covert tactics.[8] Indeed, a number of police officers reported using informants in place of undercover agents whenever the crimes they investigated did not fall into one of the statutory categories of predicate offences for which deep cover investigations may be authorized. By hindering the recruitment of organizational insiders or limiting their operational leeway, confidentiality guidelines somewhat counteract these incentives, encouraging resort to undercover agents despite the cumbersome warrant requirement and reducing police reliance on the least reliable subgroup of informants. If the police do use informants in place of undercover agents, confidentiality regulations encourage the police to use those informants whom the police bring into the organization from outside or who have connections only to the periphery of targeted organizations. This constraint may reduce some of the risk factors that make informants so difficult to control or particularly likely to engage in criminal activity. Thus informants, like undercover agents, operate in a grey zone between tolerated and impermissible levels of involvement in crime; but confidentiality regulations allow prosecutors to adjust their tolerance levels according to whether the covert operative is a trained and accountable government actor; an organizational insider with his own agenda; or a private actor whose reliability falls somewhere in between these two extremes.

Of course, confidentiality rules cannot perform these tasks without a supportive institutional context. Thus, the Ministry of the Interior works closely with prosecutors to protect informants from having to testify, while reinforcing the rule prohibiting organizational insiders from committing crimes with their erstwhile associates. Once promises of confidentiality are in place, federal law permits the Ministry of the Interior to override judicial subpoenas that would otherwise require informants to testify, but only if these informants have not themselves participated in the crimes they investigate.[9] Informants who commit crimes undercover risk losing their guarantee of confidentiality and being called to testify. The Ministry of the Interior thus performs very much the same task as

8 Strafprozessordnung (StPO) (German Criminal Procedure Code), s 110a.
9 StPO, § 96.

prosecutors in deciding whether to protect the anonymity of informants. However, the Ministry of the Interior plays this role at a much later procedural stage. Promises of confidentiality must be secured before an informant can work for the police. Otherwise he becomes an ordinary witness. By contrast, orders barring witnesses from testifying must be issued after the investigation has ended, but before trial, and they must be justified by some explanation of why the witness would be endangered if his identity became known.

Other post-investigation regulatory tools include the threat of criminal liability and the entrapment doctrine, which Germany treats as a mitigating factor that may reduce punishment, depending on the degree to which pressures and enticements contributed to the commission or severity of the offence. In principle, back-end sanctions can deter police and prosecutors from disregarding confidentiality regulations too blatantly, since informants who participate too actively in the crimes they investigate may incur criminal sanctions for themselves while reducing punishment for their targets. Of course, the deterrent impact of these adverse consequences will depend on the likelihood that the informants' role will become known. Unwarranted promises of confidentiality may significantly reduce the effectiveness of these corrective mechanisms, since such guarantees tend to protect informants' activities from discovery.

German confidentiality rules in comparative perspective

What makes confidentiality guidelines unique emerges most clearly from contrasting these guidelines with their closest analogues elsewhere. The first of these are US requirements that the police disclose the identity and role of informants who were present during the commission of charged offences. The second is the Italian requirement of a warrant for undercover investigations and covert use of informants.[10]

US case law requires disclosure of so-called 'transactional' informants who participated in or witnessed a charged offence.[11] Yet the resemblance between US disclosure requirements and German confidentiality guidelines is more apparent than real. In the United States, revelations about transactional informants protect the trial rights of criminal defendants, and specifically their right to prepare a defence. By contrast, Germany permits some informants to benefit from anonymity and protects them from having to testify—even when they are direct witnesses to a charged offence—so long as these informants meet the requirement of not having been deployed against their past or present criminal associates to investigate offences for which they themselves face criminal liability.

[10] See generally Jacqueline E Ross, 'Impediments to Transnational Cooperation in Undercover Policing: A Comparative Study of the United States and Italy', *American Journal of Comparative Law*, vol 52 (2004) 569–624.

[11] *Roviaro v United States*, 353 US 53 (1957).

German courts permit police officials who monitor informants to testify from hearsay about what informants told them they saw and heard—just as control officers who serve as liaisons between undercover agents and prosecutors may testify in place of the covert officers who witnessed charged offences.[12] Thus, the difference between the US and German approaches lies in the purpose of regulations: the US regime is designed to protect the rights of the defendant, whereas the German confidentiality guidelines make it easier for prosecutors to control the recruitment and use of compromised insiders.

German confidentiality guidelines also bear surface resemblance to warrant requirements, like those enacted in Italy and proposed by some commentators in the United States.[13] Like decisions about confidentiality promises, warrant procedures regulate informants (and undercover agents) through a system of advance approvals, permitting officials outside the police to scrutinize undercover scenarios before they are implemented. Italy limits undercover operations to the investigation of serious offences, such as drug trafficking, money laundering, and terrorism, which the governing legislation enumerates.[14] Judges must determine whether proposed investigations target crimes for which covert tactics may be authorized, and whether such tactics are truly necessary for the success of a given criminal investigation. Failure to seek a warrant will not automatically lead to exclusion of the evidence, but it may expose undercover operatives to criminal liability for participating in the crimes they investigate.

The warrant regime differs from German confidentiality regulations in a number of important respects. First, Germany entrusts the administration of confidentiality regulations to prosecutors, not neutral magistrates. Prosecutors generally have less institutional distance from the police and their investigative goals. Secondly, German prosecutors do not authorize the deployment of informants directly; rather, German prosecutors must decide whether the police may promise to keep their informants' investigative role confidential. If criminal insiders agree to testify, the police do not need to promise them secrecy, so that confidentiality regulations lose their application. Thirdly, Germany's regulatory approach for informants differs from that for undercover agents, in contrast to Italy's, which requires warrants without regard to how undercover investigations are staffed. Germany requires warrants for deep cover agents, but not for informants; confidentiality regulations fill the gap. The United States, of course, does not require warrants for any undercover investigations, as the US Supreme

[12] See Ross, 'The Place of Covert Policing', n 7 above.

[13] Christopher Slobogin, 'Deceit, Pretext, and Trickery: Investigative Lies by the Police', *Oregon Law Review*, vol 76 (1997) 775; Tracey Maclin, 'Informants and the Fourth Amendment: A Reconsideration', *Washington University Law Quarterly*, vol 74 (1996) 573.

[14] Maclin's and Slobogin's proposals differ from the Italian approach by failing to limit the range of offences the police may target through undercover operatives and by requiring the police to satisfy some defined evidentiary threshold for suspicion before they may deploy informants.

Court has held that undercover investigations do not violate any recognized expectation of privacy, for Fourth Amendment purposes.[15]

The most striking difference between German regulation of informants and US and other European approaches lies in the fact that Germany prohibits informants from participating in the crimes they investigate, but at the same time allows prosecutors to exercise informal discretion in determining the conditions under which the police may promise secrecy to criminal insiders and the capacities in which such informants may work undercover. Italy takes these judgment calls away from prosecutors since it has enacted statutory immunities that protect informants and undercover agents from criminal liability for purchasing, warehousing, and transporting firearms, supplying logistical assistance, wire-transferring proceeds from criminal activity, and creating false documents for targets and shipments of contraband. By listing permitted forms of otherwise criminal activity, Italian legislation carves out a recognized safe zone of investigative conduct. Germany, by contrast, does not purport to spell out what potentially criminal conduct informants and undercover agents may engage in undercover operations.[16] In practice, this leaves it up to German prosecutors, police, and informants to deploy criminal law notions of *mens rea*, causation and necessity in determining whether informants may steal cars, participate in burglaries, or handle stolen goods in their undercover capacity.

German confidentiality regulations make it possible for prosecutors to reduce the extent to which criminal insiders play active investigative roles that would require them to participate in criminal activity, at least where the informant is tainted by previous involvement in the crime he is used to investigate. But, as will be shown in the following discussion on the effectiveness of these regulations, confidentiality guidelines also make it possible for German prosecutors to exercise discretion in deciding who counts as a criminal insider and what counts as being implicated in the crimes one investigates, thereby defining a variable degree of operational leeway for criminal insiders while enforcing outer limits on their use. By contrast, Italian exemptions obviate the need for such discretion, insofar as statutory authorizations make it legally unproblematic for informants to play an active undercover role in investigating their prior criminal associates (so long as informants stick to the crimes they are allowed to investigate, and the acts they are statutorily authorized to commit).

[15] *Hoffa v United States*, 385 US 293, 302 (1966); *Lewis v United States*, 385 US 206 (1966).

[16] In practice, of course, German undercover agents do very much what their Italian counterparts do: they investigate a statutorily delimited category of offences—associated with organized crime—by purchasing drugs undercover, providing financial services, and offering logistical support, such as containers of all kinds, transportation assistance, warehouse space, false documentation, and lawful merchandise (like bananas) that can serve as a cover for drug cargoes. Scholars, prosecutors, and judges do not treat these activities as criminal, reasoning that undercover agents lack criminal intent and do not inflict social harm, so long as the police intervene in time to prevent drugs or other contraband from reaching the consumer. See Ross, 'The Place of Covert Policing', n 7 above.

If German prosecutors informally exercise discretion to carve out a limited investigative role for criminal insiders, their US counterparts may be said to enjoy an explicit and much more unconstrained grant of discretion in determining what informants may do undercover. This power derives from the so-called 'public authority' defence, which protects informants from criminal liability for duly authorized criminal conduct.[17] State statutes that codify this defence have little to say about the principled basis on which police and prosecutors should distinguish between permissible and impermissible law-breaking. The US Attorney-General's 'Guidelines Regarding the Use of Confidential Informants' seek to guide this discretion at the federal level, but openly acknowledge that federal investigators may license 'otherwise criminal activity', and that they may do so on grounds of investigative necessity.[18]

Confidentiality regulations are unique in requiring police and prosecutors to wrestle with the risks of delegating investigative responsibilities to criminal insiders. But if informants are generally compromised by involvement in crime, what makes it particularly problematic to use insiders in criminal organizations, against their former associates? To isolate the infirmities peculiar to insiders, it may be useful to abstract from their status as past or present criminals and to focus instead on the special challenges of using investigators to do 'field work' in their home environments.

Confidentiality regulations and their limits on organizational insiders: A social science analogy

To understand the difference between outsiders and insiders as covert operatives, it may be informative to compare undercover investigations using organizational insiders to collaborative research projects known as 'participant action' research. Teachers, administrators, or managers often conduct research on their own workplaces in order to develop new teaching or management techniques. Like police informants, organizational insiders who initiate research to improve practices in their workplace have a personal stake in the environments they investigate and 'benefit from the convenience of studying their own site', as well as from their tactical knowledge of the organization and

[17] Paul Robinson, *Criminal Law Defenses* (St. Paul, MN: West, 1984), s 142(a), 121; see, eg, NY Penal Law (McKinney 1998) s 35.05(1). The US Supreme Court has held that '[c]riminal prohibitions do not generally apply to reasonable enforcement actions by officers of the law', *Brogan v United States*, 522 US 398 (1998).

[18] The Attorney-General's Guidelines Regarding the Use of Confidential Informants (2002), available at <http://www.usdoj.gov/olp/dojguidelines.pdf>.

its practices.[19] Indeed, even researchers who are outsiders to the particular groups or organizations they study frequently share traits with their subjects. Having grown up in the neighbourhoods they study, or by belonging to the same ethnic group as their subjects, researchers and undercover agents often investigate members of communities in which they count in some way as insiders. But the parallels between social science and police infiltration extend beyond the staffing of such investigations (and the dual roles of insiders as stake-holders and investigators) to the symbiotic relationship between investigators and the phenomena they investigate. Unlike traditional research projects, which seek to avoid what many scholars regard as a contaminating influence on the studied site, 'participant action' research welcomes the investigator's input and indeed aims to involve researchers in the day-to-day activities of the studied school or business. Like covert operatives who actively assist their targets and facilitate the offences they investigate, researchers are hands-on participants in practices they study and seek to influence the settings to which they belong. This willingness to leave a footprint and to shape the phenomena under study sets participant action research off from traditional ethnography no less than it sets undercover policing off from conventional investigative tactics. In this chapter it is argued that the use of organizational insiders exacerbates the ethical and epistemological challenges of intervening actively in the environment under study.

Insiders who investigate their own communities may take some aspects of the setting for granted, making it hard for them to question or modify the way they conduct themselves. To be effective as investigators, insiders must be able to 'make the apparently familiar seem strange'[20] and must learn to act differently in some ways than they would if they had no investigative agenda—even at some cost to their authenticity as insiders. The same is true in the law enforcement context. When informants are true members of the criminal organizations they investigate, they may consider it natural to behave as others in the organization do—that is, to impose pressures, dangle enticements, lie, or manipulate.

[19] Kathryn Herr and Gary L Anderson, *The Action Research Dissertation* (New York: Sage Publications, 2005). See also N Wallerstein and B Duran, 'The Conceptual, Historical, and Practice Roots of Community Based Participatory Research and Related Participatory Traditions', in M Minkler and N Wallerstein (eds), *Community-based Participatory Research for Health* (San Francisco: Jossey-Bass, 2001) 27–54; J Zeni, 'A Guide to Ethical Decision Making for Insider Research', in J Zeni (ed), *Ethical Issues in Practitioner Research* (New York: Teachers College Press, 2001); O Spjelkavik, 'Applied Research or Action Research? Different or Complementary Methods', in D Greenwood (ed), *Action Research: From Practice to Writing in an International Action Research Development Program* (Amsterdam: John Benjamins, 1999) 117–30; P Reason and H Bradbury (eds), *Handbook of Action Research: Participative Inquiry and Practice* (Thousand Oaks, CA: Sage).

[20] Herr and Anderson, *The Action Research Dissertation,* n 19 above. See also D Tolman and M Brydon-Miller, 'Interpretive and Participatory Research Methods: Moving Toward Subjectivities' in D Tolman and M Brydon-Miller (eds), *From Subjects to Subjectivities: A Handbook of Interpretive and Participatory Methods* (New York: New York University Press, 2001) 3–11.

By contrast, undercover agents are more attuned to the norms prohibiting entrapment than the mores of the criminals they investigate. Accordingly, undercover agents would know better than informants when to deviate from organizational norms in favour of legal ones. Of course, outsiders who infiltrate an unfamiliar social setting labour under the relative disadvantage of having to 'learn the culture' and adapt to the customs of the environment they study. Yet while insiders who investigate their own communities already know how to act like a native, they must learn to act like investigators. Each type of 'researcher' must adapt to opposite demands.

The involvement of insiders matters, even when they work together with outside researchers, as the perspectives of insiders may accredit outsiders within the studied organization and assist in making sense of the social scene and in interpreting the data, while introducing new sources of unreliability into collaborative investigations. For investigators who are in some sense insiders within their studied community—such as educators investigating their own school, or police informants investigating their own gang—collaborative research creates the added complication that such ambiguous insiders will frequently have to continue to function within these communities once the research or undercover operation is over. This requires them to negotiate lasting relationships and to limit their forms of intervention to those that will allow them to preserve their position in the community in the long-run. Unlike outsiders, insiders may also have to balance competing roles within the studied setting, as they may have to function both as regular employees and as researchers. In the undercover context, this means that informants may have to continue committing crimes while helping the police gather evidence against their associates.

The analogy to participant action research makes it possible to understand why the use of organizational insiders may warrant special treatment in the law enforcement context. Like social scientists, informants who do 'field work' or 'participant observation' in their own setting already possess the inside perspective; what they lack, on the other hand, is critical distance from the milieu in which they operate and an alignment with outsiders' goals and values. Organizational insiders confront conflicts of interest between their 'research agenda' and their vested interests as established members of an organizational hierarchy. Undercover investigations, like participant action research, have to address the compatibility of these roles.

Scholars who worry about fairness to the studied communities and critics of undercover policing who worry about entrapment must attune themselves to the risk that 'collaborations between [investigators] and practitioners or communities can be co-opted' by insiders pursuing their own agendas within the studied organization and advancing their own position in relation to other stakeholders and rivals. For this reason, scholarly commentators demand that outsiders and insiders alike 'deal with bias by acknowledging [and reflecting upon their] presence in the study'. In particular, researchers must reflect on their 'position in the organizational or social hierarchy', and their 'position of power vis-à-vis other stakeholders inside and outside of the setting'.[21] But this conflict of interest between outsiders and insiders is much more problematic for informants than for participant action researchers. In the case of participant action research, other insiders can protect themselves, since such studies involve neither secrecy nor deception.

By contrast, conflicts of interest are usually unknown to other criminal insiders—namely targets—who do not know of the informants' undercover role. It is usually legitimate for organizational insiders to initiate the study, set the research agenda and to respect the behavioural norms of their setting, so long as insiders address the ethical and epistemological risks described above, in consultation with their subjects. In the law enforcement context, the responsibility for determining investigative goals and defining the bounds of acceptable conduct belongs to police and prosecutors, not to informants or targets.

Organizational insiders are particularly worrisome as informants because their established position gives them a unique ability to influence their associates, to manipulate the flow of information to the government, and thus to orient the investigation in ways that suit the informants' own purposes. The ordinary problems of informants can be described as difficulties in aligning the agent's actions and interests with those of his principal. Such difficulties derive from the government's delegation of investigative powers to private parties, who may be more difficult to control and whose interests may diverge from those of the police. However, the informational advantages of organizational insiders (including their ability to identify worthy targets), and their heightened ability to influence the plans and actions of their criminal associates, risk reversing the direction of delegation in ways that may turn informants into principals and investigators into their (unwitting) agents. Inside knowledge of the targeted organization allows such informants to manipulate the police and to reorient investigations where they wish without necessarily betraying or frustrating the investigators' intention of making a case against somebody. Instead of thinking of organizational insiders as infiltrators, one could describe them as 'exfiltrators', who sometimes arrange for the removal of rivals or other dispensable members of their organizational settings while acquiring a virtual license to remain in business themselves. When principal and agent trade roles, organizational insiders may in turn infiltrate the police, acquiring information about upcoming raids, investigative methods, and how much the government knows about their organization's activities.

[21] Herr and Anderson, *The Action Research Dissertation*, n 19 above. See also JL Kincheloe, *Teachers as Researchers: Qualitative Inquiry as a Path to Empowerment* (Philadelphia: Falmer Press, 1991); M Levin, 'Action Research Paradigms' in D Greenwood (ed), *Action Research: From Practice to Writing in an International Action Research Development Program* (Amsterdam: John Benjamins, 1991) 25–37.

German confidentiality regulations can be understood as one way of heading off the special risks attendant on using criminal insiders as covert operatives. Any system of undercover policing may have to provide some leeway for undercover agents and informants to engage in conduct that borders on the criminal; and sometimes the police will have to rely on informants rather than trained undercover agents to perform such delicate tasks. But not all informants are organizational insiders. Confidentiality regulations seek to draw the line at using organizational insiders to 'play themselves' in undercover investigations, as insiders' lack of distance from their undercover role risks diverting their activity, and the investigation as a whole, from its legitimating law enforcement goal.

Confidentiality regulation may be also thought of as a device for putting the state back in charge of the investigative agenda and of discouraging the government from allowing itself to be used by one criminal faction against another. Confidentiality guidelines impose limits on how the state can instrumentalize insiders but these regulations can also be thought about as limiting the extent to which the state may allow itself to be used, that is, the degree to which the state may license crime by delegating its informally recognized law-breaking prerogative to those who are well-placed to abuse it. To that larger end, limits on secrecy discourage the use of insiders, while providing a mechanism—namely, disclosure—for deterring or at least exposing distorting influence that secrecy helps to conceal.

How effectively do confidentiality regulations limit the undercover use of organizational insiders?

Confidentiality guidelines address themselves to the perils of permitting co-operating members of criminal organizations to commit crimes, both with the government's blessing (by participating too actively in the offences they investigate) and without (by committing offences 'on their own time' and at their own initiative), while working undercover for the government. To what extent do confidentiality guidelines succeed in curtailing the recruitment of such insiders and the practice of deploying them undercover to investigate their own accomplices for crimes in which insiders themselves took part? Do confidentiality regulations improve the ability of police and prosecutors to control the ways in which informants operate, and to reduce the dangers that they pose? How effectively do confidentiality guidelines keep informants from participating in crime?

Police informants or undercover agents?

If German police and prosecutors generally preferred staffing undercover operations with covert agents rather than informants, this would be one indicator that the government avoids assigning informants to active undercover roles that require them to participate in crime—at least when it is feasible to infiltrate an undercover agent in their stead. But both police and prosecutors gave mixed responses when asked about their selection of undercover operatives. Many indicated that they preferred informants over undercover agents, since the same features that make organizational insiders so risky also make them authentic and useful. According to one prosecutor, 'Informants are much cheaper than undercover agents; and since they don't need elaborate covers, they get you much more bang for your buck.'[22] Using informants also reduces certain pressures to end investigations prematurely. A covert policing official reported, 'For undercover agents there's always a time limit on using them for any given case. Not so with our informants.' Several officers asserted that informants were more effective than undercover agents. In one officer's view, 'Informants are always more convincing for the target. They speak the group's language, and they know how criminals talk. Of course, undercover agents are professionals and these guys are not; often their only reason for working with us is to push their rivals out of the market; but undercover agents are a lot more expensive, and there are so few of them.' According to some officials, informants may also be employed in ways that undercover agents cannot. 'Informants can be useful, because they won't hesitate to engage in the smaller illegal stuff that's taboo for undercover agents. They'll smoke a joint, or drive after they've been drinking, and do those little crimes that just belong to the setting in which they live. That's a minus and a plus; but it does make them more credible.'

Some officials saw this operational leeway as acceptable so long as the informants' activities did not attract attention. On the other hand, if arguably illegal conduct has to occur under police supervision, officers indicated that they would prefer to use undercover agents. Several police officers and prosecutors preferred using undercover agents precisely because these supervisory officials were willing to give informants much less latitude than undercover agents to participate in the crimes they investigated, thus making informants less useful for investigators. According to one police officer, 'The informant now can't buy contraband without us there to watch and observe; the undercover agent can do that on his own.' Another officer explained that 'the covert agent can release the drugs and pass them along if he has to, so long as we have control over what's going on. But there's no way an informant can do that.' A prosecutor echoed this opinion. 'The undercover agent can help change the licence plate of stolen cars, when he's investigating car thieves; but we can't allow informants to do that.' Summing up the differences between covert police and informants, a police officer reported, 'Informants can't commit crimes. They have less autonomy than undercover agents, less freedom to go along and participate in the crime being investigated.'

[22] Information provided in interviews was cross-checked by speaking to a variety of different legal actors (police, prosecutors, and judges) at different levels of government (state and federal) and by consulting statutes, guidelines and directives, as well as scholarly commentaries.

Nonetheless, prosecutors reported using informants much more widely than undercover agents.

'Hot' versus 'cold' informants

Police terminology provides another clue suggesting that the police sometimes permit informants to participate in crimes. One German police officer explained that the police distinguish between 'hot' and 'cold' informants:

> We let the 'cold informants' sign [written agreements obligating them to secrecy], but not the 'hot' ones; because the agreement makes you promise not to take part in crimes yourself. But for the 'hot' informants, the ones right smack in the middle of the crimes we're investigating, we don't have them sign those agreements; cause you simply can't avoid them taking part in crimes. We just try to have them commit the crimes under our auspices, and tell us everything afterwards.

While it thus appears that German police sometimes permit organizational insiders to participate in crime, it is by no means clear that 'hot' informants benefit from secrecy when they do so. Several prosecutors thought that the regulations made it unlikely that the police would seek guarantees of confidentiality for informants who faced pending criminal charges, even though such promises are sometimes given to those who have offended in the past. After all, the ability of police and prosecutors to use informants who were implicated in wrongdoing depends, to some extent, on their ability to reward informants with sentencing breaks. Grants of confidentiality made this difficult. Some prosecutors stated that it would not be possible to get the informant a lower sentence if he enjoyed a guarantee of confidentiality, since then one could not tell the court of his co-operation. 'You can't get someone a lower sentence if you can't reveal to the judge that he's an informant, which is the effect of our guarantee of confidentiality. So the typical motive of our informants is money, not the hope of getting a sentence reduced.'

Others disagreed. In one prosecutor's view, 'The informant can get a lower sentence despite the secrecy surrounding his identity, because you just tell the judge generally that he's working with the police, and the judge will leave it at that.' Similarly, when the pending case stemmed from informants' efforts to assist investigators, prosecutors found ways to mitigate punishment without breaching their obligations of secrecy. A prosecutor recalled an informant:

> who had gone along with a crime in order to avoid attracting suspicion from his associates. We had to prosecute him, but we picked out a defence lawyer for him and explained the situation, and then we worked together to get him a mild sentence. We could do that without even involving the judge, without telling the court that the defendant had worked for us.

In this way, police and prosecutors may reduce punishment for unrelated past offences. In practice, they find ways to work around constraints that nominally limit informants from working undercover against their former associates. A police official reported, 'If the guy on the inside is a criminal, you just make sure he gets a lower sentence or that the charges against him are dropped; once you've dealt with the past crimes, you can continue to have him make buys or introductions.' A prosecutor opined that a person could not become an informant against his own criminal organization but conceded that 'if he does, say, continue to commit thefts but on behalf of the police, he faces criminal liability. Still, we can say, let's not pursue the matter, and then give him a lower sentence for the crimes he committed [before becoming an informant].' Even if the informant continues to incur criminal liability for crimes he committed undercover, a prosecutor explained, 'you can use him to take part in future crimes once he's already been implicated in the earlier ones', since punishment for the crimes he committed undercover could be folded into punishment for past offences, with a volume discount for the later ones and a sentence reduction for the lot.

German leeway to recruit organizational insiders

For many respondents, the impossibility of promising confidentiality did not foreclose an undercover role. Although the informant may not receive a promise of secrecy, a police official explained, a person who is implicated in the crime being investigated could still be used, short-term, as an 'operational witness', to be deployed undercover against his or her associates—so long as they are willing to testify. This makes it possible for the police to use arrests as a way of working their way up the chain of distribution, using those whom they arrest to make controlled deliveries to middlemen or to make undercover purchases from suppliers.

But prosecutors do not use sentencing breaks alone to work around the principle that prohibits informants from committing crimes. Some prosecutors also indicated that they would, in fact, grant secrecy to organizational insiders, so long as these informants did not continue to take part in crimes and so long as the police paved the way for eventually withdrawing them from the group. Other prosecutors were willing to grant confidentiality to informants who had involved themselves in the targeted offence, so long as the informants were used to investigate some crime other than the one in which they had participated. Still others went further. One prosecutor stated that a member of a criminal organization could be promised confidentiality and could be deployed against his associates, 'because the crime he's going to investigate is a new crime; it's not the same as the crime in which he was involved'. Echoing this distinction, a police official explained, 'If the informant belongs to the gang we're investigating, he can't get a promise of confidentiality for anything he tells us about the crimes in which he participated, but he can still be promised confidentiality for future crimes in which he participates.' Thus informants might even be promised confidentiality for undercover work inside their own organizations. And though informants are not generally authorized to participate in crimes while investigating their organization, some prosecutors believed that an informant could retain his confidential status if he did participate in a crime, provided he did so solely for the purpose of not coming under suspicion of working with the police. A prosecutor acknowledged, 'If someone is involved in the crime it's a matter of interpretation; it depends on whether you need him.'

Indeed, even if an organizational insider could not be guaranteed confidentiality with regard to one target, he might still receive it in connection with others. According to one prosecutor, 'If someone's a member of the group, then he's a witness or a defendant and can't be an informant, at least not against his accomplices, because they will eventually figure it out; but maybe you can still use him against others.' Another prosecutor opined, 'if the informant does stray, say by shoplifting, he doesn't necessarily forfeit his guarantee of confidentiality'. One prosecutor used a contrasting case to illustrate the outer limits of informant use. 'The state protection unit at one point had infiltrated the leadership of some extremist group to such an extent that half of the leadership consisted of informants. That's going too far. Those informants practically built the organization and directed its operations.'

While the willingness of prosecutors to permit such informant roles suggests that confidentiality rules have little bite, German regulations reinforce the regulation's animating principle through a corollary that one might call the 'Rumpelstilzkin rule', according to which no person can be kept off the stand once defendants have identified him or her and called for them to testify. 'If the defendant figures out who the informant is, he can call him to testify; and the promise of confidentiality becomes meaningless', a police official explained. Thus, if the informant is too deeply involved in criminal activity with the target, the target might guess that the informant is the one who betrayed him. If the defendant or his attorney succeeds in identifying the informant as such, neither the Ministry of the Interior nor the prosecutor's promise of secrecy can protect him from having to testify.

But if sentencing breaks can induce informants to forego secrecy and to testify openly, the fear of disclosure loses its regulatory bite. The police would no longer face restrictions on how actively they used the co-operating insider or for how long. As a result, it would become possible to leave people in place for longer. Using a co-operating witness for longer could mean two different things. It could mean deploying him in a highly targeted way, to perform limited tasks which the police specified and approved in advance. Or it could mean allowing him to keep his place in the organization and to engage in criminal activity. Advocates of the former approach stated, 'the open witness can participate in crimes under police control, for the limited purpose of helping us gather evidence to prove these crimes; but this means doing a few well-defined things, like arranging meetings, until we can do the take-down; it doesn't mean that he can simply continue with business as usual'. A prosecutor explained, 'at most he can facilitate a seizure [by making a controlled delivery] or maybe let one last stolen car get through, which we can seize later on'. Other officials were more willing to allow the co-operating witness to remain in the organization in his previous capacity. 'The witness can continue his work in the criminal organization, so long as no-one gets killed. If the only harms inflicted are harms to property, there should be no problem about using her undercover—with the approval, of course, of the prosecutor.' From the perspective of the police, 'The criminal insider can be invaluable for identifying infrastructure, storage spaces, destination ports, and winnings.'

Latitude afforded to organizational insiders

Among those willing to leave co-operating witnesses inside their old organizations, there was a further division of opinion about how actively such witnesses could participate in the crimes they investigated. 'Hey, if the person is willing to testify, there's no reason why he can't continue to help the organization sell stolen property, but he should try to stay in the background and not assume any principal functions', one official stated. 'He'd have to play a subordinate role in the organization', another explained. 'He could not make too significant a contribution to the offence; but he could continue his work in the organization if the crimes being investigated are theft, fencing, selling stolen property, tax offences, and other crimes which affect the general welfare but do not endanger specific people.' Other prosecutors and police officials approved more active degrees of participation. On the one hand, a prosecutor stated, 'the open witness can go to the place where the break-in will take place, but he can't take part in the actual break-in, only the planning'. On the other hand, the prosecutor and other officials elaborated, they could permit the informant to participate in the break-in itself, if the police obtained the insurance company's advance consent to the theft, so long as the targets and the stolen goods were later seized. Yet other police officials thought that vehicle thefts could be justified even without the insurance company's consent and without the possibility of seizing the vehicles later, whenever the crime being investigated was more serious than the crimes in which the witness participated. In one officer's view, 'any property crime short of burglary can be tolerated if the witness clears it with us in advance. And if it's a terrorism investigation, even a burglary can be tolerated.' If an organizational insider were willing to testify, confidentiality regulations would lose what remains of their constraining influence.

How effectively do preconditions for confidentiality promises restrict informants' manoeuvre room?

It is by no means clear, however, whether informants who benefit from guarantees of confidentiality enjoy that much less latitude than other open witnesses—even when prosecutors are willing to set meaningful operational limits before they approve promises of secrecy. Once granted, guarantees of confidentiality can cloak many sins, given a prevailing uncertainty about what disclosures must be made to defendants. As one police officer explained:

> Right now, the only thing that's regulated is the approval of confidentiality, and how you become an informant; but not what happens to the information that you get from these guys, or what goes into the file for defence attorneys to see. There's a general principle of 'case file transparency', but nobody knows what that really means. How much do you keep out to protect the informant?

Although one prosecutor explained that, in principle, 'the fact that one used an informant should always find its way into the file, since it formed the basis for further investigative activity', another prosecutor reported that 'we just won't put the original information into the file, to avoid burning the source'. This effort to protect the confidentiality of the source pushes prosecutors to avoid questioning the source of an informant's knowledge, even though this may be important in evaluating the reliability of the informant's claims. A prosecutor elaborated: 'Questioning of informants is very limited, because we want to conceal its source; how the informant knows something is usually left very vague.' Even when the police must disclose how they obtained certain information, they may avoid telling all. One officer reported, 'With multiple secret sources one can keep one out of the file.' Unless they are too compromised to be kept secret, informants do not testify, but their handlers can testify from hearsay. At trial, the police will typically refuse to disclose favourable plea deals for informants or how much the informants were paid, although they will testify as to whether or not the informant received some form of payment for their services.

Judges confirmed that secrecy shielded problematic informants from discovery. According to one judge, informants were a 'nightmare', not because they were difficult to keep secret, but because of what the secrecy concealed, and because of what the judge perceived to be inadequate bases for such secrecy. 'Sometimes, it's not even clear from the file that there were two informants and not just one', a judge complained. 'And the orders barring informants from testifying are completely pro forma; they don't explain why, and they don't even address the inadequacy of other security measures', another judge stated. 'And then, when I did get an informant to testify, he could barely speak German—but mind you, the transcript of his answers to the handler's questions was extremely articulate. The court is always being manipulated.'

Conclusion

When states delegate responsibility for security to private actors, critics worry about who can be held accountable, and how. In particular, national security scholars and other commentators on government contend that certain tasks (such as torture) should not be privatized because they should not be performed by anyone, including government employees. Thus, the government should not be permitted to do indirectly what it may not do through its own civil servants. At the same time, these commentators argue, certain tasks should not be outsourced because they ought not to be carried out by anyone *except* government employees. As chapter 9 of this volume by Simon Chesterman shows, it remains highly contested and uncertain what the term 'inherently governmental functions' encompasses. But when the state outsources criminal investigation to private parties and licenses them to participate in crime, one may question both whether anyone ought to be permitted to commit crimes for investigative purposes, and, if so, whether the state may entrust such a task to anyone but its own specially trained personnel.

The latter concern intensifies if the private actors whom the state licenses to engage in 'otherwise criminal activity' are themselves members of the criminal organizations they investigate. Comparing the undercover role of such insiders to that of teachers and managers who study their own workplaces made it possible to identify the unique ethical and epistemological challenges that insiders face—and that outsiders must take into account when they team up with 'field workers' drawn from their research site. Like criminal insiders, workplace insiders sometimes use their research to improve their own position and influence in the organizational hierarchy, though criminal insiders do so deceptively, without revealing their investigative activity. Insiders who collaborate in participant action research also resemble criminal insiders in their capacity as privileged intermediaries between subjects and outside investigators. Having special access to the research site, lawful and unlawful insiders alike have a unique ability to filter information, guide its interpretation, and orient outside investigators towards preferred targets and subjects of inquiry. All of this can enable organizational insiders to set the investigative agenda in ways that suit their own purposes, sometimes inverting the direction of delegation by turning themselves into principals and investigators into agents.

If the analogy to participant action research points to some of the dangers of entrusting investigative tasks to organizational insiders, the signal differences between participant action research and undercover investigations suggest why these risks may be particularly acute for covert operations. Unlike participant action research, which is supposed to assist the studied organization, undercover operations are antagonistic to the aims of their targets. This heightens the conflict of interest between organizational insiders and those whom they 'study'. At the same time, the interests of the co-operating insiders are also likely to conflict more significantly with those of the outsiders with whom they co-operate (the police). In addition, the legitimacy of participant action research rests on the informed consent of its subjects. By contrast, undercover operations depend on deceit, which means that meaningful consent is impossible. At most, targets may be said to assume the risk of being infiltrated, not to agree to it. That insiders may turn 'research' on their home organizations to their own ends is also particularly problematic for criminal investigations, since criminal insiders can be expected to commit crimes and may sometimes be licensed to do so (either formally or informally). Finally, criminal investigations are meant to be controlled and directed by outsiders—the government—while participant action research is not. Allowing criminal insiders to influence or seize control of the investigation is simply illegitimate for criminal investigations.

German confidentiality regulations are unique in recognizing and addressing the special dangers of delegating law-breaking prerogatives to informants drawn from inside a targeted criminal organization. These regulations are necessary because Germany, unlike Italy and the United States, has not enacted any immunities that permit undercover agents or informants to commit crimes for investigative purposes. Accordingly, it is particularly problematic for German police to delegate investigative tasks that license informants to participate in criminal activity. Insofar as criminal insiders are most likely to be given such assignments, or to engage in criminal activity on their own account, confidentiality regulations are meant to discourage their recruitment by requiring prosecutors to withhold promises of secrecy from co-operating insiders who investigate their own criminal associates.

Unlike the US entrapment defence or the application of criminal penalties to informants, confidentiality regulations intervene in advance. But confidentiality regulations also differ from other advance constraints, like warrant requirements, in that they make it possible for Germany to regulate informants and undercover agents differently; discourage the police from using organizational insiders against their criminal associates, at least where this would require insiders to participate in criminal activity; and provide a corrective mechanism—namely disclosure of the informant's investigative role—if the police insist on deploying criminal insiders within their home environments.

What is the promise and what are the limitations of confidentiality regulations compared to alternative constraints on those to whom the government delegates investigative tasks? Warrants may be suitable for addressing threshold questions about the relation between means and ends and the evidentiary basis for selecting particular targets. Warrants are useful for evaluating the existence of probable cause, for determining whether the crimes investigated are serious enough to warrant the investigative tactic used, and for assessing the availability of less intrusive tactics. Thus, warrants are means of regulating different aspects of investigative activity, such as predication or suitability, without regard to whether these activities are carried out by private or public actors. By contrast, *ex post* mechanisms like the entrapment defence or criminal sanctions make it possible to redress abuses of delegated authority. Due to their emphasis on individual rather than collective institutional responsibility, however, criminal sanctions may be better suited to deterring gross misconduct by renegade operatives rather than to punishing individual operatives who carry out collaboratively designed tactics approved by police supervisors and prosecutors. The doctrine of entrapment,[23] in turn, may be particularly suitable for evaluating the extent of the covert operative's disruptive or distorting influence on his target environment, and thus for remedying one of the abuses that criminal insiders may commit. Yet the entrapment doctrine has little to say about the trade-off between undercover operatives, peripheral informants, and criminal insiders; nor is it designed to deal specifically with the pitfalls of outsourcing. By contrast, confidentiality guidelines address precisely those risks. Confidentiality rules prophylactically burden the recruitment of organizational insiders by withholding the cloak of secrecy from their investigative actions and effectively requiring them to testify openly once their covert role is over. As an alternative to criminal sanctions, and as a complement to the entrapment doctrine, confidentiality regulation has some potential to control the ways in which institutional actors design investigative tactics—for example, in choosing and using informants. Such regulations provide a different means of reducing informants' involvement in criminal activity and of minimizing the extent to which the police license crime by some insiders for the sake of catching others.

Interviews with German police and prosecutors suggest that they have become relatively proficient at working around rules that restrict confidentiality promises to compromised insiders. The legal system provides them with options for using informants even absent guarantees of confidentiality. Prosecutors are willing to interpret confidentiality guidelines liberally to permit the police to work closely with knowledgeable insiders, so long as harms can be minimized and the benefits are sufficiently great. Police and prosecutors may simply decide that compromised informants are just too valuable in certain cases to be dispensed with. On the other hand, the regulations may have some impact on the margins, by limiting how actively organizational insiders participate in crime and by encouraging the police to sideline compromised insiders in favour of undercover agents. To the extent that confidentiality rules provide the police with reasons to insist that co-operating insiders forego confidentiality and testify, these regulations may also counterbalance the risks of using compromised insiders with the transparency provided by open testimony. This may itself act as a check on the types of behaviour that the police are willing to tolerate. If the secret use of organizational insiders distances the police from the actions of their proxies, public airing of insiders' roles holds some prospect of making the police more accountable for the actions of their most compromised informants and for their

[23] In the United States, this is an affirmative defence; in Germany it is a mitigating factor at sentencing. In Italy, it is a theory of complicity and renders undercover agents and informants criminally liable for the offences they instigate. Under any of these theories, however, entrapment is an *ex post facto* regulatory device that intervenes, if at all, at the close of adjudication, though it may shape the design of the investigation *ex ante*. See Ross, 'The Place of Covert Policing', n 7 above.

own tactical choices in permitting such operatives to participate in crime while undercover.

German confidentiality regulation provides an instructive example of how regulators set outer limits on the outsourcing of security operations, intelligence gathering, and criminal investigations. Confidentiality rules target criminal insiders, whose informational advantage sets the police at a particularly severe tactical disadvantage and therefore makes such informants most likely to offend and most difficult to control. By outsourcing undercover assignments to criminal insiders who can manipulate the investigation to serve their own purposes, the police may effectively be delegating agenda-setting powers. To the extent criminal insiders have the power to manipulate the selection of targets, and thereby to guide police exercise of investigative discretion, the executive may be abdicating an 'inherently governmental' function in relying on criminal insiders for this type of assistance. If the police tacitly countenance criminal activity by such insiders, the police may also become complicit in the criminal aims and conduct of those to whom they outsource their law enforcement role. Confidentiality regulations are one mechanism by which the state can (attempt) to keep the police from delegating this prerogative to those who are structurally unreliable, by virtue of their position as insiders in a criminal organization, unless some compensating mechanism of accountability—like disclosure—is available.

9

Intelligence services

*Simon Chesterman**

On 14 May 2007, a senior procurement executive from the Office of the Director of National Intelligence gave a presentation to an intelligence industry conference in Colorado convened by the Defense Intelligence Agency (DIA), part of the US Department of Defense.[1] Her unclassified PowerPoint presentation, 'Procuring the Future', was posted on the DIA website, but later modified and subsequently removed. In it, she revealed that the proportion of the US intelligence budget spent on private contractors is 70 per cent. She also revealed that the amount the United States spends on such contractors is $42 billion, out of an implied total intelligence budget of $60 billion for the 2005 financial year. At its midpoint the presentation cheerily exhorted: 'We can't spy . . . if we can't buy!'[2]

Though it lags behind the privatization of military services, the privatization of intelligence has expanded dramatically with the growth in intelligence activities following the 11 September 2001 attacks on the United States.[3] In a report published three days after those attacks, the Senate Select Committee on Intelligence encouraged a 'symbiotic relationship between the Intelligence

* Many thanks to Madan Mohan and Lakshmi Ravindran for invaluable research assistance on this project and to Angelina Fisher and Christen Broecker for comments on an earlier draft. The text draws heavily upon work first published as '"We Can't Spy . . . If We Can't Buy!": The Privatization of US Intelligence Services', *European Journal of International Law*, vol 19 (2008) 1055.

[1] The Defense Intelligence Acquisition Conference was hosted by the Office of the Acquisition Executive of the Defense Intelligence Agency at Keystone Resort and Conference Center in Keystone, Colorado from 14–17 May 2007. See Defense Intelligence Agency Office of Public Affairs, 'Acquisition Conference Announces Keynote Speakers', 30 April 2007, available at <http://www.dia.mil/publicaffairs/press/press17.htm>.

[2] Terri Everett, '"Procuring the Future": 21st Century IC Acquisition', Office of the Director of National Intelligence, Defense Intelligence Acquisition Conference, 14 May 2007, available at <http://www.fas.org/irp/dni/everett.ppt>; Tim Shorrock, 'The Corporate Takeover of US Intelligence', *Salon*, 1 June 2007, available at <http://www.salon.com/news/feature/2007/06/01/intel_contractors>; RJ Hillhouse, 'Update: DNI Inadvertently Reveals Key to Classified National Intel Budget', *The Spy Who Billed Me*, 4 June 2007, available at <http://www.thespywhobilledme.com/the_spy_who_billed_me/2007/06/update_dni_inad.html>.

[3] See, eg, Ronald P Sanders, 'Letter to the Editor: The Value of Private Spies', *Washington Post*, 18 July 2007. Everett's figures suggest that since 2000 the amount spent on private contractors has more than doubled. See Everett, 'Procuring the Future', n 2 above.

Community and the private sector'.[4] In addition to dollars spent—dominated by large items such as spy satellites—this has seen an important increase in the proportion of personnel working on contract. More than 70 per cent of the Pentagon's Counterintelligence Field Activity (CIFA) unit is staffed by contractors, known as 'green badgers', who also represent the majority of personnel employed by the DIA, the Central Intelligence Agency (CIA)'s National Clandestine Service, and the National Counterterrorism Center. At the CIA's station in Islamabad, contractors reportedly outnumber government employees three to one.[5]

Controversy over government reliance on outsourcing in this area frequently coalesces around issues of cost (a contractor costs on average $250,000 per year, about double that of a government employee), 'brain-drain', and periodic allegations of self-dealing and other forms of corruption. More recently, however, the confirmation by the Director of the CIA that contractors have probably participated in 'waterboarding' (simulated drowning) of detainees at CIA interrogation facilities has sparked a renewed debate over what activities it is appropriate to delegate to contractors, and what activities should remain 'inherently governmental'.[6] (This is, of course, separate from whether such activities should be carried out in the first place—a topic that is not the focus of this chapter.)[7]

Privatization of intelligence services raises many concerns familiar to the debates over private military and security companies (PMSCs) described by Michael Likosky in chapter one. One of the key problems posed by PMSCs is their use of potentially lethal force in an environment where accountability may be legally uncertain and practically unlikely; in some circumstances, PMSCs may also affect the strategic balance of a conflict.[8] The engagement of private actors in the *collection* of intelligence exacerbates the first set of problems: it frequently encompasses a far wider range of conduct that would normally be illegal, with express or implied immunity from legal process, in an environment designed to avoid scrutiny. Engagement of such actors in *analysis* raises the second set of issues: top-level analysis is precisely intended to shape strategic

[4] 'Authorizing Appropriations for Fiscal Year 2002 for Intelligence and Intelligence-related activities of the United States Government, the Community Management Account of the Director of Central Intelligence, and the Central Intelligence Agency Retirement and Disability System and for Other Purposes', Senate Select Committee on Intelligence, Report 107-63, 14 September 2001, available at <http://www.fas.org/irp/congress/2001_rpt/srep107–63.html>.

[5] Walter Pincus, 'Lawmakers Want More Data on Contracting Out Intelligence', *Washington Post*, 7 May 2006; Patrick Radden Keefe, 'Don't Privatize Our Spies', *New York Times*, 25 June 2007.

[6] See also Sarah Percy, 'Morality and Regulation', in Simon Chesterman and Chia Lehnardt (eds), *From Mercenaries to Market: The Rise and Regulation of Private Military Companies* (Oxford: Oxford University Press, 2007).

[7] For a discussion of this point, see Simon Chesterman, 'Secrets and Lies: Intelligence Activities and the Rule of Law in Times of Crisis', *Michigan Journal of International Law*, vol 28 (2007) 553–73.

[8] See generally Chesterman and Lehnardt, *From Mercenaries to Market*, n 6 above.

policy and the more such tasks are delegated to private actors, the further they are removed from traditional accountability structures such as judicial and parliamentary oversight—and the more influence contractors may have on the executive.

The concerns raised here are similar to those discussed by Angelina Fisher in chapter three: even where there is a measure of accountability, a key question is accountability *to whom*? And, similar to the issues addressed by Alfred Aman in chapter five and by Jacqueline Ross in chapter eight, a particular difficulty lies in matching the incentives of private actors to public policy.

This chapter first surveys the manner in which US intelligence functions have been outsourced in collection activities such as electronic surveillance, rendition, and interrogation, as well as the growing reliance on private actors for analysis. It then turns to accountability issues raised by this new phenomenon, focusing on three areas: first, the necessary secrecy that limits oversight of intelligence and thus militates against further removal of such activities from democratic structures; secondly, the different incentives that exist for private, rather than public, employees; and finally, the uncertainty as to what functions should be regarded as 'inherently governmental' and thus inappropriate for delegation to private actors.

Outsourcing intelligence

The term 'intelligence' is often not well-defined. At its most general, it is used synonymously with 'information'—reflecting the importance of publicly available ('open source') material in developing policy and suggesting an appropriate analogy between much of intelligence and quality journalism. For present purposes, it will be used in two more narrow senses. The first denotes the *collection of information* that is not intended to be made public, sometimes referred to as 'secret intelligence'. This embraces two subcategories that have remained essentially unchanged since the Second World War: intelligence obtained wittingly or unwittingly from individuals, known as human intelligence, and communications intercepts and other 'signals' intelligence.[9] The second sense is a broader understanding of the term intelligence as the *analytical product* of intelligence agencies, best understood as a risk assessment intended to guide action.[10] Both areas have seen significant growth in the role of non-government employees.

[9] Michael Herman, *Intelligence Power in Peace and War* (Cambridge: Cambridge University Press, 1996) 61–81.
[10] Ibid. at 111–12.

Collection

The biggest single item of outsourcing in this area is hardware and software. Typically, this is comparable to government contracting in other areas. There are occasional scandals, such as the National Security Agency's (NSA) contract with Science Applications International Corporation (SAIC) to modernize its ability to sift vast amounts of electronic information with a proposed system known as 'Trailblazer'. Between 2002 and 2005, the project's $280 million budget ballooned to over $1 billion and the project was later described as a 'complete and abject failure'.[11] Perhaps the most spectacular scandal was Boeing's Future Imagery Architecture, a 1999 contract with the National Reconnaissance Office (NRO) to design a new generation of spy satellites. The NRO finally cancelled the project in 2005 after approximately $10 billion had been spent.[12] Nevertheless the pool of potential contractors—particularly given the requirement for security clearances—remains small. Thus, when the NSA sought a replacement to the failed Trailblazer, the contractor it retained to develop the new programme ExecuteLocus was SAIC.[13]

Somewhat more sensitive than contracts for equipment and software is direct involvement in covert operations. For example, Abraxas, a company founded by CIA veterans in McLean, Virginia, devises 'covers' for overseas case officers.[14] In Iraq, US reliance on contractors appears to have extended to recruiting and managing human intelligence sources.[15] In 2004, Aegis Defence Services Ltd, a British company, was awarded a $300 million contract that explicitly required hiring a team of analysts with 'NATO equivalent SECRET clearance'; their responsibilities include analysing 'foreign intelligence services, terrorist organizations, and their surrogates targeting DoD personnel, resources and facilities'.[16]

The reasons given by government officials for reliance on private contractors are similar to those justifying reliance on PMSCs: the need for swift increases in skilled personnel that had been scaled back during the 1990s, and the desirability of flexible, temporary increases compared to the addition of permanent government employees.[17] In addition, such hires have been used to avoid personnel ceilings imposed by Congress; it is also alleged that such outsourcing enables the intelligence agencies to avoid congressional and other oversight of specific activities. Some of these justifications clearly have merit, but oversight

[11] Keefe, 'Don't Privatize Our Spies', n 5 above.

[12] Ibid.; Philip Taubman, 'In Death of Spy Satellite Program, Lofty Plans and Unrealistic Bids', *New York Times*, 11 November 2007.

[13] Keefe, 'Don't Privatize Our Spies', n 5 above.

[14] Greg Miller, 'Spy Agencies Outsourcing to Fill Key Jobs', *Los Angeles Times*, 17 September 2006.

[15] Ibid.; James Bamford, 'This Spy for Rent', *New York Times*, 13 June 2004.

[16] Steve Fainaru and Alec Klein, 'In Iraq, a Private Realm of Intelligence-Gathering', *Washington Post*, 1 July 2007.

[17] Sanders, 'Letter to the Editor: The Value of Private Spies', n 3 above.

bodies have emphasized that 'in the long term' the intelligence community must reduce its dependence on contractors, if only for reasons of cost.[18]

This section will focus on three sets of activities where privatization is more problematic because it has allowed private actors to intrude into areas that may be construed as 'inherently governmental'. One way of defining 'inherently governmental' activities is to identify those that significantly affect 'the life, liberty, or property of private persons', in the language of a 1992 'Policy Letter' from the Office of Federal Procurement Policy.[19] Such a definition would challenge the use of private contractors in three areas: electronic intercepts, the rendition of prisoners to detention facilities, and the interrogation of prisoners.

Electronic intercepts

The controversy over warrantless electronic surveillance as part of the 'Terrorist Surveillance Program' (TSP), authorized by President Bush soon after 11 September 2001, is well-known. Interception of telephone calls by the NSA between a party in the United States and a party in a foreign country is governed by the Foreign Intelligence Surveillance Act (FISA), which allows for interception when a warrant is procured in advance or, in some circumstances, within 72 hours of beginning the intercept. A warrant may be issued if 'there is probable cause to believe that . . . the target of the electronic surveillance is a foreign power or an agent of a foreign power'.[20] Congress passed the law in 1978 following intelligence scandals; in the following years the court established to review requests for such warrants rejected just five of around 19,000 requests for wiretaps and search warrants.[21] The TSP removed this check on the NSA's activities in cases where it was suspected that one party to a phone conversation had links to a terrorist organization such as al Qaeda. The presidential authorization creating the programme is classified and it appears that even congressional intelligence committees were only partially briefed on its scope, although President Bush said in a radio address that he renewed the authorization 'approximately every 45 days'.[22] Administration lawyers defended the programme variously on the bases that Congress implicitly authorized it in the 18 September 2001 Congressional Joint Authorization for the Use of Military Force, or that the President enjoys the inherent power to authorize such activities in his constitutional role as Commander-in-Chief. Legal academics largely

[18] 'Intelligence Authorization Act for Fiscal Year 2008', Senate Select Committee on Intelligence, Report 110–75, 31 May 2007, available at <http://intelligence.senate.gov/11075.pdf>, 11.

[19] 'Inherently Governmental Functions', Office of Federal Procurement Policy, Policy Letter 92–1, 23 September 1992, available at <http://www.whitehouse.gov/omb/procurement/policy_letters/92-1_092392.html> para 5(c).

[20] US Congress, Foreign Intelligence Surveillance Act of 1978 (FSIA), 50 USC § 1805(a)(3).

[21] Carol D Leonnig, 'Secret Court's Judges Were Warned About NSA Spy Data', *Washington Post*, 9 February 2006 (citing figures from 1979 to 2004).

[22] George W Bush, 'President's Radio Address', White House, 17 December 2005, available at <http://www.nytimes.com/2005/12/17/politics/17text-bush.html>.

rejected these arguments and the programme was declared unconstitutional by a district court judge,[23] although an appeals court stayed her decision[24] and later overturned it on the basis that the plaintiffs lacked standing to bring the suit.[25] The Supreme Court turned down a subsequent appeal without comment.[26]

Congress hastily passed legislation in August 2007 to fill the legal void,[27] but as its sunset date of 1 February 2008 approached there was a debate over whether to extend it. The two major points of contention were the appropriate levels of oversight for such powers (the 2007 Act essentially substituted internal NSA processes for the requirement of FISA warrants) and, crucially, whether to grant immunity to telecommunications companies that had helped the government to conduct surveillance without warrants and thus potentially exposed themselves to civil liability.[28] President Bush authorized a 15 day extension and urged Congress to grant 'liability protection' to those companies:

> In order to be able to discover enemy – the enemy's plans, we need the co-operation of telecommunication companies. If these companies are subjected to lawsuits that could cost them billions of dollars, they won't participate; they won't help us; they won't help protect America. Liability protection is critical to securing the private sector's co-operation with our intelligence efforts.[29]

John Ashcroft, Attorney-General from 2001 to 2005 had weighed in earlier, arguing that, whatever one's view of warrantless surveillance and its legal basis, allowing litigation against co-operative telecommunications companies would be 'extraordinarily unfair'. As his by-line noted, Ashcroft now heads a consulting firm with telecommunications companies as clients.[30]

The legislation ultimately lapsed. The following week, the Bush administration asserted that the government had 'lost intelligence information' because of the failure by Democrats in Congress to pass appropriate legislation, causing some telecommunications companies to refuse to co-operate. This was retracted hours later, apparently after the last holdout among the companies agreed to co-operate

[23] *American Civil Liberties Union v National Sec. Agency*, 483 F Supp 2d 754 (ED Mich 2006), No 06-CV-10204.

[24] *American Civil Liberties Union v National Sec. Agency/Central Sec. Service*, 467 F3d 590 (6th Cir 2006), Nos 06-2095/2140.

[25] *American Civil Liberties Union v National Sec. Agency*, 493 F3d 644 (6th Cir 2007), Nos 06-2095/2140, available at <http://www.ca6.uscourts.gov/opinions.pdf/07a0253p-06.pdf>.

[26] *American Civil Liberties Union v National Sec. Agency*, 128 SCt 1334 (US 2008) (memorandum opinion), available at <http://www.supremecourtus.gov/docket/07-468.htm>.

[27] US Congress, Protect America Act, 50 USC § 1801 note, 5 August 2007.

[28] The number of 'contractor facilities' cleared by the NSA grew from 41 in 2002 to 1,265 in 2006. Keefe, 'Don't Privatize Our Spies', n 5 above.

[29] George W Bush, 'President Bush Discusses Protect America Act' (White House, Washington, DC, 13 February 2008). The companies concerned included AT&T, Sprint, and MCI. See, eg, Tim Shorrock, 'Watching What You Say', *The Nation*, 11 May 2006.

[30] John Ashcroft, 'Uncle Sam on the Line', *New York Times*, 5 November 2007.

fully, even without new authorizing legislation.[31] Five months later, Congress passed legislation essentially granting the companies immunity as part of an overhaul of FISA.[32]

Examples of potential problems in outsourcing collection in this manner are not hard to find. As a result of an 'apparent miscommunication', an Internet provider complying with a warrant to forward emails from one account instead gave the FBI emails from every account on a small domain for which it served as host. Intelligence officials refer to it as 'overproduction' when third parties provide them with more information than actually required.[33] In the case of the NSA's programme there is little reason for confidence in existing oversight measures: no warrant is required, the programme remains highly classified (and, indeed, was only revealed to the public when the *New York Times* published a story it had withheld for more than a year),[34] and the companies involved have a clear self-interest in avoiding public challenges to their actions. Legislators only became involved after the story had become public, at which point Attorney-General Alberto Gonzales said in a press conference that the administration had had 'discussions with Congress in the past—certain members of Congress—as to whether or not FISA could be amended to allow us to adequately deal with this kind of threat, and we were advised that that would be difficult, if not impossible'.[35]

Rendition

In the case of telecommunications companies, involvement of private actors was necessary as a technical matter in order to access information. With respect to private involvement in rendition, recourse to the private sector appears to have been part of a clear effort to avoid oversight.

The CIA's use of private aircraft for moving detainees between black site detention centres is now well-documented. Enterprising journalists, blogger activists, and hobbyist plane spotters combined to share information about planes

[31] Dan Eggen and Ellen Nakashima, 'Spy Law Lapse Blamed for Lost Information; Some Telecom Firms Not Cooperating for Fear of Liability, US Says', *Washington Post*, 23 February 2008; Josh Meyer, 'White House Backtracks on Lost Intelligence; Officials Acknowledge that Telecom Firms Are Furnishing All Requested Information', *Los Angeles Times*, 24 February 2008.

[32] Eric Lichtblau, 'Senate Approves Bill to Broaden Wiretap Powers', *New York Times*, 10 July 2008.

[33] Eric Lichtblau, 'Error Gave FBI Unauthorized Access to E-Mail', *New York Times*, 17 February 2008.

[34] James Risen and Eric Lichtblau, 'Bush Lets US Spy on Callers Without Courts', *New York Times*, 16 December 2005. It appears that the story was ultimately published because a forthcoming book by one of the journalists would have rendered the *Times*' discretion moot. See James Risen, *State of War: The Secret History of the CIA and the Bush Administration* (New York: Free Press, 2006).

[35] Alberto Gonzales (Attorney General) and Michael Hayden (Principal Deputy Director for National Intelligence), White House Press Briefing, 19 December 2005. Gonzales later clarified that he had intended to say that it would have been difficult, if not impossible, to obtain legislation without compromising the programme.

that are believed to have been at the heart of the 'extraordinary rendition' programme,[36] which dated back to the Clinton administration.[37] The use of proprietary or 'front' companies by the CIA is not unusual, although the reliance upon private companies for active support rather than cover is atypical. Officials who were involved in the practice suggested this was in order to protect government officials from involvement in a legally questionable process:

> 'Our policymakers would never confront the issue', said Michael Scheuer, a former CIA counterterrorism officer who has been involved with renditions and supports the practice. We would say, 'Where do you want us to take these people?' The mind-set of the bureaucracy was, 'Let someone else do the dirty work.'[38]

The rendition programme became a scandal in Europe, with a report from the European Parliament leading to a resolution recommending, among other things, that 'all European countries that have not done so should initiate independent investigations into all stopovers made by civilian aircraft carried out by the CIA'.[39]

Interrogation

In February 2008, CIA Director Michael V Hayden testified before the Senate and House that the United States had waterboarded at least three detainees.[40] He was also asked about the use of contractors. Before the Senate Select Intelligence Committee, Hayden confirmed that the CIA continued to use 'green badgers' at its secret detention facilities.[41] In testimony before the House two days later, Hayden was asked whether contractors were involved in waterboarding al Qaeda detainees. He responded by saying 'I'm not sure of the specifics. I'll give you a tentative answer: I believe so.'[42]

[36] Stephen Grey, *Ghost Plane: The True Story of the CIA Torture Program* (New York: St. Martin's Press, 2006); Jane Mayer, 'Outsourcing: The CIA's Travel Agent', *New Yorker*, 30 October 2006.

[37] Presidential Decision Directive 39, US Policy on Counterterrorism, 21 June 1995, available at <http://www.fas.org/irp/offdocs/pdd39.htm>; Richard A Clarke, *Against All Enemies: Inside America's War on Terror* (New York: Free Press, 2004) 143–4.

[38] Dana Priest, 'Jet Is an Open Secret in Terror War', *Washington Post*, 27 December 2004.

[39] 'Transportation and Illegal Detention of Prisoners: European Parliament Resolution on the Alleged Use of European Countries by the CIA for the Transportation and Illegal Detention of Prisoners', 14 February 2007, P6_TA-PROV(2007)0032 - (2006/2200(INI)), available at <http://www.europarl.europa.eu/comparl/tempcom/tdip/final_ep_resolution_en.pdf>, para 190.

[40] Scott Shane, 'CIA Chief Doubts Tactic to Interrogate Is Still Legal', *New York Times*, 8 February 2008.

[41] 'Annual Worldwide Threat Assessment', Senate Select Committee on Intelligence, 5 February 2008, available at <http://www.dni.gov/testimonies/20080205_transcript.pdf>, 26 (referring to 'greenbaggers', presumably a transcription error). See also R J Hillhouse, 'The CIA's Black Sites Have Gone Green', *The Spy Who Billed Me*, 6 February 2008, available at <http://www.thespywhobilledme.com/the_spy_who_billed_me/2008/02/the-cias-black.html>.

[42] 'Annual Worldwide Threat Assessment', House Permanent Select Committee on Intelligence, 7 February 2008, available at <http://www.dni.gov/testimonies/20080207_transcript.pdf>, 26. See also Siobhan Gorman, 'CIA Likely Let Contractors Perform Waterboarding', *Wall Street Journal*, 8 February 2008.

The involvement of private contractors in interrogation raises the most serious questions of accountability. It involves persons outside the government structure wielding extraordinary authority and discretion in an environment clearly weighted against either investigation or prosecution. Similar to the case of private military contractors, these concerns include the dubious prospects for after-the-fact accountability, but also the absence of standardized levels of training and location within a defined command structure.

These concerns were justified by revelations that prisoners had been abused at the US-run Abu Ghraib prison in Iraq. Although investigations by the US Army Criminal Investigation Command appear to have pre-dated public knowledge of the abuse in April 2004,[43] it was only after humiliating photographs of detainees were widely disseminated that serious investigations began.[44] Twelve uniformed personnel were convicted of various charges; most were given minor sentences but a handful of soldiers received multiple-year prison terms.[45] Only one person above the rank of staff sergeant faced a court-martial and was cleared of any wrongdoing; no charges have been laid for abuses other than those that were photographed.[46] No charges have been laid against contractors, despite repeated allegations that they participated in abuse. The companies Titan and CACI provided interpreters and interrogators to the US military, respectively; the commanding officer at the prison, Brigadier General Janis Karpinski (later demoted to colonel), claimed in an interview with a Spanish newspaper that she had seen a letter signed by Secretary of Defense Donald Rumsfeld allowing civilian contractors to use techniques such as sleep deprivation during interrogation.[47] A class action brought against Titan and CACI under the Alien Tort Claims Act and state tort law was lodged in 2004 and is ongoing in the US District Court for the District of Columbia.[48] The claims against Titan were dismissed as pre-empted by the Federal Tort Claims Act (FTCA) after its linguists

[43] Michael Scherer and Mark Benjamin, 'Other Government Agencies (The Abu Ghraib Files)', *Salon.com*, 14 March 2006, available at <http://www.salon.com/news/abu_ghraib/2006/03/14/introduction>, chap 5.

[44] See generally Karen J Greenberg and Joshua L Dratel (eds), *The Torture Papers: The Road to Abu Ghraib* (Cambridge: Cambridge University Press, 2005).

[45] Multiple-year terms were awarded to Cpl Charles Graner Jr (10 years prison and demotion to private), Staff Sgt Ivan Frederick of Buckingham (8½ years), and Pfc Lynndie England (3 years). Other punishments with jail time included Spc. Jeremy Sivits (1 year), Spc. Roman Krol (10 months), Spc. Armin Cruz (8 months), Spc. Sabrina Harman (6 months), Sgt. Javal Davis (6 months). Brig Gen Janis L Karpinski was demoted to colonel; Sgt Santos Cardona was given 3 months hard labour and reduction in rank to Specialist; Spc Megan Ambuhl was discharged without prison time. See 'Fast Facts: Abu Ghraib Convictions' *Associated Press*, 27 September 2005; 'Chronology of Abu Ghraib', *Washington Post*, 17 February 2006; Eric Schmitt, 'Army Dog Handler is Convicted in Detainee Abuse at Abu Ghraib', *New York Times*, 22 March 2006.

[46] Philip Gourevitch and Errol Morris, 'Exposure: Behind the Camera at Abu Ghraib', *New Yorker*, 24 March 2008, 56.

[47] 'Rumsfeld Okayed Abuses Says Former US Army General', *Reuters*, 25 November 2006.

[48] See generally 'Our Cases: Saleh et al v. Titan et al', Center for Constitutional Rights, available at <http://ccrjustice.org/ourcases/current-cases/saleh-v.-titan>.

were found to have been 'fully integrated into the military units to which they were assigned and that they performed their duties under the direct command and exclusive operational control of military personnel'.[49] As CACI interrogators were subject to a 'dual chain of command', with significant independent authority retained by CACI supervisors, the case against it was allowed to continue.[50]

There appears to be only one case of a contractor being convicted of a crime in the United States connected with interrogations during the 'war on terror'. David A Passaro was convicted of misdemeanour assault and felony assault with a dangerous weapon charges for his connection with the torture and beating to death of Abdul Wali in Afghanistan in June 2003. In February 2007, Passaro was sentenced to eight years and four months prison. His background is testimony to the danger of contracting out such interrogations: both his previous wives have alleged that he was abusive at home, and he had been fired from the police force after being arrested for beating a man in a parking lot brawl.[51] Soon after the Passaro story broke, Attorney-General John Ashcroft established a 'Detainee Abuse Task Force', but it does not appear to have brought any charges against contractors.[52]

Analysis

The involvement of contractors in analysis raises somewhat different questions from their involvement in collection of intelligence. A company's analytical work is less likely to be linked to abusive behaviour or the type of activities typically discussed in the context of PMSC accountability. And yet through participating in, and influencing, high-level decisions about national security, the consequences are troubling if they indicate a removal of such decisions from democratically accountable structures.

For the most part, the challenges that have been publicly identified tend to be at the level of personnel, notably the drain encouraged by significantly higher salaries in the private sector. A practice known as 'bidding back' sees officials leaving for industry and then being brought back in the capacity of consultant at a higher salary. Some estimate that as many as two-thirds of the Department of Homeland Security's senior personnel and experts have left for industry in recent years.[53] In a

[49] *Ibrahim v Titan Corp.*, 556 F Supp 2d 1 (DDC 2007) Civil Action Nos 04-1248 (JR), 05-1165 (JR), available at <http://ccrjustice.org/files/saleh_summaryjudgmentdec_11_07.pdf>, 21.

[50] Ibid. at 22.

[51] James Dao, 'A Man of Violence, or Just "110 Percent" Gung-Ho?' *New York Times*, 19 June 2004. See also E L Gaston, 'Mercenarism 2.0? The Rise of the Modern Private Security Industry and Its Implications for International Humanitarian Law Enforcement', *Harvard International Law Journal*, vol 49 (2008) 229.

[52] Susan Burke, 'Accountability for Corporate Complicity in Torture', *Gonzaga Journal of International Law*, vol 10 (2006) 85; 'Focus on Corporate Accountability in the "War on Terror"', Amnesty International USA, 2007, available at <http://www.amnestyusa.org/War_on_Terror/Private_Military_and_Security_Contractors/page.do?id=1101665&n1=3&n2=26&n3=157>.

[53] Keefe, 'Don't Privatize Our Spies', n 5 above; Bamford, 'This Spy for Rent', n 15 above.

2006 report the Office of the Director of National Intelligence noted that the intelligence community increasingly finds itself in competition with its contractors:

> Confronted by arbitrary staffing ceilings and uncertain funding, components are left with no choice but to use contractors for work that may be borderline 'inherently governmental'—only to find that to do that work, those same contractors recruit our own employees, already cleared and trained at government expense, and then 'lease' them back to us at considerably greater expense.[54]

From 1 June 2007, the CIA began to bar contractors from hiring former agency employees and then offering their services back to the CIA within the first year and a half of retirement.[55]

As indicated earlier, a second general concern is the cost of retaining contractors. In May 2007, the Senate Select Committee on Intelligence criticized the intelligence agencies' 'increasing reliance on contractors'.[56] The CIA subsequently announced that it would reduce the number of contractors by 10 per cent.[57]

In addition to individual contractors, firms such as Booz Allen Hamilton have established themselves as consultants to the intelligence community. Booz Allen currently employs a former CIA director (R James Woolsey), a former executive director of the President's Foreign Intelligence Advisory Board (Joan Dempsey), and a former director of the National Reconnaissance Office (Keith Hall). Mike McConnell headed the NSA and then went to Booz Allen in 1996 as a Senior Vice President working on intelligence and national security issues; in 2007 President Bush appointed him as Director of National Intelligence.[58] The firm's website includes dedicated channels for job applicants with security clearances.[59]

Although there are occasional breathless accounts of contractor involvement in high-level analytical documents such as the President's Daily Brief,[60] it is enough to note for present purposes that even the perception of a conflict of interest should raise questions about the involvement of the corporate sector in the analytical functions of the intelligence services. It might be argued that this is

[54] 'Strategic Human Capital Plan', Office of the Director of National Intelligence, 22 June 2006, available at <http://www.odni.gov/publications/DNIHumanCapitalStrategicPlan18October2006.pdf>, 6.

[55] Walter Pincus and Stephen Barr, 'CIA Plans Cutbacks, Limits on Contractor Staffing', *Washington Post*, 11 June 2007.

[56] Senate Select Committee on Intelligence, 'Intelligence Authorization Act for Fiscal Year 2008', n 18 above, 11.

[57] Keefe, 'Don't Privatize Our Spies', n 5 above; Mark Tarallo, 'Hayden Wants Fewer CIA Contractors', *Federal Computer Week*, 25 June 2007.

[58] Tim Shorrock, 'The Spy Who Came In from the Boardroom', *Salon*, 8 January 2007, available at <http://www.salon.com/news/feature/2007/01/08/mcconnell>.

[59] See, eg, Booz Allen Hamilton, 'Career Opportunities for Cleared Professionals', available at <http://www.boozallen.com/careers/9001843/cleared_intelligence_opportunities>.

[60] See, eg, R J Hillhouse, 'Corporate Content and the President's Daily Brief', *The Spy Who Billed Me*, 23 July 2007, available at <http://www.thespywhobilledme.com/the_spy_who_billed_me/2007/07/corporate-conte.html>.

little different from the influence of wealth on US politics more generally, although as the next section argues, the secrecy, incentive structures, and potentially abusive powers of the intelligence community warrant special care in regularizing the participation of private actors.

Accountability

As in the case of private military and security companies, obvious accountability issues arise when private actors wield potentially lethal force under the actual or apparent authority of the state but outside formal oversight structures. This section will not rehearse such arguments but will instead focus on three areas specific to the privatization of intelligence: secrecy, incentives, and the difficulty of defining what activities should be regarded as 'inherently governmental'.

Secrecy

Oversight of intelligence services is always difficult given the secrecy necessary for many of their activities to be carried out effectively.[61] In the case of privatization of these services within the US intelligence community, however, secrecy appears to have compounded ignorance.

In May 2007—the same month as the 'We can't spy . . . if we can't buy!' presentation—the House Permanent Select Committee on Intelligence reported that

> Intelligence Community leaders do not have an adequate understanding of the size and composition of the contractor work force, a consistent and well-articulated method for assessing contractor performance, or strategies for managing a combined staff-contractor workforce. In addition, the Committee is concerned that the Intelligence Community does not have a clear definition of what functions are 'inherently governmental' and, as a result, whether there are contractors performing inherently governmental functions.[62]

Legislators subsequently called for the Department of Defense to compile a database of all intelligence-related contracts,[63] and for a Government Accountability Office investigation of contractors in Iraq.[64]

[61] See, eg, Fred Schreier, 'The Need for Efficient and Legitimate Intelligence', in Hans Born and Marina Caparini (eds), *Democratic Control of Intelligence Services: Containing Rogue Elephants* (Aldershot: Ashgate, 2007).

[62] 'Intelligence Authorization Act for Fiscal Year 2008', House of Representatives, Permanent Select Committee on Intelligence, Report 110–131, 7 May 2007, available at <http://intelligence.house.gov/Media/PDFS/IAAFY08.pdf>, 42; See also 'Intelligence Authorization Act for Fiscal Year 2008', House of Representatives, Conference Report, Report 110–478, Washington, DC: 6 December 2007, available at <http://frwebgate.access.gpo.gov/cgi-bin/getdoc.cgi?dbname=110_cong_reports&docid=f:hr478.110.pdf>, 68.

[63] Walter Pincus, 'Defense Agency Proposes Outsourcing More Spying', *Washington Post*, 19 August 2007.

[64] Fainaru and Klein, 'In Iraq, a Private Realm of Intelligence-Gathering'.

Reports have been commissioned before. In fact, only one month before the House report, a year-long examination of outsourcing by US intelligence agencies was held up by the Director of National Intelligence, and then reclassified as a national secret.[65] The secrecy was justified on the basis that the United States does not reveal the cost and size of its intelligence operations, although recent disclosures on that topic by senior officials belie this explanation.

In December 2007, legislation approved by the House-Senate Conference on the Intelligence Authorization Act called on the Office of the Director of National Intelligence (ODNI) to produce a report by 31 March 2008 'describing the personal services activities performed by contractors across the intelligence community, the impact of such contractors on the intelligence community workforce, plans for conversion of contractor employment into government employment, and the accountability mechanisms that govern the performance of such contractors'.[66] Similar language was included in the Intelligence Authorization Act for Fiscal Year 2008 but the legislation was vetoed by President Bush due to provisions intended to prohibit waterboarding by the CIA. An effort to override the veto failed on 11 March 2008.[67]

Such information as does exist about the involvement of contractors often remains classified. Much is available to the contractors themselves, however, who are able to lobby members of Congress using that information. SAIC, for example, spent well over a million dollars in each of the past ten years on lobbying; in that period it was awarded between one and $3 billion in government contracts annually.[68] Earmarks, in which members of congress add provisions to legislation directing funds to specific projects, have long been acknowledged in the intelligence sector but rarely made public. In some cases a list of the amounts of projects might be made available, but redacting the names of companies.[69] In November 2007 Congress broke with tradition by releasing information about $80 million worth of earmarks included in a defence appropriations bill.[70]

As is frequently the case, this new found transparency was driven in significant part by scandal. The previous year Randy 'Duke' Cunningham, a Republican

[65] Scott Shane, 'Government Keeps a Secret After Studying Spy Agencies', *New York Times*, 26 April 2007; R J Hillhouse, 'Who Runs the CIA? Outsiders for Hire', *Washington Post*, 8 July 2007.

[66] Conference Report, 'Intelligence Authorization Act for Fiscal Year 2008', n 62 above, 11.

[67] See details at <http://www.opencongress.org/bill/110-h2082/show>.

[68] Shorrock, 'The Corporate Takeover', n 2 above; Donald L Barlett and James B Steele, 'Washington's $8 Billion Shadow', *Vanity Fair*, March 2007.

[69] Shorrock, 'The Corporate Takeover', n 2 above.

[70] Roxana Tiron, 'Congress Discloses Intel Earmarks for First Time', *The Hill*, 24 November 2007; see 'Making Appropriations for the Department of Defense for the Fiscal Year Ending 30 September 2008, and for Other Purposes', House of Representatives, Conference Report, Report 110–434, 6 November 2007, available at <http://frwebgate.access.gpo.gov/cgi-bin/getdoc.cgi?dbname=110_cong_reports&docid=f:hr434.110.pdf>, 378–9.

Congressman from California, had been sentenced to eight years in prison for accepting $2 million in bribes from MZM, a defence contractor. Cunningham had used his position on the House appropriations and intelligence committees to win MZM tens of millions of dollars' worth of contracts with the CIA and the Pentagon's CIFA office. In a related case, Kyle 'Dusty' Foggo, a former executive director of the CIA (its third-ranking official), was indicted for conspiring with former MZM CEO Brent Wilkes (who inexplicably lacked a folksy nickname) to direct contracts to the company.[71]

In addition to undermining effective oversight either by formal or informal means, such as media scrutiny,[72] access to secrets creates the possibility of abuse of those secrets. In 2006 the Boeing Corporation, a major defence contractor, agreed to a $565 million civil settlement arising from its use of sensitive bid information to win rocket launch contracts. The information had been provided by an engineer formerly employed by a competitor for the contracts who had moved to the Department of Defense.[73]

Incentives

The abuse of sensitive information is suggestive of the potential conflict of interests on the part of private actors engaged in intelligence activities. Discussions of this issue frequently paint a somewhat idealized picture of the patriotism and competence of full-time government employees, but there are reasonable grounds to be wary of inserting a profit motive into intelligence activities. The former head of the CIA's clandestine service has been quoted as saying that 'There's a commercial side to it that I frankly don't like . . . I would much prefer to see staff case officers who are in the chain of command and making a day-in and day-out conscious decision as civil servants in the intelligence business.'[74]

It is also arguable that the freedom to outsource alters the incentives of the intelligence agencies themselves. John Gannon, a former CIA Deputy Director for Intelligence and now head of BAE Systems' Global Analysis Group, has noted that this freedom offers flexibility but also avoids the need to justify a full-time employee and allocate responsibility, thereby breeding duplication and inhibiting collaboration. In the 1980s, 'what we discovered was that having smaller numbers forced collaboration, and collaboration was a good thing. As you soon as you start throwing money at the intelligence community, not only

[71] Shorrock, 'The Corporate Takeover', n 1 above.

[72] See, eg, Marina Caparini, 'Controlling and Overseeing Intelligence Services in Democratic States'in Born and Caparini (eds), *Democratic Control of Intelligence Services*, n 61 above; Chesterman, 'Secrets and Lies', n 7 above.

[73] Semiannual Report to the Congress, 1 April 2006-30 September 2006, Inspector General, United States Department of Defense, 2006, available at <http://www.dodig.osd.mil/sar/SAR>, 55.

[74] Miller, 'Spy Agencies Outsourcing', n 14 above, (quoting James L Pavitt).

does it lead to more contractors, it also leads to individual units thinking "We want to get one of our own."'[75] This in turn makes it harder to contain costs.[76]

It is possible, of course, that a profit motive may encourage *better* behaviour through the operation of a kind of market. There is evidence that this may be happening gradually in the context of PMSCs, particularly through professionalization of the industry and the creation of industry associations such as the British Association of Private Security Companies and the International Peace Operations Association. This is largely being driven by self-interest as some actors seek to establish themselves as 'legitimate' and thereby raise the costs of entry for competitors while enabling the charging of higher fees for similar services.[77]

Markets can indeed be an effective form of regulation, but operate best where there is competition, an expectation of repeat encounters, and a free flow of information. It is far from clear that these qualities apply to the commercial military sector;[78] there is even more reason to be wary of embracing it in the realm of intelligence.

Competition is severely restricted by the requirement that intelligence contractors meet security clearances. The process of granting new clearances is famously inefficient[79] while the government frequently needs to hire people quickly. This was exacerbated in April 2006 when the Department of Defense stopped processing new clearance applications following a funding dispute with the Office of Personnel Management.[80] The 'market' thus tends to be dominated by former military and civilian officials who already have such clearances, exacerbating the 'brain drain' problems cited earlier and creating predictable monopoly-type problems.

Though this has led to established relationships with a select group of firms, in respect of individuals being retained to collect human intelligence—particularly interrogators and interpreters connected to the 'Global War on Terror'—the need to get personnel on the ground and results back home has negated considerations of repeat encounters. As in the case of PMSCs, the assumption that such activities are atypical reduces the incentive to use any leverage that does exist to require adequate training or oversight.[81]

[75] Sebastian Abbot, 'The Outsourcing of US Intelligence Analysis', *News 21*, 28 July 2006, available at <http://newsinitiative.org/story/2006/07/28/the_outsourcing_of_u_s_intelligence> (quoting John Gannon).

[76] Robert O'Harrow, Jr, 'Costs Skyrocket as DHS Runs Up No-Bid Contracts', *Washington Post*, 28 June 2007.

[77] Simon Chesterman and Chia Lehnardt, 'Conclusion: From Mercenaries to Market', in Chesterman and Lehnardt, *From Mercenaries to Market*, 254–5, n 6 above.

[78] Ibid. at 254.

[79] This appears to have affected even the Director of National Intelligence. See Lawrence Wright, 'The Spymaster', *New Yorker*, 21 January 2008, 42.

[80] Abbot, 'The Outsourcing of US Intelligence Analysis', n 75 above.

[81] See, eg, Martha Minow, 'Outsourcing Power: How Privatizing Military Efforts Challenges Accountability, Professionalism, and Democracy', *Boston College Law Review*, vol 46 (2005) 1005–16.

Finally, and most obviously, the secrecy necessary for certain intelligence operations undermines the possibility of information flowing freely. In some circumstances there may be collusion in avoiding oversight, as when activities—such as rendition—are outsourced precisely for this reason. More generally, the movement of a limited number of individuals between the government and private intelligence worlds may encourage a form of regulatory capture when government employees are nominally tasked with overseeing former colleagues and future employers.

'Inherently governmental' functions

The simplest way of containing some of the problems outlined in this chapter would be to forbid certain activities from being delegated or outsourced to private actors at all. Intelligence services have a chequered history of abuse, but their legitimate activities tend to be justified in established democracies by reference to their grounding in the rule of law—a relatively recent requirement in some states[82]—and the existence of an accountability chain to democratic institutions.[83]

In the United States, this question is framed in the language of 'inherently governmental' functions, which are presumed to be carried out by government employees only. Debates concerning public functions in the United States frequently emphasize not the need to maintain certain functions in public hands but rather to justify passing them to the government in the first place;[84] the definition of 'inherently governmental' has thus emerged not as a sphere to be protected but rather as an exception to the more general push to privatization. Legislation adopted by Congress in 1998 as part of a larger privatization effort

[82] Britain, for example, operated its Security Service (MI5) until 1989 on the basis of a one-page administrative directive issued in 1952: The Maxwell-Fyfe Directive (issued by the UK Home Secretary, Sir David Maxwell-Fyfe, to the Director-General MI5, 1952), reprinted in Laurence Lustgarten and Ian Leigh, *In from the Cold: National Security and Parliamentary Democracy* (Oxford: Clarendon Press, 1994) 517; Laurence Lustgarten and Ian Leigh, 'The Security Service Act 1989', *Modern Law Review*, vol 52 (1989). The Secret Intelligence Service (MI6) only found a legislative basis in 1994. John Wadham, 'The Intelligence Services Act 1994', *Modern Law Review*, vol 57 (1994).

[83] See generally Born and Caparini (eds), *Democratic Control of Intelligence Services: Containing Rogue Elephants*, n 61 above.

[84] 'Government Contractors: Are Service Contractors Performing Inherently Governmental Functions?', US General Accounting Office, GAO/GGD-92-11, 18 November 1991, available at <http://archive.gao.gov/t2pbat7/145453.pdf>, 2 ('Concern about which federal agency activities are inherently governmental functions is not new. It goes back as far as the early days of the nation, as evidenced, for example, by the discussion in the Federalist Papers among the framers of the Constitution over what functions are appropriate for the federal government to exercise.'); see also Mohab Tarek Khattab, 'Revised Circular A-76: Embracing Flawed Methodologies', *Public Contract Law Journal*, vol 34 (2005). For historical context, see James Madison, *The Federalist*, No 44, 25 January 1788, available at <http://www.law.emory.edu/law-library/research/ready-reference/us-federal-law-and-documents/historical-documents-the-federalist-papers/the-federalist-no-44.html>.

required government agencies to identify 'inherently governmental' functions in order to enable cost comparisons between private bids and public budgets for everything else.[85] An 'inherently governmental' function was defined as a 'function that is so intimately related to the public interest as to require performance by Federal Government employees'.[86]

The Government Accountability Office noted in a 2002 report that there had been some uncertainty about how to apply this broad definition, but argued that it was

> clear that government workers need to perform certain warfighting, judicial, enforcement, regulatory, and policy-making functions . . . Certain other capabilities, . . . such as those directly linked to national security, also must be retained in-house to help ensure effective mission execution.[87]

Uncertainties about the limits continue, however, and the Department of Defense in particular has failed to adopt or apply consistently a clear interpretation.[88]

The executive has adopted various guidelines seeking to elaborate a definition of 'inherently governmental' functions. The 1983 version of an Office of Management and Budget (OMB) circular on this topic stated that '[c]ertain functions are inherently Governmental in nature, being so intimately related to the public interest as to mandate performance only by Federal employees'.[89] The definition was elaborated as including 'those activities which require either the exercise of discretion in applying Government authority or the use of value judgment in making decisions for the Government' and were said normally to fall into two categories:

> (1) The act of governing; ie, the discretionary exercise of Government authority. Examples include criminal investigations, prosecutions and other judicial functions; management of Government programmes requiring value judgments, as in direction of the national defense; management and direction of the Armed Services, activities performed exclusively by military personnel who are subject to deployment in a combat, combat support or combat service support role; conduct of foreign relations; selection of

[85] US Congress, Federal Activities Inventory Reform Act of 1998, 31 USC § 501 (2000); Minow, 'Outsourcing Power', 1015, n 81 above.

[86] US Congress, Federal Activities Inventory Reform Act of 1998, PL 105–270, codified at 31 USC § 501 (1998), Section 5.

[87] 'Improving the Sourcing Decisions of the Federal Government', US General Accounting Office, GAO-02-847T, 27 September 2002, available at <http://www.gao.gov/new.items/d02847t.pdf>, 21.

[88] Steven L Schooner, 'Contractor Atrocities at Abu Ghraib: Compromised Accountability in a Streamlined, Outsourced Government', *Stanford Law and Policy Review*, vol 16 (2005) 554–7.

[89] OMB Circular No A-76: Performance of Commercial Activities (superseded), White House Office of Management and Budget, 1983, para (b), quoted in William V Luneburg, 'Contracting by the Federal Government for Legal Services: A Legal and Empirical Analysis', *Notre Dame Law Review*, vol 63 (1988) 419 fn 91.

programme priorities; direction of Federal employees; regulation of the use of space, oceans, navigable rivers and other natural resources; *direction of intelligence and counter-intelligence operations;* and regulation of industry and commerce, including food and drugs.
(2) Monetary transactions and entitlements, such as tax collection and revenue disbursements; control of the treasury accounts and money supply; and the administration of public trusts.[90]

A 1992 'Policy Letter' from the Office of Federal Procurement Policy defined inherently governmental 'as a matter of policy' by essentially repeating the text above, which was elaborated as including 'the interpretation and execution of the laws of the United States so as to . . . significantly affect the life, liberty, or property of private persons'.[91] The illustrative list of examples provided in an appendix included the 'direction *and control* of intelligence and counter-intelligence operations'.[92] The 1999 revision of OMB Circular No A-76 maintained the 1983 language.[93]

The policy is now codified in the 2003 revision of OMB Circular No. A-76.[94] This kept the general definition in place,[95] but opened up significant loopholes by allowing for activities to be performed by contractors 'where the contractor does not have the authority to decide on the course of action, but is tasked to develop options or implement a course of action, with agency oversight'.[96] The revision also dropped any reference to intelligence or counter-intelligence operations. Another aspect of the Circular worthy of note is the ability of the Defense Department to 'determine if this circular applies to the Department of Defense during times of a declared war or military mobilization'.[97] It is not clear whether this provision has been implemented.

The ODNI in its 2006 'Five Year Strategic Human Capital Plan' noted that OMB had requested it to conduct a study to determine if contractors were engaged in intelligence community work that is '"inherently governmental" and

[90] OMB Circular No A-76, 1983 (emphasis added).
[91] Policy Letter 92–1: Inherently Governmental Functions, para 5(c).
[92] Ibid. at Appendix A, para 8 (emphasis added).
[93] OMB Circular No A-76 (Revised) (superseded): Performance of Commercial Activities, White House Office of Management and Budget, 1999, available at <http://www.whitehouse.gov/omb/circulars/a076/a076.html>.
[94] OMB Circular No A-76 (Revised): Performance of Commercial Activities, White House Office of Management and Budget, 29 May 2003 available at <http://www.whitehouse.gov/omb/circulars/a076/a76_incl_tech_correction.pdf>.
[95] Ibid. at Attachment A: Inventory Process, para B(1)(a) ('An inherently governmental activity is an activity that is so intimately related to the public interest as to mandate performance by government personnel. These activities require the exercise of substantial discretion in applying government authority and/or in making decisions for the government. Inherently governmental activities normally fall into two categories: the exercise of sovereign government authority or the establishment of procedures and processes related to the oversight of monetary transactions or entitlements.')
[96] Ibid. at Attachment A: Inventory Process, para B(1)(c).
[97] Ibid. at para 5(h).

hence improper'.[98] The study was said to be underway as an effort to determine the optimum mix of civilian, military, and contractor personnel, but was ultimately classified secret and, apparently, buried. In June 2007, the CIA announced its own plans to review the use of contractors, including the identification of jobs that should be performed only by government personnel.[99]

In the absence of strong political direction, there is little prospect of intelligence agencies adopting a robust definition of 'inherently governmental' functions. In any case, the significance of this limitation is diminished by the ability to outsource even inherently governmental functions in so far as they may be construed merely as implementing policy with some form of oversight.

With respect to the activities considered in the first section of this chapter, electronic surveillance by telecommunications companies may be an acceptable or necessary delegation of the implementation of government policy, although in some circumstances it might have fallen foul of the broader 'control' of intelligence operations test included in the 1992 Policy Letter. Rendition might also be construed as mere implementation of government policy, although it may violate other laws—notably including those of the territories through which CIA transport planes have passed.[100] There would, however, seem to be some prospect for agreement at the political level that interrogation of detainees falls 'squarely within the definition of an inherently governmental activity'.[101] Analysis by private contractors is somewhat trickier: clearly if it amounted to direction or the exercise of government discretion this would cross the line, but in most circumstances it would be easy to construe the work as merely as 'develop[ing] options'.[102]

[98] Strategic Human Capital Plan, n 54 above, 14.

[99] Stephen Barr, 'This CIA Mission—Better Contract-Workforce Management—Isn't Classified', *Washington Post*, 11 June 2007.

[100] The Venice Commission found rendition to be in violation of arts 2, 3, and 5 of the European Convention on Human Rights. See Monica Hakimi, 'The Council of Europe Addresses CIA Rendition and Detention Program', *American Journal of International Law*, vol 101 (2007). The European Parliament also noted that the CIA flights may be in violation of the Chicago Convention on Civil Aviation. Extraordinary Rendition: European Parliament Resolution on the Alleged Use of European Countries by the CIA for the Transportation and Illegal Detention of Prisoners, Adopted Midway Through the Work of the Temporary Committee, 2007, P6_TA(2006)0316 - (2006/2027 (INI)), available at <http://www.europarl.europa.eu/sides/getDoc.do?pubRef=-//EP//TEXT+TA+P6-TA-2006-0316+0+DOC+XML+V0//EN&language=en>. See also 'Transportation and Illegal Detention of Prisoners', n 39 above.

[101] Dianne Feinstein, Letter to the Honorable Michael B Mukasey, Attorney General of the United States, 6 February 2008, available at <http://tpmmuckraker.talkingpointsmemo.com/2008/02/wsj_contractors_likely_involve.php>; Gorman, 'CIA Likely Let Contractors Perform Waterboarding', n 42 above. The Senate Intelligence Committee has proposed banning the CIA from using private contractors to interrogate detainees. The restriction would be introduced as a part of a new bill authorizing intelligence expenditure in 2009 and would restrict the CIA to interrogation techniques that have been approved by the military and allow the International Red Cross access to all their prisoners. Similar restrictions imposed by the 2008 Intelligence Authorization Bill were vetoed by President Bush. See 'Notes from the War on Terror', *New York Times*, 2 May 2008.

[102] See n 95 above.

Uncertainty in this area appears to be intentional and thus exacerbates the accountability challenges posed by secrecy and problematic incentives. At the very least the responsibility to determine what is and is not 'inherently governmental' should itself be an 'inherently governmental' task.[103]

Conclusion

The assertion in the presentation cited at the beginning of this chapter—that private contractors are essential to the intelligence community's work—is at least partly accurate. Procuring hardware and software from the private sector, and engaging in electronic surveillance through the co-operation of telecommunications companies may be the only way to carry out such functions effectively. In some situations, however, outsourcing has been undertaken precisely to avoid oversight, as in the case of rendition. In others, it has placed the life or liberty of persons in the hands of private actors, as in the case of interrogation. Outsourcing has also, on occasion, opened the formulation of national security policy susceptible to actual or apparent influence.

Consideration of these issues has tended to focus on overblown costs, drains on government personnel, and episodic outrage at scandals in the form of corruption or, more recently, abuse. Addressing the problems raised by privatization of intelligence services requires engaging with the barriers to accountability considered in this chapter. The secrecy of some—but not all—of these activities is necessary, but requires a corresponding limitation on their further removal from public scrutiny. The incentives for corporate actors do not support a market regulatory approach to the problem. Clarity could most effectively be achieved by a transparent definition of what functions should be 'inherently governmental'—for example, actions that significantly affect the life, liberty, or property of private persons—although this requires political capital that is unlikely to be spent in the absence of scandal.

[103] See also Minow, 'Outsourcing Power', 1016, n 80 above. Contrast Khattab, 'Revised Circular A-76: Embracing Flawed Methodologies', n 84 above, 516 (arguing that a revision of OMB Circular No A-76 should be entrusted to 'private sector outsourcing experts'). See also 'Defense Federal Acquisition Regulation Supplement (DFARS)', *Federal Register*, vol 71, no 116 (2006) 34826-7 ('It is the responsibility of the combatant commander to ensure that the private security contract mission statements do not authorize the performance of any inherently Governmental military functions, such as preemptive attacks, or any other types of attacks. Otherwise, civilians who accompany the US Armed Forces lose their law of war protections from direct attack if and for such time as they take a direct part in hostilities'), quoted in *Matter of Brian X Scott*, US Government Accountability Office, B-298370 and B-298490, 18 August 2006, available at <http://www.gao.gov/decisions/bidpro/298370.htm>.

Such a scandal in the form of Blackwater's activities in Iraq pushed the United States and Iraq to revisit the accountability of private military companies.[104] Despite revelations that contractors employed by the US government appear to have engaged in torture, in the form of waterboarding, this was insufficient to start a major debate on the topic. Instead, reforms—if any—seem most likely to come because each of those torturers cost the US taxpayer double the salary of a Federal employee.

[104] 'Blackwater's Impunity', *New York Times*, 16 May 2008.

10

Peacekeeping

*Chia Lehnardt**

Private military and security companies (PMSCs), anticipating the end of the 'Iraq bubble', seek to tap new business opportunities. Involved in peacekeeping operations since the 1990s, the industry has stepped up efforts to lobby for a more active involvement. Already in 2003 the US industry association International Peace Operations Association (IPOA) issued a concept paper setting out how the private military sector could support the United Nations Mission in the Democratic Republic of Congo (MONUC).[1] The idea was also discussed in governmental circles. In a study outlining options for regulation of the sector, the British government floated the possibility of a greater involvement in UN operations.[2] The mere notion of lending legitimacy to PMSCs in such a manner was so repugnant to some that the idea was quickly shelved.[3] In the past few years, however, the security environment in fragile states has continued to grow more complex. Personnel of humanitarian organizations and international organizations frequently become targets of attack by criminals, terrorists or insurgents.[4] As a result, the demand for commercial security has grown, and although the perception of PMSCs in the broader public remains predominantly negative, the stigma of mercenarism is slowly evaporating.

Implicit and explicit acceptance of PMSCs by non-governmental organizations (NGOs), international organizations, and governments has allowed the companies to present a fundamental problem of UN peace operations—the lack of sufficient deployable resources—as a question of demand and supply. Their

* This chapter draws upon text first published as 'Privatisierter Frieden? Die Rolle privater Militärfirmen in UN-Peacekeeping', *Vereinte Nationen*, vol 56, no 2 (2008) 60.

[1] 'Supporting the MONUC Mandate with Private Services in the Democratic Republic of Congo', IPAO Concept Paper, January 2003, available at <http://www.ipoaonline.org>.

[2] Foreign and Commonwealth Office, 'Private Military Companies: Options for Regulations', Green Paper HC 577, February 2002, 4, 19.

[3] Paul Waugh and Nigel Morris, 'Mercenaries as Peace-keepers Plan under Fire', *Independent*, 14 February 2002.

[4] See, eg, UN Office for the Coordination of Humanitarian Affairs, 'Guidelines for Humanitarian Organisations on Interacting with Military and Other Security Actors in Iraq', 20 October 2004, available at <http://www.unhcr.org/refworld/docid/4289f2f74.html>; Report of the Secretary-General on Safety and Security of United Nations Personnel, 2000, UN Doc A/55/494.

efforts to present themselves as the solution to problems facing peacekeeping operations not only aims at opening up new business opportunities, but also at taking advantage of the enormous image boost a greater and more visible involvement in UN operations would entail. It is in this vein that the IPOA established a 'peace operations institute' advocating a 'private alternative to a standing United Nations peacekeeping force'[5] and the General Director of the British Association of Private Security Companies remarked, if half-jokingly, that branding PMSCs the 'dogs of war' was no longer appropriate; instead he preferred the term 'pussycats of peace'.[6]

Such advances still meet with disapproval, scepticism and outright hostility, not least by the UN Working Group on Mercenaries.[7] Nonetheless, it cannot be overlooked that they address a fundamental problem facing UN operations. Despite the mixed reputation PMSCs have earned in Iraq, given the continuing discrepancy between operational requirements on the one hand and the willingness of member states to commit the necessary resources on the other, PMSC lobbying efforts are increasingly supported by academics and practitioners.[8] They are particularly welcomed in circles where PMSCs are seen not only as a solution to the political, financial and institutional constraints on the ability of the United Nations to respond quickly and efficiently to crises, but also as a welcome alternative to an inefficient, unaccountable, and costly world organization.

As a consequence, it is sometimes suggested that an increasing utilization of the private sector would demonstrate 'a growing pragmatism among policy makers' and indicate 'that they place a greater value on humanitarian results', narrowly framing the discussion as one that is essentially about the choice between genocide and PMSC involvement.[9] Yet it is frequently unclear what functions, in the context of peacekeeping operations, PMSCs have taken on thus far and what

[5] Christopher M Rochester, 'A Private Alternative to a Standing United Nations Peacekeeping Force', IPOA Peace Operations Institute, White Paper, 2007, available at <http://peaceops.org/poi/images/stories/poi_wp_privatealternative.pdf>.

[6] 'War Dogs Rebranded as "Pussycats of Peace"', *Economist*, 19 November 2006.

[7] On the position of the two Special Rapporteurs and the Working Group see Viktor-Yves Ghebali, 'The United Nations and the Dilemma of Outsourcing Peacekeeping Operations', in Alan Bryden and Marina Caparini (eds), *Private Actors and Security Governance* (Münster: Lit Verlag 2006) 213.

[8] See, eg, Kevin O'Brien, 'What Should and What Should not be Regulated', in Simon Chesterman and Chia Lehnardt (eds), *From Mercenaries to Market. The Rise and Regulation of Private Military Companies* (Oxford: Oxford University Press, 2007) 45; Andrew Bearpark and Sabrina Schultz, 'The Future of the Market' in Chesterman and Lenhardt (eds), *From Mercenaries to Market*, 239; Alrik van den Berg, 'Effective Peacekeeping and the Privatization of Security', in Thomas Jäger and Gerhard Kümmel (eds), *Private Military and Security Companies: Chances, Problems, Pitfalls and Prospects* (Wiesbaden: VS Verlag für Sozialwissenschaften, 2007) 293; Steve Mantaux, 'Des Chiens de Guerre Pour le Maintien de la Paix?', *Jeune Afrique*, No 2393 (November 2006); Oldrich Bures, 'Private Military Companies: A Second Best Peacekeeping Option?' *International Peacekeeping*, vol 12 (2005) 533.

[9] See Anna Leander and Rens van Munster, 'Private Security Contractors in the Debate about Darfur: Reflecting and Reinforcing Neo-Liberal Governmentality', *International Relations*, vol 21 (2007) 201.

options for further roles are proposed. In addition, the presence of PMSCs in peacekeeping operations raises a number of legal issues that have to date received insufficient attention in the discussion.[10] These aspects shall be considered in turn.

The role of PMSCs in multilateral peacekeeping operations

The notion of peacekeeping operations denotes a number of very different activities, some of which PMSCs have undertaken under contract with a member state or with the UN directly. Those activities range from 'second rank' activities, such as the building of barracks or transport of supplies, to more sensitive tasks, including the provision of intelligence or training of militaries, to functions involving the use of force.

The US-based PMSC Pacific Architect Engineers (PAE), hired by the US government, provided logistic support to the Economic Community of West African States Monitoring Group in Sierra Leone, including helicopter services, communication facilities, vehicles and general repairs, and maintenance.[11] The same company provided supplies to blue helmets in Sierra Leone and East Timor. PAE and DynCorp, again hired by the US State Department, contribute to the building of infrastructure and transports to peacekeeping troops of the African Union in Sudan.[12] The United Nations relies on International Charter Incorporated of Oregon for heavy airlifting jobs and to bring UN troops into areas of operation.[13] PMSCs also undertake mine clearance work under the auspices of the UN Office for Project Services and the UN Mine Action Coordination Centre in many conflict zones, for example for the UN Interim Force in Lebanon funded by the United Arab Emirates,[14] and since 2005 in southern Sudan.

PMSCs are also tasked with more sensitive functions, such as monitoring, intelligence collection, and policing functions. In 2001, the UN Transitional Administration in East Timor hired two South African PMSCs, KZN Security and Empower Loss Control Services, to provide local intelligence.[15] The US government has used the US-based company DynCorp and subsequently PAE

[10] An exception is Nigel D White and Sorcha MacLeod, 'EU Operations and Private Military Contractors: Issues of Corporate and Institutional Responsibility', *European Journal of International Law*, vol 19 (2008) 965.

[11] 'Lessons from ECOWAS Peacekeeping Operations: 1990–2004', Report of the ECOWAS Workshop, 23 March 2005, available at <http://www.un.org/unowa/unowa/reports/ecowas110205.pdf>, 32.

[12] Colum Lynch, '3200 Peacekeepers Pledged on Mission to Darfur', *Washington Post*, 21 October 2004.

[13] Traci Hukill, 'Firms Seek to Sell UN on Privatized Peacekeeping', *National Journal*, 18 May 2004.

[14] 'Leg Blast Mine-clearer Honoured', BBC News, 16 May 2007, available at <http://news.bbc.co.uk/1/hi/england/tees/6661389.stm>.

[15] Peter W Singer, *Corporate Warriors. The Rise of the Privatized Military Industry* (Ithaca: Cornell University Press, 2005) 183.

to recruit and manage civil police personnel and monitors to be deployed in peacekeeping operations. For example, the personnel constituting the International Police Task Force for the United Nations Mission in Bosnia Herzegovina were recruited by DynCorp, as was the unarmed personnel for the Organisation for Security and Cooperation in Europe Kosovo Verification Mission.[16] PAE is under contract with the State Department to provide staff to the Civilian Protection Monitoring Team in Sudan, which is tasked with monitoring human rights, investigating complaints about human rights abuses and issuing reports.[17] Moreover, PMSCs have been involved, again on behalf of the United States, in the disarmament of former combatants, security sector reform, capacity-building programmes to develop African peacekeeping capabilities, and military aid. The Global Peace Operations Initiative, initiated in 2005 for five years, aims at training 75,000 soldiers for peace missions. MPRI is one of three companies providing peacekeeping support training in this programme.[18] For the UN Mission in Liberia (UNMIL), the demobilization of militias and the restructuring of Liberia's armed forces were outsourced to DynCorp in 2005.

In a few instances PMSC employees have also been contracted directly by the United Nations as security guards for site protection. The UN Protection Force (UNPROFOR), deployed between 1992 and 1995 in what was then the Former Republic of Yugoslavia, relied on five PMSCs whose personnel not only carried out functions typical of civilian personnel—as drivers, IT experts, or engineers—but were also deployed as armed security guards and personnel securing borders.[19] Private military personnel also worked for what is now called the UN Mission in Côte d'Ivoire, MONUC, the UN Mission in Sierra Leone and the UN Mission in Kosovo (UNMIK).[20]

There appears to be no administrative regulation concerning the question of which functions under a Security Council mandate might be outsourced or not. Indeed, PMSCs have not only provided services in support of such a mandate, but also carried out some of its more ancillary aspects constituting peace consolidating measures or post-conflict measures, such as the recruitment and training of troops in Liberia for UNMIL or the clearing of mines for the UN Mission in Sudan. The line between functions that might be outsourced and activities that must be carried out by UN troops appears to be between the

[16] Jonathan Steele, 'US gives Kosovo Monitoring Job to Mercenaries', *Guardian*, 31 October 1998.

[17] Pratap Chatterjee, 'Darfur Diplomacy: Enter the Contractors', *CorpWatch*, 21 October 2004, available at <http://www.corpwatch.org/article.php?id=11598>.

[18] 'L-3 Communications MPRI Awarded Global Peace Operations Initiative Contract', *GlobalSecurity.org*, 17 May 2007, available at <http://www.globalsecurity.org/military/library/news/2007/05/mil-070517-l-3comm01.htm>.

[19] 'Memorandum from ArmorGroup Services Limited: A Contractor's View', UK House of Commons, Select Committee on Foreign Affairs Minutes of Evidence, 23 July 2002, Appendix 6, paras 73–80.

[20] Report of the Secretary-General on Outsourcing Practices, 2004, UN Doc A/59/227.

relatively mundane, if important activities on the one hand, and the actual foot-soldiering—the maintenance of buffer zones and demilitarized areas through armed patrolling—on the other hand. This can be problematic with regard to armed protection services PMSCs provide, such as site protection. If the peace mission operates in a hostile environment and the robust use of force is integral to the operation, the distinction between carrying out the mandate and providing armed 'support' for the mandate might be accurate from a legal point of view, but rather artificial in practice.

PMSC personnel in international law

A principal rationale underlying this delineation between PMSCs carrying out aspects of the mandate on the one hand and merely providing support for a mandate on the other, seems to be the idea that PMSCs must not engage in hostilities. To the extent that such a distinction is made however, it is one which in practice can be extremely difficult to sustain. From an international humanitarian law perspective this is particularly problematic in cases where the threshold of armed conflict is crossed. If engaged in situations of armed conflict, UN blue helmets are combatants,[21] whereas private military personnel not integrated in the military chain of command or otherwise made part of the UN force are not.[22] Only combatants have the right to participate directly in the hostilities.[23] If PMSC employees, despite their status as civilians, take direct part in the hostilities they become unprivileged belligerents and upon capture may be treated as criminals under the domestic law of the captor. Armed defence of civilian persons or objects is in principle covered by the right to self-defence or to defence of others, which are rights anyone has regardless of status. Therefore the exercise of these rights does not amount to direct participation. However, the question of which actions are necessary for the defence, and thus covered by the right to self-defence or to defence of others, can be difficult to answer.

International responsibility for misconduct

If PMSC personnel violate interests protected by international law—for example, by shooting indiscriminately at civilians or engaging in acts that would

[21] Secretary-General's Bulletin on Observance by United Nations Forces of International Humanitarian Law, 1999, UN Doc ST/SGB/1999/13, ss 1.1, 3.

[22] On the qualification of PMSC personnel under international humanitarian law see Christian Schaller, 'Private Security and Military Companies under the International Law of Armed Conflict', in Jäger and Kümmel (eds), *Private Military and Security Companies*, 345.

[23] Protocol Additional to the Geneva Conventions of 12 August 1949, and relating to the Protection of Victims of International Armed Conflicts, 8 June 1977, 1125 UNTS 3.

otherwise constitute human rights violations—the question arises over who bears responsibility for such acts: the UN, its member states, both, or none of them?[24] The answer to these questions is particularly difficult for at least two reasons. Relationships not between two, but three actors—the United Nations, states, and the PMSC employee—must be considered. Moreover, while it is accepted that international organizations can in principle incur international responsibility, the efforts of the International Law Commission (ILC) to formulate rules on the responsibilities of international organizations are complicated by the fact that there is much less case law and practice from which principles can be drawn than in the context of state responsibility.[25] Therefore, many of the legal issues discussed in the following analysis regarding UN responsibility remain to be tested.

Attribution of PMSC conduct to the UN

The point of departure for an examination of UN responsibility is that the United Nations, as an abstract entity, primarily acts through its organs and is thus responsible for their conduct. Yet, although peacekeeping operations are established as subsidiary organs of either the General Assembly[26] or the Security Council[27] in accordance with articles 22 or 29 of the UN Charter, they are a special case. Peacekeeping forces are made up, as will be explained more fully below, of national contingents provided by states. Therefore, the status of peacekeeping forces as subsidiary organs of the UN does not imply, in the

[24] In principle, both the UN and states can be bound by international humanitarian law and human rights law, although the precise extent of an international organization's obligations under international law and states' obligations outside their own territories is still a matter of uncertainty. While a detailed analysis of this question is outside the scope of this chapter, for the purposes of the following analysis it will be assumed that the state of nationality of PMSC employees, the state funding the use of PMSCs in an UN operation, and the home state of the company as such are neither subject to human rights law nor to international humanitarian law in the area where the mission operates. On the question of jurisdiction in the context of international co-operation generally see *Matthews v United Kingdom*, App no 24833/94, 18 February 1990, para 34 (European Court of Human Rights (ECtHR)); on the question of jurisdiction in the context of multilateral peace operations see *Behrami and Behrami v France & Saramati v France and ors*, App nos 71412/01 and 78166/01, 2 May 2007, paras 116, 151 (ECtHR); on the obligations of the UN as an international organization see *Interpretation of the Agreement of 25 March 1951 between the WHO and Egypt*, Advisory Opinion, ICJ Reports 1980, para 37; Secretary-General's Bulletin, n 21 above, s 1.1.; White and MacLeod, 'EU Operations and Private Military Contractors', n 10 above, 672.

[25] See Draft Articles on the Responsibility of International Organizations, International Law Commission, 2008, UN Doc A/CN.4/L.725.

[26] The First United Nations Emergency Force (UNEF) was established by the General Assembly. See UN General Assembly, 7 November 1956, UN Doc A/RES/1001 (ES-I); Status Agreement with Egypt, UN Treaty Series vol 260, 62.

[27] See UN General Assembly, Model Agreement Between the United Nations and Member States Contributing Personnel and Equipment to the United Nations Peacekeeping Operations, 1991, UN Doc A/46/185, art IV.

absence of additional factors, UN responsibility for the conduct of PMSC personnel who are part of the mission.[28]

If PMSC personnel are not part of a UN organ acting for the UN, the issue turns on the question whether PMSC employees can be considered agents of the UN. According to the International Court of Justice (ICJ), international organizations act not only through their organs but also through their 'agents' and are responsible for the conduct of both,[29] an approach adopted by the ILC in its draft articles.[30] It is not entirely clear who, precisely, aside from UN officials, falls into that category. The definition the ILC adopted—an agent is any 'official and other persons or entities through whom the organization acts'[31]—appears circular. The draft echoes part of the ICJ's paraphrasing in the context of privileges and immunities of UN agents, which reads in full:

> The Court understands the word 'agent' in the most liberal sense, that is to say, any person who, whether paid official or not, and whether permanently employed or not, has been charged by an organ of the Organization with carrying out, or helping to carry out, one of its functions—in short, any person through whom it acts.[32]

This definition appears very broad, as any person contributing to a peacekeeping operation could be considered an agent of the UN, triggering its responsibility regardless of the activity involved or the control exercised on the part of the UN. Whether just any PMSC contracted by the UN is also an agent of the organization is questionable.[33] At a minimum, if private military personnel are tasked directly by the UN with aspects of the Security Council mandate establishing the peacekeeping operation,[34] the UN deploys PMSC employees to fulfil its

[28] Giorgio Gaja, Second Report on Responsibility of International Organizations, 2004, UN Doc A/Cn.4/541, para 35. Even though it relied extensively on ILC documents, the ECtHR assumed that the UN bears responsibility for conduct of peacekeeping forces on the basis that peacekeeping missions are established as subsidiary organs, see *Behrami*, n 24 above, para 143.

[29] *Reparation for Injuries Suffered in the Service of the United Nations*, Advisory Opinion, ICJ Reports 1949, 177; *Difference Relating to Immunity from Legal Process of a Special Rapporteur of the Commission on Human Rights*, Advisory Opinion, ICJ Reports, 1999, para 66; Clyde Eagleton, 'International Organizations and the Law of Responsibility', *Recueil des cours*, vol 76 (1950-I) 323, 387.

[30] Draft Articles on Responsibility of International Organizations, ILC, 2004, UN Doc A/CN.4/L.648, art 4(1) ('The conduct of an organ or agent of an international organization in the performance of functions of that organ or agent shall be considered as an act of that organization under international law whatever position the organ or agent holds in respect of the organization.')

[31] Ibid. at art 4 (2). [32] *Reparations for Injuries*, 29 above, 177.

[33] For a different view, see White and MacLeod, 'EU Operations and Private Military Contractors', n 10 above, 976.

[34] The UN General Conditions of Contracts for Services stipulate that the contractor's personnel 'shall not be considered in any respect as being the employees or the agents of the United Nations.' General Conditions of Contract: Contracts for the Provision of Services, United Nations, revised January 2008, available at <http://www.un.org/Depts/ptd/pdf/general_condition_services.pdf>, s 1.2. If from an international law perspective PMSC personnel are agents of the UN, such provisions are by themselves not relevant in relations with third parties.

functions and thus acts through them. Accordingly, any misconduct on their part will be seen as UN conduct, regardless of their formal status or whether they are integrated in the peacekeeping force or not. Beyond this category of persons, the ICJ, for the purposes of responsibility, considers at least 'experts on mission' as agents of the UN.[35] Here the Court appears to grant the UN wide discretion as to whom the organization may grant that status,[36] which is appropriate as the designation as an 'expert on mission' not only implies functional immunity and certain privileges[37] but also UN responsibility for any misconduct of the expert. The UN regards, for example, members of formed police units or military observers as 'experts on mission'. While according individual and corporate contractors the status and privileges of 'experts on mission' is possible, it seems that generally the UN does not consider PMSC personnel as such.[38]

If PMSC personnel are neither 'experts on mission' nor tasked with functions that are part of the Security Council mandate (for example, services provided 'in support' of the mandate), the second scenario in which their conduct might be attributed to the UN is where PMSC personnel are under UN command. This can be the case where they are part of the UN force either because they belong to the troops contributed by a member state to the UN operation, or by virtue of the Status of Forces Agreement (SOFA) or Status of Mission Agreement (SOMA), or other agreements (such as a Memorandum of Understanding (MoU)) concluded between the UN and the host state or the troop-contributing state.[39]

If PMSC personnel are part of the mission by virtue of their membership in a national contingent, establishing whether they are, in fact, under UN command can be problematic. The fact that UN forces are composed of national contingents supplied by member states of the UN results in a dual character of members of UN forces: while remaining in the service of their state, for the period of assignment to the operation they are also considered international personnel under the authority of the UN.[40] Here, the question of responsibility is resolved according to the principle of effectiveness. It is not the formal designation as an organ that is decisive, but rather which entity exercises effective

[35] *Difference Relating to Immunity from Legal Process*, n 29 above, paras 60, 66.

[36] *Applicability of Article VI, Section 22, of the Convention on the Privileges and Immunities of the United Nations*, Advisory Opinion, ICJ Reports, 1989, paras 45, 48.

[37] Convention on the Privileges and Immunities of the United Nations, 13 February 1946, 1 UN Treaty Ser 15, February 1947 art VI, s 22.

[38] Confidential communication with UN official.

[39] At least military personnel working for UNPROFOR who were armed were covered by the MoU (personal communication of author). The same is true for contractors doing mine-clearing work in the Suez Channel in 1956. See Finn Seyerstedt, 'United Nations Forces: Some Legal Problems', *British Yearbook of International Law*, vol 37 (1961) 351, 355.

[40] Model Agreement Between the UN and Member States Contributing Personnel and Equipment to UN Peacekeeping Operations, n 27 above, art VII.

control over the conduct in question.[41] This means that the fact that member states retain only control over disciplinary matters and criminal affairs is not relevant for the purposes of attribution. The command structure is decisive.[42] The level of command conferred to the UN is usually set out in the participating state agreement or Transfer of Authority and is typically as follows: While contributing states retain the right to decide to withdraw their troops from a mission, the commander of the UN force is appointed by, and takes orders only from, UN organs. Although his or her commands are not issued directly to the members of the force but channelled through the national commanders of the contingents, they take immediate effect without national authorities being involved.[43] National commanders may take orders in operational matters only from the UN commander.[44] At the same time, in day-to-day operations, it might well be that the national commander must concretize the mandate without seeking orders from the UN commander. Yet even then it is assumed that he or she is operating in an international capacity as UN personnel.[45]

In sum, while powers concerning personnel matters rest with the states, operational control is vested with the UN with the chain of command running through the UN commander and the commanders of national contingents. If PMSC personnel are integrated in the troops contributed by member states or otherwise under the command of the UN, in principle, the latter is responsible

[41] Moshe Hirsch, *The Responsibility of International Organizations Toward Third Parties: Some Basic Principles* (Dordrecht: Nijhoff, 1995) 64; Pierre Klein, La *Responsabilité des Organisations Internationals: Dans les Orders Juridiques Internes et en Droit des Gens* (Brussels: Bruylant, 1998) 380; Report of the Secretary General on Financing of the United Nations Protection Force, the United Nations Confidence Restoration Operation in Croatia, the United Nations Preventive Deployment Force and the United Nations Peace Forces Headquarters, 1996, UN Doc A/51/389, para 16; Responsibility of International Organizations: Titles and Text of Draft Articles 4, 5, 6, and 7, ILC, art 5; R *(on the application of Al-Jedda) (FC) v Secretary of State for Defence* UKHL 58 (2007) para 22 (House of Lords). The practice of the UN to accept responsibility for combat-related damages in peacekeeping operations (see below) indicates that here the test of 'effective control' to be exercised by an international organization for the purposes of attribution is less stringent than the one codified in the Articles on State Responsibility, ILC, 2001, UN Doc A/56/10, art 8; see also Christian Tomuschat, 'The International Responsibility of the European Union', in E Cannizaro (ed), *The European Union as an Actor in International Relations* (The Hague: Kluwer 2002) 177, 180; C F Amerasinghe, *Principles of the Institutional Law of International Organizations* (2nd edn; Cambridge: Cambridge University Press, 2005) 400. For a different view on the relevant test see *Behrami*, n 24 above, para 133, where the court claims without much support that 'the key question is whether the UNSC retained ultimate authority and control so that operational command only was delegated'.

[42] Gaja, 'Second Report on the Responsibility of International Organizations', n 28 above, para 40.

[43] See, eg, UNEF Regulations, 1957, UN Doc ST/SGB/UNEF 1, arts 6, 31; ONUC Regulations, 1963, UN Doc ST/SGB/ONUC/1, arts 6, 26.

[44] Seyerstedt, 'United Nations Forces', n 39 above, 406–11; *NK v Austria*, 77 ILR 470, 26 February 1979 (Austrian Superior Provincial Court of Vienna).

[45] Model Agreement Between the UN and Member State Contributing Personnel and Equipment to UN Peacekeeping Operations, n 27 above, para 9. Derek W Bowett, *United Nations Forces: A Legal Study of United Nations Forces* (London: Stevens 1964) 352 (arguing that for the period of their service national commanders are subject to art 100 of the UN Charter).

for their misconduct. This is recognized in practice by the UN, which assumes responsibility for combat-related damages amounting to violations of international humanitarian law.[46] The presumption that members of the UN force act under UN control can of course be rebutted if the national commander maintains a back channel communication link with his or her government, which is frequently the case where robust use of force is at issue. Consequently, where it can be established that PMSC personnel acted on the instructions of, and thus under the control of, the sending state, that state would be responsible for the conduct in question.[47]

Attribution of PMSC conduct to the contributing state

If the PMSC is hired by a member state to exercise elements of governmental authority outside UN command, that member state will be responsible on the basis of the principle codified in article 5 of the ILC Articles on State Responsibility.[48] The notion of 'governmental authority', however, is inordinately difficult to define.[49] It probably includes disarmament of combatants or recruitment of armed forces, but not, for example, mine clearance. The hiring state would also be responsible if it instructed the company to commit international law violations or controlled the employees in the course of the violation.[50]

If it has been established that the UN is responsible, judicial enforcement of its responsibility will often be precluded on account of the immunity of the organization[51] and the lack of jurisdiction of, for example, the European Court of Human Rights (ECtHR) over entities other than states.[52] The question of

[46] Financing of the UN Protection Force; Daphna Shraga, 'UN Peacekeeping Operations: Applicability of International Humanitarian Law and Responsibility for Operation-Related Damage', *American Journal of International Law*, vol 94 (2000) 407.

[47] Hirsch, *Responsibility of International Organizations*, n 41 above, 64–5; Marten Zwanenburg, *Accountability of Peace Support Operations* (Leiden: Nijhoff 2005) 101; *M M-M et al v the State of The Netherlands*, case no 265618, 10 September 2008 (District Court of The Hague) para 4.16.1, English translation available at <http://zoeken.rechtspraak.nl/resultpage.aspx?snelzoeken=true&searchtype=ljn&ljn=Bf0182&u_ljn=Bf0182>.

[48] ILC Articles on State Responsibility, n 41 above, art 5 ('The conduct of a person or entity which is not an organ of the State under article 4 but which is empowered by the law of that State to exercise elements of the governmental authority shall be considered an act of the State under international law, provided the person or entity is acting in that capacity in the particular instance.')

[49] Chia Lehnardt, 'Private Military Companies and State Responsibility', in Chesterman and Lehnardt (eds), *From Mercenaries to Market*, n 8 above, 144.

[50] ILC Articles on State Responsibility, n 41 above, art 8.

[51] Charter of the United Nations, 26 June 1945, 1 UNTS XVI, art 105(1). See *Association of Citizens Mothers of Srebenica and ors v the State of the Netherlands and the United Nations*, case no 295247, 10 July 2008 (District Court of The Hague) para 5.9; English translation available at <http://zoeken.rechtspraak.nl/resultpage.aspx?snelzoeken=true&searchtype=ljn&ljn=BD6796&u_ljn=BD6796>.

[52] See Behrami, n 24 above.

whether states can incur concurrent or subsidiary responsibility is therefore of great importance.[53] While the ECtHR, in a case concerning acts committed in the context of KFOR and UNMIK, did not even consider this hypothesis,[54] the question whether dual attribution of the same act is possible in principle is subject to dispute.[55] The better view is probably to exclude attribution to member states where the relevant conduct took place under UN command so as not to provide states with an additional incentive to interfere with UN command. Given that states retain disciplinary powers and criminal jurisdiction over members of their troop contingents, it is rather the issue of subsidiary responsibility on the basis of due diligence that requires further consideration.

Responsibility on the basis of the principle of due diligence

Even if one takes the view that the relevant PMSC conduct is exclusively attributed to the UN, the contributing state can still incur responsibility if that conduct was accompanied by omissions on its part demonstrating failure to exercise due diligence in attempting to prevent or respond to the violation of international law.[56] Human rights treaties have established the principle of due diligence with regard to human rights conventions obligating states to 'ensure', 'protect' or 'secure' rights.[57] Such provisions have been held to require states to take positive measures in order to prevent the violation of rights by non-state actors.[58] The principle is less established in the context of international humanitarian law,

[53] This question concerns state responsibility for breach of obligations binding on member states of the UN, rather than on the UN itself. It is therefore separate from the issue of responsibility of member states for the financial liabilities incurred by the international organization by virtue of their membership, which was the subject of the Tin Council cases (eg, *Maclaine Watson & Co Ltd v International Tin Council* (No 2), 80 ILR 110 (1988) (English Court of Appeals)); see Giogio Gaja, 'Fourth Report on Responsibility of International Organizations', 2006, UN Doc A/CN.4/564/Add.2, para 75.

[54] See *Behrami*, n 24 above.

[55] Luigi Condorelli, 'Le Statute des Forces de l'ONU et le Droit International Humanitaire', *Rivista di Diritto Internazionale*, vol 78 (1995) 881 (arguing for the possibility of dual attribution); Pierre Bodeau-Livinec, Gionata P Buzzini, and Santiago Villalpando, 'Comment on *Behrami and Behrami v France*', *American Journal Of International Law*, vol 102 (2008) 323, 327; Gaja, Second Report on the Responsibility of International Organizations, n 28 above, para 48; Report of the International Law Commission, Yearbook of the International Law Commission (2004) vol II(2) 101, para 4; but see Henry G Schermers and Niels M Blokker, *International Institutional Law* (4th edn; Boston/Leiden: Nijhoff, 2003) para 1585; *M M-M and ors v the State of The Netherlands* (District Court of The Hague) para 4.1.

[56] Zwanenburg, *Accountability of Peace Support Operations*, n 47 above, 107.

[57] See, eg, European Convention for the Protection of Human Rights and Fundamental Freedoms, 4 November 1950, 213 UNTS 22, art 1; International Covenant on Civil and Political Rights, 19 December 1966, 99 UNTS 171, UN Doc A/6316 (1966) art 1(2); American Convention on Human Rights (1969) 22 November 1969, 1144 UNTS 123, art 1.

[58] For an overview, see August Reinisch, 'The Changing International Framework for Dealing with Non-state Actors', in Philip Alston (ed), *Non-State Actors and Human Rights* (Oxford: Oxford University Press, 2005) 79–80.

although the textual basis can be found in the wording of article 1 of the Geneva Conventions.[59] Whether the UN can become responsible on the basis of that principle where the PMSC conduct is not attributable to it is unclear. Although there is no jurisprudence or practice to that effect, there is no reason to foreclose that possibility if the relevant omission concerns an action within the competence of the UN.

On the basis of the due diligence principle, it is arguable that a state contributing obviously untrained and undisciplined private military personnel to the UN operation will incur responsibility for lack of due diligence.[60] Another obvious necessity for preventing violations of international law is adequate regulation of, and control of, personnel deployed in an unstable environment. States have been reluctant to establish effective legislative control mechanisms over PMSCs.[61] As a result, there appears to be a preference for self-regulation as the sole accountability mechanism and a tendency to rely on this idea more seriously than would be appropriate from an international law perspective. The industry has encouraged this trend by establishing lobbying associations and committing to codes of conduct. Such measures, while perhaps laudable, are insufficient and fall well short of international legal imperatives to which states and the UN are subject. Self-regulation can only build on existing regulation and does not absolve the hiring state or the UN of the responsibility to exercise adequate control over PMSCs. Precisely because there is a lack of efficient regulation and control of PMSCs through states, it is essential for the UN to ensure that PMSCs carrying out functions in UN peacekeeping operations respect applicable law. A necessary preliminary step is the establishment of a standardized procedure through which the UN selects PMSCs for a given task. Such a procedure should, at a minimum, include the participation of the Department of Peacekeeping Operations and the Department of Security and could, for example, rely on a database of PMSCs meeting certain criteria and that have been reliable in the past.[62] In addition, contracts should include clauses ensuring respect for applicable laws, including human rights, international humanitarian law, and the principle of sovereign equality of states.

The principal problem is likely to be ensuring adequate control of private military personnel. In cases where PMSCs operate in a relatively benign environment and carry out activities not involving the use of force, mere reporting

[59] Report on Expert Meeting on Private Military Contractors,University Centre for International Humanitarian Law, Geneva, 29–30 August 2005, 44; *Case Concerning Armed Activities in the Territory of the Congo (Democratic Republic of the Congo v Uganda)*, Judgment, ICJ Reports, 2005, paras 172, 178, 179; Zwanenburg, *Accountability of Peace Support Operations*, n 47 above, 108.

[60] Zwanenburg, *Accountability of Peace Support Operations*, n 47 above, 111.

[61] Marina Caparini, 'Domestic Regulation: Licensing Regimes for the Export of Military Goods and Services', in Chesterman and Lehnardt (eds), *From Mercenaries to Market*, n 8 above, 158.

[62] See James Cockayne, 'Commercial Security in Humanitarian and Post-Conflict Settings: An Exploratory Study', International Peace Academy, March 2006, iii.

requirements and supervision through UN personnel might be adequate. The situation would be different, however, in cases where PMSCs provide armed security services. Here, their integration into UN troops, or at least in the military chain of command, becomes indispensable and would be necessary for them to acquire combatant status. Such measures, however, would bring the more fundamental problem to the fore: the risk of commercial actors taking part in hostilities is unlikely to be accepted by most member states or the broader public.

Another aspect of the obligation to 'ensure' human rights and international humanitarian law is the obligation to respond adequately to a violation of international law. Accordingly, there must be effective sanctioning mechanisms in place that are used in cases of misconduct, sometimes including criminal prosecution. As stated above, the UN does not have jurisdiction over peacekeeping personnel. Jurisdiction over members of national contingents is vested exclusively in troop-contributing states. Equally, if the company is hired directly by the UN, the UN can terminate the contract or demand the removal of the alleged wrongdoer from the area of operation, but it has no further means at its disposal to ensure adequate sanctioning of any violation of international law. Thus, in the end, the obligation to effectively sanction PMSC misconduct is likely to rest solely on the host state and the contributing state. If the rule of law has broken down in the area of operation, the host state is frequently not in a position to exercise effective jurisdiction. Moreover, if PMSC personnel are covered by the SOFA or SOMA—and consequently exempted from the host state's jurisdiction as UN 'experts on mission'—such prosecution would be excluded on legal grounds.[63] The problem, then, is that there is no basis under international law for criminal jurisdiction unless the alleged crime constitutes a 'grave breach' of the Geneva Conventions or the state that hires and contributes PMSC personnel is also the state of nationality of the alleged offender. The state of nationality, which under international law could assert criminal jurisdiction, is as such neither subject to human rights law for lack of extraterritorial jurisdiction over the population in the host state nor subject to international humanitarian law as it is not party to the conflict.

Provided international law allows the hiring state, as the state of nationality, to exercise jurisdiction over the PMSC employee, criminal prosecution is likely to meet considerable obstacles, as illustrated by efforts in the United States to subject PMSC personnel contracted by US agencies to US jurisdiction. If the domestic law does allow for the prosecution of crimes committed extraterritorially, the exercise of that competence might be hindered by lack of willingness to commit the resources to investigate the incident in an inherently

[63] See Model Status of Forces Agreement for Peacekeeping Operations, 1990, UN Doc 4/45/594, art VI; Convention on the Privileges and Immunities of the United Nations, n 37 above, arts V–VI.

unstable environment. Despite those problems, it should be noted that deferring questions of accountability and sanctioning to industry associations by evoking justifications based largely on economic efficiency or bureaucratic ease (for example, because an 'added layer of UN bureaucracy would dilute the advantages of the industry',[64] and 'empowering a trade association like the IPOA would save the difficulty of recreating an oversight organization from scratch',[65] as suggested by the IPAO), would amount to a failure by the hiring state to meet its international obligations.

PMSCs on the frontlines?

The above analysis demonstrates that the deployment of PMSCs in peace operations is not only politically problematic, but also fraught with unresolved legal tensions.

It is sometimes suggested that PMSCs should be deployed as UN blue helmets with a robust mandate, as a rapid deployment force immediately after the cessation of hostilities and before the arrival of UN blue helmets, or even as UN-mandated or UN-led troops carrying out military sanctions.[66] Greater military efficiency, reduction of costs, and the circumvention of political and procedural constraints of the UN are seen as the main arguments for such options,[67] with Executive Outcome's intervention in Sierra Leone in 1996 frequently presented as an illustration of the advantages of PMSCs replacing national troops. Although most PMSCs presently appear unwilling to engage directly in combat operations and would probably reject the notion of their employees operating on the basis of a robust mandate or carrying out military sanctions, some companies as well as the IPOA have actively advocated for the idea,[68] suggesting that in some circles the idea is not dismissed outright but seen at least as the desirable outcome of a long-term development.

64 IPOA White Paper, n 5 above, 47. 65 Ibid. at 59.

66 See, eg, James Wither, 'European Security and Private Military Companies: The Prospects for Privatized "Battlegroups"', *Connections*, vol 4 (2005) 107, 117; IPOA Concept Paper, n 1 above, 5; Peter Gantz, 'The Private Sector's Role in Peacekeeping and Peace Enforcement', *Refugees International*, November 2003, available at <http://www.globalpolicy.org/component/content/article/199/41034.html>; Doug Brooks, 'Messiahs or Mercenaries? The Future of Private Military Services', *International Peacekeeping*, vol 7 (2000) 129; Singer, *Corporate Warriors*, n 15 above, 189.

67 See, eg, van den Berg, 'Effective Peacekeeping', n 8 above, 304.

68 IPOA White Paper, n 5 above, 51; Doug Brooks, 'Hope for the Hopeless Continent: Mercenaries', *Traders: Journal for the Southern African Region*, no 3 (2000), available at <http://www.sandline.com/hotlinks/00_Brooks.pdf>. Greystone Ltd, a subsidiary of the US firm previously known as Blackwater (now Xe) offers at its website: 'The Greystone peacekeeping solution provides a flexible force with the ability to provide a properly trained force in a short period of time. . . . The program consists of personnel specializing in crowd control and less than lethal techniques and military personnel for the less stable areas of operation'. 'Humanitarian Aid/Peacekeeping', Greystone Ltd. website, available at <http://www.greystone-ltd.com/humanitarianPeace.html>.

Nonetheless, it is unlikely that such proposals would be realized in the near future. With regard to a UN force composed of PMSC personnel enforcing military sanctions, it is very doubtful whether it would be permissible to substitute the standing force foreseen in article 43 of the UN Charter with troops composed of PMSCs. Secondly, article 48 of the UN Charter stipulates that Security Council decisions under Chapter VII of the Charter shall be carried out by member states. Given the wording and the purpose of the provision, and in view of the fundamental importance of the maintenance of international peace and security as the overarching purpose of the UN, it would be a long stretch to argue that states could delegate this task to PMSCs. With regard to peacekeeping operations, it is important to consider the impact of a larger and more active presence of PMSCs on the character of an operation that is, broadly speaking, based on the principle of minimum use of force.[69] The mere fact that PMSCs are prepared to take a more aggressive posture against spoilers does not sidestep the political considerations that shape the formulation of the mandate through the Security Council and any agreement on rules of engagement.

On the contrary, it is inconceivable that the Security Council would send a private force into the field with a vaguely worded mandate, leaving its interpretation partly or entirely to the company. Regardless of the envisaged relationship between the Council and the private force and the command structure—an aspect not even mentioned by those advocating a greater role for PMSCs—the UN will in principle be responsible for peacekeeping operations and states for military interventions authorized by the Security Council.[70] This alone is reason enough for the Security Council to be wary of attempts on the part of PMSCs to obtain a broader authorization to use force. If this is accepted, it is hard to see how the alleged comparative advantage of military efficiency is supposed to play out in a peacekeeping operation. Moreover, if the situation on the ground changes and the mandate must be modified accordingly—as was the case in 1999 in East Timor—it is questionable whether the presence of a company operating on a contract that must be renegotiated and adapted would be an

[69] With regard to the principle of impartiality of the operation, it is of note that companies and the IPOA have argued that PMSCs are particularly well-suited to be perceived as non-partisan by parties to the conflict as they are commercial actors and as such non-political. Carrie M Schenkel, 'Finding Suitable Peacekeepers: Who Do You Want to Keep Your Peace?', *Journal of International Peace Operations*, vol 2, no 3 (2006), available at <http://www.ipoaonline.org>. Similarly, in 2006, Blackwater/Xe put itself forward for a military involvement in Darfur, Sudan, arguing that it would be seen by the Sudan government as 'neutral and non-interventionist'. Willis Witter, 'Private Firms Eye Darfur', *Washington Times*, 2 October 2006; see also Louise Morup, 'Strengthening African Security Capacities', DIIS Brief, 16 August 2004, available at <http://www.diis.dk/graphics/Publications/Briefs2004/lom_africansecurity.pdf>, 7.

[70] The latter point is generally accepted: Gaja, Second Report on the Responsibility of International Organizations, n 28 above, para 32; Kirsten Schmalenbach, *Die Haftung Internationaler Organisationen* (Frankfurt: Peter Lang, 2004) 202. For a different view, see Dan Sarooshi, *The United Nations and the Development of Collective Security: The Delegation by the UN Security Council of its Chapter VII Powers* (Oxford: Oxford University Press 1999) 163; *Behrami*, n 24 above, para 133.

asset or a burden—although it is not impossible to provide for these types of unforeseen events and to apportion the risks accordingly. Nevertheless, the main reason PMSCs are unlikely to play a greater role in the foreseeable future is the still deeply rooted aversion within and outside the UN to commercial military actors.[71]

The use of PMSCs in UN peace operations is therefore far from being a simple question of 'marrying the UN's legitimacy with the effectiveness of private military companies'.[72] In fact, even existing outsourcing practices can be considered problematic in both these respects. Some functions are arguably performed more professionally and effectively by PMSCs than by some poorly trained peacekeeping troops. Indeed, PMSCs can be valuable in carrying out technical tasks, such as mine clearance or the building of barracks. Yet assessing what is effective is a much more complex exercise when it comes to functions carrying political implications. This was pointed out in 2006 by then Under-Secretary-General for Peacekeeping Operations Jean-Marie Guéhenno when he argued that states cannot 'get off the hook by committing to tragic situations by just handing over the job to private companies.'[73] PMSCs are by definition not legitimate political actors, and there is very little in an operation aimed at stabilizing a fragile peace in a post-conflict situation that is merely technical. Providing security in unstable regions is a highly sensitive task, as is training or recruiting troops. This is not to say that peacekeeping troops contributed by states are inherently more competent to fulfil such roles. But the very fact that politically sensitive functions are outsourced to commercial companies raises questions about the credibility of the commitment of the international community and, more fundamentally, about the UN's perceived legitimacy, which is essential to its effective functioning.

Conclusion

In a sense, 'outsourcing' has always been the *modus operandi* of UN peacekeeping operations, which in the absence of UN standing troops rely on the troops supplied by member states. Yet recourse to commercial firms is outsourcing of a different quality and raises significant political and legal issues, only a few of which could be touched upon here. Nonetheless, it should be borne in mind that the choice is not between sufficiently staffed and equipped troops on the one hand and PMSCs on the other. Rather, the discussion is

[71] Email communication with David Harland, then Head of the DPKO Best Practices Unit, September 2007; Sarah Percy, 'Morality and Regulation', in Chesterman and Lehnardt (eds), *From Mercenaries to Market*, n 8 above, 11.

[72] van den Berg, 'Effective Peacekeeping', n 8 above, 304.

[73] Frank Langfitt, 'Private military firm pitches its services in Darfur', *National Public Radio*, 26 May 2006, available at <http://www.npr.org/templates/story/story.php?storyid=5433902>.

situated in a context of the failure of key states to respond efficiently to crises and to provide sufficient and timely political, material and military support to UN operations. The dilemma is illustrated by a situation in 1996 facing Kofi Annan, then Under-Secretary-General for Peacekeeping. In a refugee camp in Goma (then Zaïre) members of militias were hiding among Rwandan refugees, making work difficult for the UNHCR and other aid workers. When the additional troops requested from member states were not forthcoming Annan considered the hiring of a private firm to separate fighters from refugees, eventually deciding against it, saying, 'the world is not ready yet for privatized peace'.[74]

With peacekeeping forces stretched thin, it is difficult to argue that only purely technical functions should be outsourced to PMSCs. Moreover, given that states have begun to outsource 'diplomatic activities',[75] even the argument that at least some activities are better left to the public sector appears to be open to challenge. However, whether or not states choose to continue outsourcing peacekeeping functions to the private sector, more attention must be paid to the consequences of outsourcing parts of or an entire operation to PMSCs. The example of Iraq illustrates the many legal issues raised by the presence of PMSCs in fragile states that need to be addressed before considering a greater role in UN operations generally. More important, perhaps, is that the implications of involving PMSCs in peace operations extend beyond questions of law or operational feasibility. The question is not only whether the world is ready to privatize peace, but also what would be left of an international community which outsources the first promise of the UN Charter to private companies.

[74] 'Secretary-General Reflects on "Intervention" in Thirty-Fifth Annual Ditchley Foundation Lecture', 26 June 1998, UN Press Release SG/SM/6613/Rev.1.

[75] The British company Control Risks was contracted to help 'to restructure the Palestinian decision-making process' involving 'an element of diplomatic work in facilitating a dialogue between the various Palestinian security forces.' Security & Defence Agenda, 'The Private Security Phenomenon: Policy Implications and Issues', December 2006, 8.

11

Conclusion: Private security, public order

Simon Chesterman & Angelina Fisher

On the morning of Sunday, 16 September 2007, US Agency for International Development and State Department officials were meeting in a guarded compound in central Baghdad. At ten minutes to noon, a bomb exploded on the road a few hundred yards from the compound, prompting a decision to evacuate. The company contracted to ensure the security of State Department employees, Blackwater, bundled the diplomats into one convoy while a second went ahead to ensure a clear path back to the International Zone of Iraq, known more commonly as the Green Zone.

This second convoy, comprising four vehicles, was attempting to stop traffic at Nisour Square when gunfire broke out. Though Blackwater initially claimed that its personnel had been fired upon, this was not supported by subsequent investigations by the Iraqi government, the Pentagon, or the Federal Bureau of Investigation (FBI), all of whom concluded that Blackwater had used excessive force. Seventeen Iraqi civilians were killed in the incident; according to a report in the *New York Times* one Blackwater guard continued shooting after 'cease fire' was called out several times, stopping only when another guard turned a weapon on him.[1]

For a year it looked as though no consequences would follow. The Iraqi government threatened to expel Blackwater then quietly backed down. The State Department extended Blackwater's contract. In December 2008, however, one of the Blackwater guards pleaded guilty to manslaughter; five others have been charged with the same and other offences. In January 2009, Iraq announced that it would not renew Blackwater's license to operate. The State Department then notified Blackwater that its contract would not be extended again. The following month, Blackwater changed its name to Xe and announced a new focus on training rather than security services.

Such consequences are the exception rather than the rule. For the most part, private military and security companies (PMSCs) operate with minimal oversight and little prospect of meaningful accountability for their actions. As we

[1] James Glanz and Sabrina Tavernise, 'Blackwater Shooting Scene Was Chaotic', *New York Times*, 28 September 2007.

argued in *From Mercenaries to Market*, however, this is not because they operate in a legal vacuum. Rather, accountability deficits are caused by a lack of political will, an absence of effective institutions, and a reluctance to take seriously market incentives that might encourage good, and punish bad, behaviour.[2]

This volume has shown that such problems are not new; nor are they unique to the military and security sector. As Michael Likosky suggested in chapter one of this volume, privatization today is a continuation of colonial privatization, with imperial flags being replaced by corporate logos. And, as the discussion of other industries in the book demonstrated, accountability gaps plaguing the private military and security sector have been encountered in the course of outsourcing of other public services as well. Apart from the long (and once-respected) tradition of mercenarism,[3] privatization of other sectors offers some lessons applicable to current policy discussions on the governance of notionally 'private' actors exercising public functions, and where to draw the line as to which of such functions should be kept within genuinely 'public' hands.

Governance

Even when rudimentary accountability structures are in place, they may be ineffective or misdirected. As Olivier De Schutter demonstrated in chapter two, the international regime for legal accountability is patchy at best and may not capture the growing instances of PMSCs being retained by other non-state actors. Internationally, responsibility is usually placed on the state in which private companies operate (the 'host state'). Often, however, the state has weak or non-existent governance structures and may be unable, and in some cases unwilling, to satisfy its international responsibility. De Schutter argues that international legal responsibility should therefore be shifted to the state of incorporation (the 'home state'), but international law is yet to solidify such a shift.

In any case, as discussed by Angelina Fisher in chapter three, the international regime only provides for accountability 'up' to the state. Rarely is accountability directed towards those most affected by conduct (Iraqi civilians, for example). The circumstances under which victims of a private company's abuse may seek redress are, for the moment, extremely limited.

To ensure meaningful accountability both 'up' to the state and 'down' to the people affected by privatization, states must take action *prior* to privatization. As Daphne Barak-Erez argued in chapter four, initial consideration must be given

[2] Simon Chesterman and Chia Lehnardt, 'Conclusion: From Mercenaries to Market', in Simon Chesterman and Chia Lehnardt (eds), *From Mercenaries to Market: The Rise and Regulation of Private Military Companies* (Oxford: Oxford University Press, 2007) 251.

[3] See, eg, Simon Chesterman, 'Leashing the Dogs of War: The Rise and Regulation of Private Military Companies', *Carnegie Reporter*, vol 5, no 1 (2008) 36.

to whether particular functions should be privatized at all. Once this initial threshold is crossed one must consider the process through which the decision to privatize is made. Among other things, governments should be required to offer public justifications for the outsourcing of functions and establish procedures that are transparent when awarding contracts—points emphasized by Alfred Aman in chapter five.

Transparency and public participation are essential components of meaningful accountability, as Aman, Barak-Erez, and Mariana Mota Prado each showed. But the justification for outsourcing is also important because, as Prado noted in chapter six, reasons for privatization will affect states' regulatory choices. For example, it is commonly asserted—frequently with little evidence—that privatization will be cheaper in absolute terms or more efficient in the allocation of resources. This is not always the case, however. Governments may also privatize to avoid political scrutiny or regulatory barriers, or because they lack the capacity to perform a certain function themselves. If cost-saving is a dominant concern it will militate against robust administrative oversight; if the avoidance of public scrutiny is part of the reason for outsourcing it reduces the likelihood of transparent and effective review mechanisms. Where a government turns to a company because it lacks capacity itself, cultivating meaningful competition may be impossible.

In deciding on an appropriate accountability mechanism, a range of tools must be considered. Supplementing traditional tools such as the criminal law, administrative law, licensing provisions, and contractual terms, the other sectors considered in this volume suggest ways in which incentive structures can shape behaviour. Fisher, for example, argued for the creation of grievance mechanisms via purely private initiatives or public-private partnerships, while Rebecca DeWinter-Schmitt's discussion of the apparel industry in chapter seven showed the potential impact of nominally voluntary codes of conduct. To be effective, both the voluntary codes and the grievance mechanisms require multi-stakeholder participation, strong operational standards, independent verification of their implementation (in case of codes) and transparency of process (in case of grievance mechanisms), enforcement provisions, and public reporting.

These elements are not yet present in self-regulation of the private military and security sector. Three weeks after the Nisour Square incident, for example, the International Peace Operations Association (IPOA) authorized the first investigation under its code of conduct. Two days later, Blackwater withdrew from IPOA and announced that it was setting up its own association, the 'Global Peace and Security Operations Institute'. The boilerplate website includes a few platitudes but makes it clear that Blackwater is the only member of this institute and that it does not have a code of conduct. IPOA's code remains essentially untested.

Another avenue down which accountability may be sought is the financing of the private market. As Likosky argued in chapter one, focusing only on the contractor, or even on the government doing the contracting, may ignore a range of actors with incentives that may shape behaviour in good or bad ways. The financing and insuring of privatized actors in particular appears to be a productive area for further research.

Limits

Underlying the question of what governance regime should apply to privatized public functions is the issue of whether some things cannot, or should not, be privatized in the first place. The justifications for such limits tend to fall into two categories. First, some functions may be difficult to regulate in a *legal* sense if they are removed from public hands. Secondly, some functions are so connected to the public interest that they require oversight by a public entity accountable through a *political* process. The United States is something of an unusual case in this area, as debates over privatization sometimes run in the opposite direction to, say, Europe. Whereas such debates normally consider the appropriateness of transferring public functions to private actors, in the United States the legal and political environment frames many such questions as whether those functions should be public in the first place. As Simon Chesterman described in chapter nine, this means that the 'inherently governmental' label operates not as a protected area of public interest so much as an increasingly narrow exception to the presumption that all aspects of government should be considered for privatization.

Legal accountability concerns militate against outsourcing where secrecy and potential for abuse operate together. This is true both in the case of intelligence, as Chesterman showed, but also police informants. In chapter eight of this volume Jacqueline Ross offered an example of how some regulators have used compensating mechanisms of accountability to set outer limits on the outsourcing of public functions to those who are 'structurally unreliable'. However, as Aman noted, the question of what functions should remain beyond the pale of privatization is, and should be, a political determination. As Chesterman suggested, the determination of what is 'inherently governmental' might reasonably be seen as a governmental function.

The need for *political accountability* clearly applies to the formulation of government policy. As Aman argued, some questions are so fundamental that they require collective responses: democratic institutions are intended to serve such a purpose. The conduct of hostilities is one of the gravest decisions any government can make and would thus fall squarely into this category. There are, nevertheless, serious discussions within the United Nations of outsourcing peacekeeping functions, as Chia Lehnardt outlined in chapter ten. This is being driven in part by demand, as existing peacekeeping resources are stretched beyond the willingness of member states to contribute troops. Yet it is also being encouraged to some extent by the possibility of supply, as PMSCs see in peacekeeping the possibility of a form of redemption—in Andy Bearpark's phrase, replacing the 'dogs of war' with the 'pussycats of peace'.[4]

Whose security, whose order?

Much as Blackwater has sought to rebrand itself as 'Xe', so the industry appears to be responding to market pressures to disaggregate legitimate from illegitimate activities. How these boundaries will be determined depends on who is involved in the conversation. For the most part, governments have evinced little interest in taking a lead role. The most energetic at the international level has been Switzerland, working together with the International Committee of the Red Cross. This 'Swiss initiative' culminated in the Montreux Document, which essentially reiterates existing obligations of states, PMSCs, and their personnel under international law during armed conflict. The document also describes 73 'good practices' designed to assist states in complying with these obligations.[5] Although 17 states have signed up to the Montreux Document, the document explicitly states that it does not create legal obligations. The most aggressive at the domestic level has been South Africa, which adopted legislation aimed at ending its troubled history of mercenarism—but which inadvertently threatened to end the careers of 600 South Africans in the British armed forces and made even humanitarian work in conflict zones legally precarious.[6]

Between these extremes, the privatization of security has continued apace. It is striking that industry has taken such a lead role in debates over regulation, except when governments are forced to act by scandal. And even in response to scandal the industry may play an outsize role. Three weeks after the Nisour Square incident, half a dozen FBI investigators prepared to fly to Baghdad to examine the crime scene and interview witnesses. Under its State Department contract, initial plans provided for the investigators' security and transportation outside the Green Zone to be provided by. . . Blackwater. Following protests, the FBI announced that in order to avoid 'even the appearance' of a conflict of interest their agents would be protected by US government personnel.

[4] 'War Dogs Rebranded as "Pussycats of Peace"', *Economist*, 19 November 2006.

[5] Montreux Document on Pertinent International Legal Obligations and Good Practices for States Related to Operations of Private Military and Security Companies During Armed Conflict, 2008, UN Doc A/63/467-S/2008/636, Annex.

[6] The Prohibition of Mercenary Activities and Regulation of Certain Activities in Country of Armed Conflict Act, 2006 (Act No 27, 2006), assented to and signed by President Thabo Mbeki on 12 November 2007.

Index

The manufacturer's authorised representative in the EU for product safety is Oxford University Press España S.A. of el Parque Empresarial San Fernando de Henares, Avenida de Castilla, 2 – 28830 Madrid (www.oup.es/en or product.safety@oup.com). OUP España S.A. also acts as importer into Spain of products made by the manufacturer.

www.ingramcontent.com/pod-product-compliance
Lightning Source LLC
Chambersburg PA
CBHW071300180926
51613CB00001B/78
9780199574124